# SOCIALIST MANAGEMENT
# AND PLANNING

INTERNATIONAL DEVELOPMENT

RESEARCH CENTER

*Studies in Development: No. 2*

BY NICOLAS SPULBER

# Socialist Management & Planning

## TOPICS IN COMPARATIVE SOCIALIST ECONOMICS

····•──◄◈►──•····

INDIANA UNIVERSITY PRESS

*Bloomington & London*

TO JEANETTE AND JOSEPH R.
*in friendship and gratitude*

# Contents

# Foreword

PROFESSOR SPULBER's volume on the focal question of development
performance and planning transitions in socialist-type economies
formally initiates a substantial publications program at the International Development Research Center. It was developed in one of several research programs. Others cluster about the subject fields of
planning theory and practice, rural modernization, human resources
and international organization, mainly in relation to development
processes and with primary emphasis on the low-income nations. Beginning in 1967–68, interrelated studies have been launched in each
of these areas, involving in every case a series of cognate individual
projects conducted by research scholars from several disciplines. The
present work is the second book-length publication to be issued under
Center auspices; a previous volume, *World Population: The View
Ahead* appeared in 1968.

The chapters below have implications far beyond their immediate
subject matter. The outcome of Socialist agrarian policy, for example,
has both recognized relevance for the Indian development planner
and vivid immediacy for the Latin American intellectual espousing
radical reform on the land. The history of agrarian organization in the
underdeveloped nations during the past quarter century would almost
surely have been very different from what it has been in fact, had
Communist agrarian claims been better matched by fulfillment. Trade
and aid among the Communist nations provide a fresh comparative
basis for gauging the extent to which economic relations between the
underdeveloped regions and the West have been "imperialistic"—
still a rallying cry for hundreds of millions—or mutually beneficial.
The great and still evolving issue in our time of "plan or no plan,"

xi

seen here in cool empirical review, is found to resolve itself into some generic—and ideologically more mundane—essentials: the outcome of inevitable confrontation between social controls and private incentives; technical capabilities that extend the effective scope of the central planner and technical limitations that constrain him; the persistent weight of historical social patterns and resource endowments in socialist no less than in non-socialist polities. Or finally—the lode is rich and deeply mined here—the comparative growth performance of the Communist economies, their self-stabilizing and destabilizing tendencies, the possibility or impossibility of their systemic convergence to "mixed" or centrally controlled-cum-market–guided prototypes, are vital not only to the third of the world's population directly involved. All seem certain, in addition, to have fateful impact upon development decisions being made throughout Asia, Africa and Latin America, and upon the prospects for international peace everywhere.

The prospective interest of the following essays derives from all of these perspectives: the importance of the Communist economies in themselves, their outreaching significance to other regions and alternative or rival systems, their richness from comparativist-theoretical viewpoints. Written by a distinguished authority in the field of socialist economics, the essays bring fresh ideas, insights and judgment to each such perspective. Nor have either the dictates of objective scholarship or the uses of open opinion been slighted here.

For numerous reasons, therefore, the appearance of this volume marks a Center occasion of special pride and anticipation.

GEORGE J. STOLNITZ
*Director*
*International Development Research Center*

*December 14, 1970*

# Introduction

THESE ESSAYS comprise an examination of the key directions of change in planning, management, and performance control in "Soviet-type" socialist economies, and an assessment of those changes with particular reference to shifts in the choice of economic objectives and in the instruments used to attain them under socialism.

Students interested in socialist economics, comparative economic systems, and systemic change in general should find some new materials in the essays. The standard textbooks on comparative economic systems do not examine alternative patterns of planning and management under socialism, the logic of recurrent socialist economic reforms, or the nature of the changes in their operating principles; they do not attempt to treat the socialist economies simultaneously, but focus usually on a certain phase of the Soviet experience only or, at best, on the Soviet and some specific phase of the Yugoslav experiment. Broader syntheses such as Peter Wiles' *Political Economy of Communism* and Benjamin Ward's *The Socialist Economy: A Study of Organizational Alternatives* set up ideal models which admittedly provide only limited and indirect clues to variations implemented or implementable in Comunist-led socialist economies. The "comparatist" student may better grasp the gamut of possible changes in the management of centrally directed socialist economies through the application of system control theory (Essay 1), the analyses of specific schemes of decentralization (Essays 2 and 4), the examination of specific shifts in the organizational patterns of certain sectors (Essays 5 and 6) and the discussion of various aspects of "systemic convergence" (concluding comments of Essay 9). He may further deepen his understanding of the options and changes in socialist economic policies through the examination of the Soviet and Chinese strategies of economic development (Essay 3), of the difficulties of establishing a socialist "second world-market" (Essay 7), of the conflicts among socialist countries at various levels of development (Essay 8) and of the problems raised by the processes of their "modernization" (Essay 9). The essays are grouped into three parts: Steering Mechanisms and Economic Policy, Systemic Changes and Sectoral Dilemmas, and Development and the International Economy.

I have used interchangeably the terms "socialist economy of a Soviet-type" and "centrally directed socialist economy" (CDSE) to mean an economy with nationalized non-labor production factors, managed as a *single,* unified multi-branch, multi-plant *corporation.* In their day-to-day operations, however, the component parts of the unified national corporation are autonomous within specified limits (those limits having changed at various historical junctures). The theoretical owners of this complex—i.e., its nominal shareholders—are its workers, who sell their services to the state-owned enterprises through the market and, as consumers, are free to buy the consumer goods produced. Management of the corporation is interlocked with the country's administration. The central organs of coordination, decision, and control constitute the "government" of both the country *and* the corporation. In the framework of a corporation, centralization means management by edict, whereas decentralization implies delegation of diverse decision-making authority along vertically descending nodes. The scope of central management may be different under various forms of decentralization; under all, however, central management establishes the goals of the corporation, allots to each branch or division a specific role and the means for carrying it out, and sets the limits within which each managerial function is discharged. The corporate form of a CDSE may be broken only when the interlocking functions of direct economic management and state administration are separated and when, within the economic sphere itself, the direct connection between the center and the periphery (the enterprises) is severed. Under Stalin, the USSR "corporation" as well as the other CDSE's of Eastern Europe and Asia were managed by edict. Only a single socialist country—Yugoslavia—has progressively disentangled direct economic management from the state administration, and the economic life of the enterprises (collectively-owned) from central edicts. Since the death of Stalin, and more particularly since the 1960's, various significant changes have occurred within the corporate framework of most socialist societies and there have even been moves toward dismantling this framework. It is these changes and attempts, as they affect each economy as a whole, that are discussed primarily in Part I.

In the West the USSR, China, Poland, etc., are usually referred to as communist countries—the term alluding, of course, to political rule by the Communist party—and Britain is sometimes loosely referred to as a socialist country. On the other hand, in the Sino-Soviet "socialist camp" the term socialist is used only with respect to countries that have nationalized the non-labor production factors and that, furthermore, are supposed to make a transition economically toward communism. In Marxian terminology, socialism is indeed only a "transitional" stage from capitalism to communism, i.e., from a class society to a classless society and from an economy of scarcity to an economy of abundance in which, by definition, the problem of allocating scarce resources in relation to infinite wants would cease to exist. (Marx implies that the transitional stage would first be reached by the most advanced capitalist countries, which would draw after them, precisely because of their vast international involvement, the world as a whole. The contrary took place, in fact.) Be that as it may, the regimes of the "socialist camp" do not call themselves communist; only the USSR claims that it has started to "build" communism. One way out of these semantic tangles, but an awkward one for this discussion, would be to place the term socialist in quotation marks so as to distinguish it from both the current Western and the Eastern connotations. However, this has not seemed expedient. Hereafter, we shall use the term socialist to refer to CDSE's or to evolving Soviet-type economies, such as Yugoslavia, which have passed through various permutations but whose internal "circuitry" (i.e., "couplings" of basic component elements) is still significantly different from that of capitalism.

In its fundamental, traditionally accepted definition, socialism—as a broad political movement with well-specified goals—aims at the eradication of "inequity" in income distribution and of "anarchy" in production (insofar as the latter is deemed to result from random decisions of private-profit seekers). To achieve their goals the socialists have advocated the abolition of property earnings (i.e., rent, interest, and profit)—hence the substitution of collective ownership for private ownership of the means of production, as well as the replacement of the spontaneous play of market forces by centralized economic guidance and control. But, obviously, private ownership of the means of production may be supplanted by state-ownership or group-ownership or by a variety of combinations of these. Economic steering may take diverse forms under vastly expanded governmental activity, with crucial consequences not only for income distribution, but also for the quality and quantity of the product mix and for the stimuli applied to generate national output.

Exactly by whom and in which ways could and should the *entrepreneurial* (or executive-managerial) function and the *operational* (or operative-managerial) function be discharged in socialist societies? For simplicity, let us define the entrepreneurial function as the task of determining the main avenues of economic growth, and the operational function as the task of combining inputs and of producing outputs in some accordance with demand intensities and supply scarcities. In the CDSE's, the entrepreneurial function (with its adjunct the investment strategies) as well as a part of the operational-managerial tasks (including decisions on factor combinations, outputs, and pricing) have been placed at the apex of the party-state decision-making pyramid. Furthermore, within that system, an investment policy stressing the priority development of industry in general and of heavy industry in particular was adopted by Stalin, with the assumption that it would be valid not only for the USSR but for any socialist country in the world. Finally, in the Bolshevik type of party organization and of party-state relationships, the party's Central Committee was meant to be in each country—as Rosa Luxemburg observed perceptively in *Leninism or Marxism?*—"the only thinking element" while all other groupings were to be "its executive limbs." During the Stalin era, each Central Committee in all the socialist countries ultimately relinquished its powers to a single leader and, as Rosa Luxemburg had predicted, Bolshevism led to a "person-oriented" type of society, with extravagant "personality cults" for each party-state leader. But the Yugoslav experience—from the 1940's to the 1960's—

shows that even "person-oriented" types of societies may, in case of deep crises, reverse the processes of power concentration. As it evolved through the 1950's and the 1960's, socialist Yugoslavia passed through various forms of guided-market socialism, largely leading to the removal of state and politics from investment and to an independent role for the enterprises. The methods of economic management thus raise complex problems, not only for the economy as a whole but also within each of its sectors, where various dilemmas confront the policy-maker concerning policies, instruments, and the institutional arrangement in which they must be applied. The examination of some of these problems and dilemmas is the primary object of Part II.

Under the direction of Communist parties, the socialist organization of the economy has taken place within the framework of long-established national states evolving at widely different levels of economic development. If traditional revolutionary socialism intended to negate the nation, current organizational socialism seems totally unable to dispense with it. In each of the contemporary socialist countries, collective ownership has, indeed, been placed at the service of national power. Individual profit-making has been replaced by a new all-encompassing goal of national growth and autarkic development at the "fastest" rate possible. The capacity for economic growth, however, differs so radically from one national collectivity to another —say, from Albania to the USSR—that it would be unreasonable to expect the economic gap between them ever to be narrowed by the autarkic efforts of each, no matter how heroic these efforts may be. Hence, among the socialist states conflicts have arisen that are hardly different in scope and intensity from those among states with different systemic organizations. An examination of the nature of these conflicts and of the specific institutional arrangements within which they have occurred is the focus of Part III.

Some of the essays included in this volume are entirely new, others draw on my previous studies published in various journals here and abroad. Entirely new are Essays 1, 4, and 8. Essays 3 and 6 have been presented in closely related forms—the former in *Soviet Studies*, the latter in *Law and Contemporary Problems*. They are, however, updated and enlarged in this book. I thank the publishers of those journals for permission to re-use some of the materials as I saw fit. The other essays present, in part, ideas familiar to those acquainted with my previous work. None of my earlier essays, however, have been used in the original forms; they have served only as underlying materials, necessary for building a new, integrated thesis.

In the final preparation of the manuscript for publication I have been assisted immeasurably by a line-by-line examination and criticism of the earlier drafts of this book undertaken by Professors George J. Stolnitz of Indiana University and Arthur W. Wright of the University of Massachusetts. More general comments were made by Professors Robert W. Campbell and Leslie Singer of Indiana University and Frederic L. Pryor of Swarthmore College, who have helped eliminate a number of errors and obscurities. I am indebted to the International Development Research Center of Indiana University for a generous grant and to Professor George J. Stolnitz, in his capacity of Director of the Center, for continuous support and encouragement. I am finally indebted to the secretarial personnel of both the Center and the Department of Economics for skillful secretarial help. I alone bear full responsibility for any controversial views or for any mistakes remaining in this work.

Indiana University                                          Nicolas Spulber
Bloomington, Indiana

# I
## STEERING MECHANISMS
## AND ECONOMIC POLICY

## INTRODUCTORY NOTE

INCREASINGLY since Stalin's death, various socialist countries have come to question and reject in differing degrees his policy choices, institutional arrangements, and even the formerly unquestioned pre-eminence of the USSR among the socialist countries.

The Soviet centralized economic steering system devised under Stalin in the late 1920's and the 1930's, and faithfully copied by the other socialist countries in the late 1940's, has undergone modifications, particularly since the 1960's. The basic issues involved paradoxically bring to mind the predicament of the interwar European capitalist policy-makers and the dilemmas that confronted them, which the French labeled: *"Étatisme, dirigisme ou libéralisme?"* (in free translation, "Statism, fiscal and monetary steering, or market-determination?").

The changes taking place in some socialist countries, above all in the USSR itself, are designed to improve the functioning of the Soviet-type all-inclusive state but to leave unaffected its fundamental characteristics of interlocking political-economic leadership at the top and manifold centralized interventions in the economy. "Statism" is not questioned; the changes concern only the nature and volume of edicts to be sent down the "corporate" managerial pyramid, the areas of decisions to be effected by the centrally appointed supervisory agencies of the enterprises (i.e., the direct "actuators" of their technical activities, and of their input, output, and distribution patterns), and particularly the mechanisms to be established for "identifying" (i.e., checking and comparing) the performance of the enterprises. Another type of change, developing in other socialist countries, aims at both modifying and limiting the role of the party-state apex in the

3

economy. Some of these changes crack but do not break the traditional Soviet-type political-economic framework. Such changes, in Hungary, for instance, have led to guided-market socialism—i.e., socialist *"dirigisme"*—in which a significantly reduced dose of central decisions (preferably implementable through fiscal and monetary channels) are blended with managerial efforts toward efficiency in the public-owned enterprises through the establishment of market relationships. Finally, a third type of change has taken place in Yugoslavia, through a number of stages, from 1952 on. There, the interlocking political and economic ties have been progressively eroded; state, collective-owned, and, up to a point, private enterprises have been left free to engage in market-determined relationships; and the market rather than a plan provides the coordinating mechanisms of economic activities.

The three essays that follow focus respectively on some fundamental aspects of the Soviet-type economic steering system and its possible variations, the ramifications of investment pooling and disbursing methods, particularly with regard to impacts of managerial incentives and of a "critical investable mass," and a comparison between the Soviet and the "Maoist" strategies of economic growth. The first essay deals therefore with changes in control mechanisms and institutional arrangements and suggests a possible classification of the socialist countries in accordance with system changes. The second essay deals with changes in investment allocation procedures and their possible impact on managerial incentives and overall performance. The third essay deals with developmental policies, i.e., priority choices concerning sectors, branches, and regions, and related problems.

# [ CHAPTER 1 ]

## Scope & Logic of Economic Reforms

ORIGINALLY, control theory and control mechanisms dealt simply with the control of individual parameters such as temperature and pressure in thermo-dynamics; but as controls have become increasingly complex, their function has progressed first to the automatic control of single units, then to the control of multi-unit complexes, and finally to computer-based control systems, i.e., integrated man-computer organizations of various configurations aimed at controlling a broad spectrum of events.

Control systems now perform a vast and varied array of functions, among which one may theoretically include the centralized planning and management of an economy as a whole. Like any other system, an economy could in principle be completely "governed" on the basis of a pre-established code or program ("plan") in whose general framework certain self-adjusting mechanisms would be left to operate within predetermined ranges. The idea of central "computerized" control is particularly appealing to certain Soviet economists: Lenin's conception of the socialist economy as an entity run on the basis of a single, unitary plan indeed implies, as Rosa Luxemburg noted, an all-powerful center of decision-making. It is, in fact, this conception that Stalin erected into a dogma and tried to approximate in practice through increasingly comprehensive centrally determined plans. But enormous problems arise in practice when policy-makers and planners try to determine the appropriate ranges and the proper levels at which self-adjusting mechanisms should be left to operate within such a centrally "governed" economy.

A simple model of what the electrical engineers call a "governor," or a "servomechanism"—and the system-control theorists call a "cybernetic" system—may allow us better to visualize some of the problems which such "control" raises. A conventional servomechanism is a feedback control system usually represented by a block diagram as in Fig. 1.1:

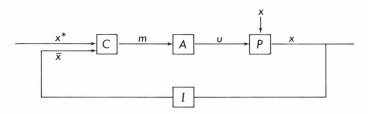

*Fig. 1.1 A Conventional Servomechanism*

In this servomechanism the performance of plant P is controlled by a system comprising a computer C, an actuator A, and an identifier I. The controlled quantity is the output x of P; the instruction or command signal $x^*$ is what the output of P should be; the actuator A supplies P with the input u; a "rectified" signal m is issued by C after the actual measurements $\bar{x}$ of P's performance, supplied by the identifier I, are compared with the command signal $x^*$. On the basis of the difference between the two, C instructs A to bring $\bar{x}$ closer to requirements.[1]

A servomechanism supposes the existence of a predetermined code, a decision-making force, a transformational structure in which incoming elements are processed into outgoing elements, and a feedback. A complex cybernetic system implies for its part the existence of subsystems into which the entire system resolves; its interconnected subsystems channel mutual information, influence each other, and tend to achieve a self-adaptive process for the system as a whole.

By extension, a centrally directed socialist economy (CDSE) may also be visualized as a cybernetic system. Taking our simple diagram as a starting point, we may say that in a CDSE, the directives of the system's manipulators must be fed to a computer center C—the central planning board. The latter must issue instructions to the supervisory agencies—the actuators A, the industrial ministries and their divisions and departments, which in turn authorize P's resource utilization in accordance with fixed norms which they determine. P's output is afterwards checked by various "identifying" mechanisms: planning committees, statistical services, supervisory agencies, banks, and sometimes the market (e.g., for labor and consumer goods). Through feedback connections they supply their information to the computing center, where the data are compared with the original instructions, and whence a rectified signal, as needed, is issued to the actuators.[2]

In large control systems—e.g., power systems, transportation systems, industrial branches, and the national economy as a whole—the system's manipulators need not know all the characteristics of the processes they wish to control. Any large system contains an enormous number of elements, all of which cannot and need not be examined analytically. What is possible and necessary, however, is to find the specific "global parameters" (like pressure and temperature in thermo-dynamics) and attempt to describe the given system in terms of those parameters. Therefore the system's manipulators need to know only those characteristics of the processes to be controlled that are dictated by the goals they have set for the system as a whole. Their instructions $x^*$ may be viewed as a collection of $n$ quantities $x^*_1, \ldots, x^*_n$ representing the coordinates of the vector $x^*$ as to what the desired outputs of plant P must be, i.e., $x^* = (x^*_1, \ldots, x^*_n)$. The several inputs of C into A and of A into P may be similary unified in vectors m and u, so that $m = (m_1, \ldots, m_j)$ and $u = (u_1, \ldots, u_k)$. In the course of implementation the desired outputs will be required at certain points in time, or x will be required to equal $x^*_i$ ($i = 1, \ldots, n$), where $x^*_i$ is a specified function of time. For optimal results, the system will have to perform in such a way that x will match $x^*$ regardless of changes of the parameters within the plant or external disturbances $z = (z_1, \ldots, z_s)$, which may affect P.[3]

The establishment of a centralized planning and control mechanism within an economy raises, besides the problems of designing a multi-loop system with numerous internal, internal-external and external-internal feedbacks (with the socio-economic and technological environment in which the system operates), numerous problems as to the degree of freedom (or of self-adjustment) to be left at each hierarchial level. The system cannot and does not function in practice as a purely mechanistic and deterministic device: central impulsions do not reverberate passively throughout the system. As control is extended to the entire production apparatus (under the assumption that, without it, its output quantity, quality, and mix would not be satisfactory), the performance of the system as a whole may prove wanting in a variety of respects. The established relationship between actuators and plants may turn out to be inappropriate, the discrepancy between $x^*$ and $\bar{x}$ may be increasing, loops for adjusting parameters automatically to make $\bar{x}$ equal $x^*$ may malfunction or cease to operate, and so on. Hence new objectives may have to be formulated, the actuators may have to be reorganized, the relationship between them and the plants may have to be reworked, the identifying mechanisms may have to be replaced (e.g., with market-automated controls), and the whole performance may have to be retested under new conditions. In practice then, the transition from non-market to market-guided controls may, in certain circumstances, be forced upon the manipulators of CDSE's, no matter how strong their own distaste for market mechanisms.

The study of control in a complex cybernetic system necessarily embraces analyses of its objectives, of the design and connection among its components, of the forms and content of the instructions issued by the system's manipulators to the system's "coordinators," actuators, and plants, and an assessment of the system's performance through various identifying mechanisms. Each of these fundamental and closely interrelated aspects can be adjusted to improve the "performance index" (i.e., the index measuring the extent to which the objectives are fulfilled under the given conditions of operation) and control the variables of the process (e.g., principal and secondary process inputs and outputs, states, constraints, disturbances, etc.).

Within this context we propose now to discuss the present and prospective Soviet adaptation and attempts at optimization of their "corporate" control system, the scope and nature of economic reforms in the rest of the socialist camp, the evolving socialist concepts on the relationship between unified management and nationalization, and finally the limitations of a "cybernetic" model, as far as various aspects of planning and management are concerned.

## DIRECTIONS OF SOVIET ADAPTATION

Soviet economic reforms carried out at various periods since the late 1920's, have traditionally entailed streamlining of the system's components design, alteration of the instructions' forms and content, and various adjustments of the identifying mechanisms. The postulated necessity of a highly centralized control system to enforce the policy-makers' priorities for industrial development and the effort of achieving in practice a tight mechanistic and deterministic system have not changed significantly, at least until Stalin's death in 1953.

Reforms of the system's components have dealt primarily with the structure of the actuators of the enterprises and with the type of connections among them and the center of the corporation. Various reforms during the Stalin era were to consolidate actuator jurisdictions vertically, along all-union ministerial lines. In the late 1950's, during Khrushchev's tenure, regional or territorial supervisory agencies were substituted for the nationally unified ministerial organizations. After Khrushchev's fall, the ministerial organizations were again established. Each system has incorporated within it some basic elements of the other. In the ministerial system, the branch-of-industry principle of organization has included territorial divisions within both the ministries and the planning committees. In the system of territorial councils of the national economy (*sovnarkhozy*), the planning committees expanded their branch-of-industry divisions and assumed many of the functions of the previous ministries. Both systems have manifested a certain incapacity to deal simultaneously and equally effectively with departmental and regional problems. Under the ministerial system, departmental barriers have traditionally led to duplications of activities in various ministries, and, under the *sovnarkhoz* system, regional barriers have led to localized distortions of the national interest and have thwarted the goals of the top policy-makers and central planners.[4] In the more complex relation of the actuators with the center of command, the organ of responsibility for allocation of investable funds has been shifted in various ways from the state budget office to the banks. (In either situation, however, decisions on the actual physical allocation of resources have remained of primary significance.)

Reforms of instructions have been planned to reduce their volume, complexity, specificity, and ranking with a view toward eliminating the multiplicity of signals that leads to disturbance or, in the language of information theory, "signal corruption." An enormous amount of redundant information still continues to circulate within the vast reaches of the Soviet state bureaucracy. According to V. A. Trapezni-kov, an examination of information-reporting within a ministry in the late 1960's showed that, for a number of divisions in that min-istry, "unnecessary information"—i.e., information for which nobody, from the lower production level up to the ministry itself, could ascribe a purpose—amounted to 90 per cent of the total information trans-ferred to the superior levels; each month the unnecessary informa-tion submitted from the lower to the upper level amounted to thou-sands of statistic-filled pages, reprinted several times along the chain of command.[5] Furthermore, the selection of some specific perform-ance indicator for assessing output has led to innumerable difficulties. The policy-makers have traditionally employed gross value of output as the "success indicator," but since the 1960's its increasingly obvious shortcomings have forced a shift toward another "success indicator"— the "profits" made by the enterprises.[6] For this reason, among others, prices have had to be rendered more meaningful than they have been in the past, though the system's manipulators still view them primar-ily as "messengers" of priorities rather than as scarcity indicators. Finally, as far as choice of identifiers is concerned, strong reliance has always been placed on direct rather than on roundabout controls and on non-market mechanisms rather than on market or other spon-taneous mechanisms.

In this perspective, what are the principal directions of Soviet adap-tation toward optimization of its control system? The main thrust takes distinctive shape along two axes, one of which might be called "optimal planning" and the other, "optimal system design." To clarify these points, let us consider again our schema of management and control. We can easily visualize how the three layers—policy-making bodies, supervisory management ("actuators"), and plant or enter-prise operational management—could be prospectively related in ways somewhat different from those used in the past. Let us assume that at the level of the production enterprise we are already in the twenty-first century—i.e., that we are already dealing with fully automated plants without workers or managers. The processes occurring there could be fully described by deterministic mathematical models, or by what is called system engineering. At the second level, where machines and materials would have to be allocated for optimal fulfillment of policy edicts, man and computers would jointly perform increasingly higher-level information processing functions in order to predict alternatives for various contingencies and to modify as needed internal network parameters so as to optimize performance. Their activities would involve rapid processing of stochastic flows of information which may throw off balance actuators and identifiers. Finally, at the top layer, where the system's manipulators would have to determine the directions of growth, product development, cost-price policies, etc., only some decisions could be made with the help of programming techniques. The criterion function would often be very complex, non-measurable, or non-quantifiable, and directional change would therefore have to be instituted on the basis of such socio-economic and political considerations as patterns of development for lagging areas, types of connections between the towns and the countryside, standards of living of various social strata, etc., none of which is fully describable by mathematical models.

The Soviet partisans of the "optimal planning" school—most of them mathematical economists of the Central Economic Mathematical Institute of the Academy of Sciences—suggest that the main thrust of Soviet research or system adaptation and optimization should be oriented toward the mathematization and model formulation of planning operations and of the planning system in general, with a view toward its continuous improvement. Decisive in this school of thought are, on the one hand, the problem of planning proper—that is, the problem of prediction and optimal solution of norms of investment and consumption, effectiveness of capital outlays, etc.[7]—and, on the other hand, the problem of automation of plan calculations requiring adequate designation of responsibility in the plan, determination of sequence in principal plan functions, standardization of instructions, and formalization of all the operations connected with the national plan.[8] The optimal planning school would in effect assign to the top decision-making layer the power to establish the criteria (e.g., profitability) and optimal parameters (e.g., planned prices, investment, efficiency norms, etc.) which the planners and project-makers would then use for preparing plan variants.

The Soviet partisans of an "optimal functioning system"—certain mathematical economists and some "cyberneticians" associated with the Scientific Council for Optimal Planning and Management of the USSR Academy of Sciences—intend to deal with problems much more ambitious in scope. They are interested in the study and design of optimal control systems for the economy and eventually of optimal controls for the entire social macro-system, including all of its subsystems and their interactions. Hence, some are interested in designing an optimal control system for the socialist economy as a whole along with self-adaptive control systems at various subordinate levels (e.g., branches, regions).[9] Others intend to deal with the social macrosystem whose subsystems are alleged to be "nature" (resources and environment), the economy (the "processor" of resources), and the society (the web of social relations, which, according to Marxian theories, is engendered by the "modes of production"—i.e., production techniques changing with various systems at various levels of development). As E. Z. Maiminas puts it, "the economy mediates a certain part of the hypothetical flow 'nature—society' "[10] (see Fig. 1.2). In research regarding optimally functioning systems, attention has been centered particularly on mathematical model-building, information theory, management science, and systems theory in general. The Soviet contributions to the theory of optimal systems in mathematics and engineering—for instance, the contributions of A. A. Fel'dbaum—are highly imaginative and of international renown.[11]

Let us note in conclusion that the partisans of optimal planning reject the theory of an "optimally functioning economy" as "not fully worked out at the present time."[12] (We should recall nevertheless that, in the West as in the East, increasingly ambitious projects are being attempted in the study of man-machines systems, at the very frontier of "optimal planning" and "optimal functioning systems.") Both Soviet schools agree, however, on the needs of developing a "unified system of optimal planning, accounting and control" based on a state-wide

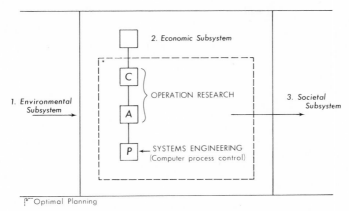

*Fig. 1.2 The Social Macro-system*

network of computer centers encompassing all levels of management, from the individual enterprises to the organs of national economic planning.[13] Much remains to be done toward the development of such a network: Soviet engineers are not certain if its development should start with the individual enterprises and firms and proceed upward, or start with the development of a national system and move downward to the development of branch and finally enterprise systems, or both; furthermore, the current Soviet computer equipment is extremely inadequate for the wild hopes it has already evoked.

## ECONOMIC REFORMS IN EASTERN EUROPE

The simple "governor" model with which we started our discussion may help us examine systemic reforms not only in the Soviet Union but also in the rest of the socialist camp. In the 1960's, the socialist camp could be divided into three groups of countries: (1) those which, like East Germany, are bent primarily on improving the single-corporation steering mechanisms; (2) those which, like Yugoslavia (and briefly, in 1968, Czechoslovakia) rejected the single-corporation system as unworkable; and finally (3) those which, like Mao's China, affirm in principle (though not in practice) that nothing must be changed in the "Stalinist" model and in its type of managment, by edict.

(1) The East Germans have long complained about rigidity and lack of imagination in the designing of "actuators" and in the definition of their role, in the use of "identifying" mechanisms and in the utilization of the market, in the volume of edicts and the resultant deluge of paper forms ("Papierflut") at each managerial level. They have accordingly redesigned and expanded the role of the actuators creating, "conglomerates" of sorts, with decisive executive powers vested in the management of the leading enterprise of the group. They have further increased the market connections among conglomerates, and have attempted to reduce drastically the volume of instructions, to stave the "Papierflut," and simultaneously to improve planning operations and data processing by developing a national network of computer systems for planning accounting and control. The East Germans have been emulated in many of these respects by the Russians, the Bulgarians, and the Rumanians.

(2) Step-by-step the Yugoslavs have come to reject the idea of the single, unified, all-embracing national corporation. After modeling their steering mechanisms on the Soviet concepts of the single corporation from 1945 to 1952, they developed a so-called New System from 1953 to 1964 and a so-called Reformed System in 1965. In both the New and Reformed systems they disconnected the three specific circuits which operate a Soviet-type, edict-managed national corporation and established entirely new connections among the enterprises and among some of their former "actuators." They have allowed the state-, collectively-, or privately-owned enterprises to establish, as needed, voluntary professional associations, direct connections with drastically changed banks (truly commercial banks, organized as profit-sharing institutions with capital subscribed by enterprises and governmental bodies, no longer the Soviet-type administrative agencies combining the role of banks of issue and banks for commerce), and direct connections with the suppliers and the consumers, leaving top policy-makers to "plan" only the broad directions of the country's growth. The enterprises have been left free to plan and finance their investments: they may reinvest in their own

firms, lend to other enterprises, or become shareholders of banks. The national plan has thus become not an operational plan comprised of the sum of the plans for the enterprises, as in a CDSE, but a broadly indicative framework of national goals.[14] In Essay 4 we shall return to the problems connected with the management of such state-owned or collective-owned enterprises. Let us note here only that the shift from the "New" to the "Reformed" system implied a drastic curtailment of the central government role in the pooling and disbursing of investments. In the "Reformed" system the relations between the center and the enterprises have been relaxed: they do not differ significantly from the analogous relations in any planned Western economy, such as France.[15]

The Hungarian regime also has tried, with some success since 1968, to establish more flexible relations between the enterprises and their "associations" (which are not voluntary), the bank (which is not a purely commercial bank), the central plan (whose role has been substantially scaled down), and suppliers and distributors. As in the earlier Yugoslav New System, the Hungarian central plan no longer contains binding instructions for the enterprises, now set free to work out their own targets according to market conditions within the broad framework of established taxes, price and wage policies, profit regulations, and foreign exchange rates. Short-term credits are extended to enterprises in conformity with thin credit ratings and general market conditions, whereas long-term credits are granted primarily to correspond to central objectives and efficiency of investment. The reform, however, has not dismantled the Soviet-type corporate structure and its interlocking administrative-economic functions at the apex of the party-state.[16] Finally the Czechs seemed to be ready, during their short-lived liberal socialist period (January-August 1968), to eventually overtake the Hungarians and telescope into one broad reform many of the measures taken piecemeal by the Yugoslavs in their two reforms.

(3) Mao's China, for its part, has proclaimed its absolute fidelity to Stalin's edict-management system and has rejected as "revisionism" any changes in the form, scope, and nature of the actuators, in the form, scope, and nature of the identifiers, and in the volume and specific nature of the central instructions. Even a shift from one indi-

cator to another—viz., from gross value of output to "profits" (at administered prices)—is denounced as "return to capitalism." Actually, as we shall see in detail in essays 3 and 8, Mao's China has also enlarged the range of the traditional Stalinist economic policy options and has made innovations in both its own domestic strategy of development and its international strategy regarding relations between the most-developed and the less-developed countries.

## RELATIONSHIPS BETWEEN UNIFIED MANAGEMENT AND NATIONALISM

In the Marx-Lenin tradition, the indispensable requisite for unified economic management on the basis of a single economic plan is the state's appropriation of the "commanding heights" of the economy through the socialization (or nationalization) of the large industries, banks, transport, and communication. Socialization has been viewed as a means of unified management, "rationalized" economic control, increased capital accumulation and sustained economic growth. During Stalin's planning era, from the 1920's to the early 1950's, and in Eastern Europe from the late 1940's to the early 1950's, these were unquestioned articles of faith. Consequently, the Communist leaders of Eastern Europe tried to copy as faithfully as possible the Soviet "model" of edict management and centralized planning. Massive nationalizations throughout these economies were accompanied by systematic blunting or elimination of market mechanism. Conversely, after certain failures in centralized planning, particularly in the early 1950's and again in the early 1960's, the extent of nationalizations was questioned as *simultaneously* were the objectives of the state control over the economy, the forms of its management, and the role of various mechanisms as identifiers of its true performance. Now, any modifications of the old planning system, along with devolution of entrepreneurial tasks to leaders of administratively designed amalgamations (e.g., in East Germany), widening application of market mechanisms and of "controlled" uses of the "profit" motive (in the USSR and some East European countries), and possible de-socializations in services, are all rejected by Mao as "return to capitalism."

Actually, excepting Yugoslavia and only partly Hungary and Czecho-slovakia (and that temporarily only), none of these countries have gone over the threshold which separates a Soviet-type "corporate" economy from a market-directed one (albeit one evolving with so-cialized property relations). The Chinese criticisms stem, in part at least, from the false premise, previously accepted in the whole of the "camp," that there exists indeed only a single pattern of management and planning which can be defined as socialist: edict-management in the Stalin manner.

The attempts at modification of the Stalin-type system of economic control throughout Eastern Europe, have, for their part, opened the way toward a more objective appraisal not only of that system but also of the one that preceded it—namely, in the USSR the New Eco-nomic Policy of the 1920's and in Eastern Europe the "recovery" pe-riod of 1945–49. Previously, the recovery-period management and planning, based on wide functioning of the market mechanisms in economies with large non-nationalized sectors, were deemed to be "in-ferior" in various ways to the Stalin model of organization. Indeed, the Communist leaders considered the early recovery plans as im-perfect frameworks for "true" planning, since, allegedly, true plan-ning could not be achieved without vast socializations and without the elimination of the market. Since the mid-1960's, however, the early system of management and planning—in which state enter-prises were not yet cut from the market and in which the economy as a whole had not yet severed its ties with the world market—has increasingly been viewed, particularly in some countries which least needed severe structural reshufflings, as much more efficient and open to broad technological change than Stalin's system which re-placed it. Planning, during recovery, was precisely "merely a frame-work of nationalized management" in which costs, prices, and profits played their usual role in the broad guidance of the operational de-cisions taken within the enterprises and by their managers. Some Czechoslovak economists, for instance, perceptively suggested that the East European recovery period during the mid-1940's was similar in numerous ways to the Soviet recovery period of the early 1920's, before Stalin's reduction of the market to a vestigial role. Just as the East Europeans are rediscovering the neglected virtues of their 1940's and the validity of some of the criticisms directed at that time against wholesale centralization, wholesale socialization, and massive pre-emption of the market mechanism, so some Russians, at least, are re-discovering various seminal economic ideas of their 1920's. The import of these rediscoveries is that they underline serious doubts (if not in-creasing convictions) that the Stalinist path was, even in the 1920's and 1930's, neither the only one open nor the only one appropriate to follow in the organization of national unified management and planning of socialist economies.

## EDICTS IN A MULTI-LOOP SYSTEM

Lenin's audacious conception of complete guidance and control of the whole economy as a "single factory"[17]—a conception which Stalin tried to implement mechanistically, through bending instructions and increasingly detailed central edicts—fails to take into account that the economy consists of numerous interconnected subsystems in which not only central decisions, but also internal couplings and feedbacks determine the performance of the system as a whole.

In an economy—as in any complex cybernetic system—central im-pulsions do not reverberate passively throughout the system; the con-nections between the system's operators—top decision-makers, plan-ners, supervisors, and operational managers—may indeed vary in numerous ways and may in turn affect performance in numerous ways. Except for some overall goals, directives cannot and do not flow in an economy as in a simple servomechanism.

Further, in a complex multi-loop system, efforts must be continu-ously made to adjust numerous discrepancies between macro- and micro-goals—i.e., various forms of "negotiations" must be instituted between the different operators of the system during plan formula-tion and plan implementation. A rigid framework stunts the self-adaptive capacities of the system as a whole.

Plan formulation, execution, and control cannot be based on cri-teria of allocation and standards of performance only. They must allow for decision-making within given ranges at various levels and must take account of the ways in which incentives interplay within these decision-making ranges. In short, even a highly centralized planning system cannot function in practice as a completely deterministic device, no matter how much the system's manipulators would like it to do so.

Stalin's management system represented in a sense—as the ex-Stalinist Roger Garaudy has rightly pointed out—the culmination of Taylor's mechanistic and deterministic conception of management. Taylor, recalls Garaudy, used to answer his workers when they suggested organizational changes in their work: "Thought slows down the reflexes. I forbid you to think. Others are paid for that." Now, remarks Garaudy, the computer technology posits an *anti-Taylor system*. Technically, it becomes impossible to ignore the subjectivity of the persons directed: this subjectivity becomes indeed an essential factor in the proper functioning of a complex cybernetic system.[18] Some Soviet "cyberneticians" and, above all, the traditional Soviet economists do not, however, accept Garaudy's contentions. They continue to conceive of Soviet centralized management *cum* computers, as a super-perfected Taylor system.

It is to the implications of some of these key questions that we turn in the essays that follow: Essay 2 takes up particularly the interconnections between central pricing, investment, credit policies, and operative managerial incentives; Essay 3 examines variations in the formulation of the policy-makers objectives; and Essay 4 discusses managerial relationships within a centralized and decentralized socialist framework.

# [ CHAPTER 2 ]

## *Ramifications in Investment Policies*

THE MULTIPLE ramifications of any attempt to improve the "perform-ance index" of the single Soviet corporation may be clearly viewed in the case of investments policies and instruments. It is also in this field that one can best observe the complex interplay between edicts and incentives and the difficulties of overcoming doctrinaire posi-tions and patterns of decision-making firmly established during the Stalin era.

In capitalist or socialist market-directed economies, the rate of capital formation is dependent on the supply of savings and the net capital imports, and, in capitalist economies only, on private invest-ment demand more than on public demand; both supply and de-mand, however, are subject to the influences of governmental poli-cies. In centrally planned, edict-managed economies of the Soviet type, the supply of savings and demand of investment are, in the main, government determined. The principal elements used to con-trol capital formation and insure its conformity to policy-makers' goals and priorities are central determination of the level and pattern of investment; determination of the quantity and structure of capital goods output, of the volume and structure of imports, and of their prices, as well as direct allocation of scarce supplies; and regulation of cash-flow channels. Moreover, direct controls over and within ex-tensive state and collective-cooperative sectors permit checks on all the phases of capital formation.

To secure a high rate of growth for certain outputs the policy-makers of a CDSE may vary the ratio of investment to income, manipulate its sectoral allocations and basic technological choices, order input and output combinations, and finally choose from a variety of instruments for mobilizing or disbursing investment funds. But the true problem is, of course, how to ascertain the optimal investment level, technology structure, and financing, so as to achieve the highest rate of growth of the selected outputs, maintain a close correspondence between executive and operational decisions, and avoid stifling any lower-level initiative.

During Stalin's era, the final solutions of these variables seemed to have been established once and for all. The investment level was to be maintained at 20 to 30 per cent of the country's net material product (national product excluding services); the socialist policy-makers were always to promote preferential development of the producer-goods branches; prices were to be centrally manipulated to insure attainment of the goals; and within this framework the development of managerial incentives was only secondary. Since the mid-1950's, however, the simple Stalinist answers, arrived at through internecine party fights in the 1920's and 1930's, appeared increasingly unsatisfactory: clearly, at certain moments, rising consumption and decreasing investments may enhance productivity; the respective rates of growth of producer and consumer goods may and should vary; prices cannot be distorted at will and confined only to the role of docile messengers of the policy-maker and planner; managerial incentives may significantly affect output mix and quality.

Specific measures were therefore taken in the late 1950's and the early 1960's in the USSR, and duplicated by Eastern European countries, (1) to discard some old assumptions and formulate new answers to the questions of investment allocation; (2) to shift instruments in an attempt to change incentives at the operational managerial level; (3) to "rationalize" the price structures. After examining these measures below, I shall consider the increasing significance of size, endowment, and developmental level of the socialist countries when several of their economies strive to grow along parallel lines, and finally, I shall conclude with some remarks on the overall efficiency of the measures taken.

## MARXIAN GROWTH THEORY AND SOVIET INVESTMENTS

Up to the 1950's Soviet economists avoided discussing either the *criteria* of capital allocation or the *pattern* of investment decided centrally. Such judgments were deemed to be in the province of the policy-makers and planners, guided by a predetermined strategy of development based on the Marxian theory of economic growth. According to the traditional Soviet interpretation of the Marxian growth theory (that is, Marx's celebrated schema of "simple and enlarged reproduction" presented in *Capital*),[1] the transition from a stationary state ("simple reproduction") to growth ("enlarged reproduction") at progressively higher rates is premised upon a growing volume of new investment, full employment of the available stock of capital resources and manpower, and a faster growth rate for producer goods than for consumer goods. This latter requirement was deemed to represent the fundamental "law" of development of capitalism and socialism alike. The establishment of an advanced technology as a foundation for the state economy was further viewed as requiring the introduction of capital-intensive methods of production in certain leading sectors, which in time would help restructure the other productive branches.

Accordingly, in the USSR and Eastern Europe (including Yugoslavia up to 1955) investment efforts were geared toward the rapid expansion of plant capacity and output in industry, particularly in the "key" producer-goods branches, namely, iron and steel, electricity, and machinery. Resources were allocated on the basis of the technological relationships among top-priority construction projects in these leading branches and the needs of the industries supporting those projects. According to official statistics, in the 1950's, investment as a percentage of the net material product varied from 20 per cent in Bulgaria and Poland to over 27 per cent in the USSR. Productive investment accounted officially for 65 per cent of total investments in the USSR, 75 per cent in Czechoslovakia and Yugoslavia, and as much as 85 per cent in the other East European countries. Investment in industrial expansion alone absorbed about one-third of the total investments in Yugoslavia, as much as 40–45 per cent in Poland, Hungary, and the USSR, and over 55–60 per cent of the total in Bulgaria and Rumania.

Then, during the middle 1950's, the economists started to re-examine with increased boldness both the implicit criteria used in capital allocation and the explicit formulations and exegeses of the official strategy of allocation. At the end of the 1950's, Stalin's successors— followed by the East Europeans excepting Yugoslavia, whose separation by then was firmly established—had to adopt officially a crucial set of recommendations to planners and project designers, entitled "Economic Effectiveness of Capital Investments and New Technology." In this document, for the first time since the 1920's, so-called Coefficients of Relative Effectiveness or payoff periods (periods in which an investment is "recouped" via savings in operating costs) were openly sanctioned as criteria of allocation. The significance of the revised recommendations is that the Soviet policy-makers thus publicly overrode the doctrinaire reluctance to recognize that capital is productive, that rates of return on investment must be determined and compared, and that a yardstick closely resembling a going interest rate must be devised and used as an investment guide in socialist economies.[2]

At the turn of the 1960's, the massive postwar restructuring of the European socialist economies ended, and the unusually high growth rates of the 1950's started to decline, particularly in the most-industrialized countries. Decrease in total product resulting from, *inter alia*, disparities between output gains in the privileged sectors with commissioned new plants and loss of momentum in the deprived branches with worn-out equipment; discrepancies within the preferred sectors themselves, between the basic material- and metal-producing industries and the continuously expanding manufacturing industries requiring these raw materials; exhaustion of the idle capacity, previously available, by the vast structural change and massive labor absorption; reduced productivity resulting from lack of incentives in a policy geared toward the leading industrial links only—all precipitated a re-examination of the sacrosanct "law" of priority development of producer-goods sectors.

By the mid-1960's, the Soviet Union's economists and ideologists were openly divided into four contending schools. The first school interpreted the "law" as embodying Marx's own conditions for economic growth—an erroneous interpretation of Marx's model since it is perfectly possible for the growth rate of producer goods output to be lower than that of consumer goods while satisfying Marx's conditions of "expanded reproduction." The second school contended that the "law" becomes effective in the case of technological progress as the "organic composition of capital" (interpreted as a rising stock of capital to man-hours of currently employed labor) necessarily increases—an orthodox interpretation of the "law" in agreement with Lenin's own reading of Marx's schema, but often at odds with the facts, since technological progress may be achieved through replacement of worn-out equipment, at a zero rate of growth of this sector. The third school affirmed that the "law" becomes effective when material coefficients increase under a condition of technological progress—an erroneous assumption also since increases in labor productivity during a technical revolution can permit a decrease in both capital outlays and new materials required to produce the same amount of output. Finally, a fourth school asserted that the "law" simply reflected the basic contradiction between present consumption and investment—a sound statement of fact which, however, cannot be directly incorporated into Marx's model if one chooses to keep his original assumptions.[3]

Be that as it may, the *Pravda* itself published an article by A. Arzumanian in which the partisans of the "law" were taken to task for failing to notice, as had been pointed out often before in the West, that personal consumption is also "a component of reproduction and a prerequisite for growth"; that there exists some limit to the share of the means of production in total output; and that technological progress consists not necessarily in a "steady arithmetical increase in the output of producer goods" but in the decrease of capital outlays and raw material inputs required to produce the same amount of output. If officially the policy-makers have neither accepted the demise of the "law" nor dealt with all the implications of this· demise, they have, nonetheless, recognized that the alleged law has been seriously challenged. They have started, indeed, to stress that the planner has "a certain freedom of choice" in fixing the growth rates of producer and consumer goods, respectively; that under some conditions consumer-goods production may grow faster; and that, at the current level of development of the USSR, the two sectors may perhaps grow apace. As we shall see in the next essay, the Chinese were forced to discard the strategy of emphasizing producer goods earlier than were the Russians; the Chinese did it, however, without officially revising the "law," but rather by asserting that they were upholding it.

## CHANGES OF SOVIET ECONOMIC INSTRUMENTS

The instruments for pooling and disbursing investable funds in the Soviet Union have been, until the 1960's, confined to those selected during Stalin's time, under the assumption that, in the single state corporation, pooling and financing of investment must take place only to and from a single center—the state budget bureau. The budget bureau was viewed as the clearing house of most if not all investable financial resources of the corporation. The "surplus" of the economy had to be fed back into the state budget, so that the priorities in the policy-makers' strategy of development could be properly provided for. There was no awareness that a more comprehensive combination of instruments for pooling and disbursing resources existed even within the narrow framework dictated by this assumed need of a unique investment organ and, above all, that each combination might possibly elicit different managerial motivations and therefore produce diverse impacts on the country's economic performance. Accordingly, up to the 1960's, the national budgets of the USSR and East Europe consistently garnered the largest share of their economy's surplus either as massive profit taxes—in both the capital goods and the consumer goods sector—or as turnover tax levied on the final outputs reaching the consumer. In turn, these taxes were used to finance capital formation, mostly as government grants to the state enterprises. Plowed-back profits, sinking funds, and bank loans played only a subsidiary role in investment financing. Thus, during the 1950's, from 55 to 65 per cent of the budget receipts of the Soviet Union and from 85 to 90 per cent of the budget receipts of some of the other countries were accounted for by deductions from profits and turnover tax. In the Soviet Union during the mid-1950's, close to 70 per cent of the profits of heavy industry, over 75 per cent of the profits of industry as a whole, and over 81 per cent of the profits of the economy as a whole were channeled into the state budget. On the other side of the ledger over 75 per cent of the state gross fixed capital formation was financed by grants from the budget to industry, some 8 per cent by profits retained within the enterprises, 15 per cent by depreciation allowances, and the balance by secondary sources. A similar type of financing was practiced in the other East European countries.[4]

By contrast, in Yugoslavia, where direct controls over the central pooling and disbursing of investment were progressively subordinated to indirect controls and more extensive bank financing, some 60 per cent of the income of the enterprises was still siphoned off into federal, republican and local agencies in the 1950's. But while macro-decisions concerning allocations were made by the state authorities and were embodied in the national plan, micro-decisions concerning the disbursement of investments were made by the banks and implemented via a system of competitive bidding among the enterprises for loans with special provisions for integration of their own resources. Roughly one-half of investments were financed in this way; one-quarter or less were directly financed by the enterprises from plowed-back profits and depreciation allowances; and, finally, the balance was made up by various funds earmarked for housing and so-called non-economic projects.[5]

Following the Yugoslav system up to a point—a system which the Yugoslavs were to abandon in the mid-1960's, as noted previously—the Soviet policy-makers, soon emulated by other East European leaders, decided also to shift from direct to indirect methods of investment control in order to encourage initiative at lower levels, avoid tying up resources unproductively, and stimulate economic growth. Accordingly, through a series of measures known as the "New System of Planning and Economic Incentives,"—in short, New Economic Management or NEM—the Soviets and, in varying degrees, the other East European countries scaled down the role of the state budget office as investment clearing house, expanded the investment roles of the banking system and of the enterprises themselves, and simultaneously overhauled their credit systems and modified income-tax regulations.

By curtailing the role of the budget office in investment and by expanding in given ways the roles of the banks and of the enterprises, the policy-makers aimed at both preserving the central guidance of the economy and generating what they believed would be more satisfactory responses to their directives. Accordingly, steering of the enterprises was to be strengthened by extension of credits instead of grants, within the limits set centrally; by enhancement at the enterprise level, of the significance of "profits" from actual sales, rather than the traditional gross value of output, as the success indicator of an enterprise's performance; and by augmentation of the operational managements "profit-mindedness' through expanded profit-sharing systems. Thus, a part of capital investment and of working capital became available to the enterprises as repayable loans, each enterprise, moreover, being expected to pay a charge on the value of all capital it tied up in production. Such charges were to induce managers to calculate carefully the rate of return and the urgency of their projects, force them to speed up the utilization of their new productive capacity, lessen the demand for investable resources, and free a greater share of the national product for consumption. In project making and in commissioning new plants, in borrowing or in depositing, managers would have to take into account openly established interest rates.

It should be noted that the NEM, and particularly the resultant shift from budget bureaucracy to bank bureaucracy was achieved without reshuffling the traditional Soviet-type institutional arrangement—though it did cause some serious soul-searching, since it officially promulgated "capital charges" (i.e., interest rates), the profit motive, and "profit-mindedness." Institutionally, however, the shift in emphasis implied only that the bank's credit plan was set to become a more significant operational element than in the past, within the broad framework set by the central directives. The shift did not entail decentralization in investment decisions; these decisions continue to be made centrally, just as before, at the apex of the party and rarely at lower levels within certain share-in profits limits.

## SOVIET PRICE RATIONALIZATION

No meaningful economic criteria can be devised for rational allocation of resources, no meaningful evaluations can be made of capital
stock or of the charges the enterprises should pay for the capital they
tie up in production, and no "profit-mindedness" can be generated
at any managerial level if cost-price relationships are blurred by arbitrary manipulations, and if value calculations remain subservient to
decisions that are based on engineering standards and reinforced by
physical allocations of key supplies. At the heart of the "rationalization" of Soviet policies for capital budgeting, incentives, and so on,
lie the price system and the role the policy-makers and planners
are willing to let it play.

Soviet and East European approaches to planning and financing
have been enmeshed in restrictive assumptions concerning the role of
prices and the market, assumptions which the Soviet policy-makers
and planners are only now discarding, partially and with considerable
reluctance. A pivotal assumption was that a qualitative difference
exists under socialism between prices of producer goods and prices
of consumer goods. Producer-goods prices were deemed to be only
accounting devices, attached not to commodities in the usual sense
of the term but to "quasi-commodities" which may change hands but
continue to belong to the same owner (the state); on the other hand,
market prices were considered applicable to consumer goods, the
only "true" commodities in a socialist economy. Market prices alone,
therefore, must be the instrument for collecting the "surplus" of the
economy as a whole.[6] Money, within the state sector, was to serve
merely as a medium of exchange, since it would be used for trans-
ferring only specified goods at predetermined prices according to
explicit plans.

Within the context of their own decisions on the division of the
national product into investment and consumption in physical terms,
input and output mixes, and foreign trade and foreign exchange, the
planners' main financial problem was to insure that the total value of
producer goods, including defense and government services, was
equal to accumulation (that is, the total of the funds earmarked for

new fixed-capital formation, addition to stocks, including state reserves and work in progress, and additions to reserves of gold and
foreign exchange), while the value of consumer goods was planned
to match personal income. If the retail prices were fixed at the level
which cleared the market for the consumer goods available as a
whole, the state regained as "social surplus"—mainly as profit markup
and turnover tax—its outlays on investment, defense, and services.
There was little point in letting turnover tax enter into the determination of producer-goods prices since such inclusion would have implied an equal rise in budgetary receipts and in the cost of investment.

Profits rates varied sharply for a number of reasons. Each price
reform was intended to establish a uniform rate of profit throughout
all industries, but the very formulation of new prices distorted them.
Two explanations will suffice. First, the reformed prices were constructed on the basis of planned costs—but even before the application of these prices, the actual cost structure started to diverge from
the scheduled costs. Secondly, price calculations were made in stages,
starting, say, with primary sectors and moving to manufacture of
materials, semi-finished, and final products, allowing for price interaction along the chosen technological axis, but failing to take account
of all feedback effects. By the time each price formulation approached
completion (usually over a period of 20 to 30 months), the new prices
already failed to correspond to the set goal of a uniform rate of profit.
Once introduced, prices remained immutable until a new reform, at
least five years later. During the interim, costs impinged in continuously changing ways on profit margins. By the end of the reform
period, the variability in profit margins from, say, minus 10 per cent
to over 50 per cent demonstrated the ineffectiveness of each reform.

In certain Western countries, payments to suppliers in the 1950's
fluctuated around 50–60 per cent of total sales (i.e., the "gross value of
output"), wages 20 per cent or less, and "surplus" 20–30 per cent. In
the industrial costs structure of the USSR and various East European
countries, payment to suppliers amounted to 70–80 per cent, wages
and supplements to 13–21 per cent, depreciation allowances to 3–5
per cent, and all other outlays to 3–5 per cent. In some countries, such
as Poland, price increases for raw materials boosted the share of payments to suppliers, while in other countries, like East Germany and

Bulgaria, a policy of systematic subsidization reduced this relative share. Comparison of data for the area as a whole with Western cost data shows, however, that the socialist camp countries paid significantly *higher* relative shares to suppliers and surplus than did the West, and a far *lower* share for wages and supplements.

In all these countries, the price manipulations voided the usefulness of prices as scarcity indicators and profits as either measurements of enterprise efficiency or incentives for the operational manager. The manager could substitute a scarce resource with a low price for an abundant one with a high price and achieve efficiency from a bookkeeping point of view while, in fact, wasting resources and decreasing the efficiency of the economy as a whole. The directors could weight their product mix toward the goods that were priced high relative to their actual costs. The weakness of the system was also evidenced by the low quality of output. The consumers were forced either to resign themselves to inferior goods or to refuse the purchase. No special incentive encouraged technological changes, since any changes would have upset production patterns and schedules and jeopardized fulfillment of the output and profit plan.

Uncertainty as to the constellation of prices that will obtain when a given investment comes to fruition plus the irrationality of the existing price constellation plague all investment decisions. Moreover, the prevailing price irrationality affects the implementation of investment decisions no matter what their criteria. Price "rationalization" is undoubtedly one of the thorniest economic problems confronting the Soviet and East European polciy-makers and planners. A number of steps have been taken, especially since the mid-1960's, toward some partial solutions: charges have been placed on capital to make opportunity costs more meaningful, investment loans have been urged in lieu of grants, actual profits from sales have been made a prime indicator of enterprise performance, and so on. But the Soviet and East European economists are still divided over how to fix and allocate administratively the "net income" of the society—i.e., its "surplus" ($m$ in the Marxian scheme of reproduction)—in relation to payments to suppliers ($c$) or wages ($w$) or their sum.

The Soviet economists are divided roughly into three main schools of thought: supporters of a "straight value" concept of planned price, advocating that the surplus be built into price proportionately to wage costs; supporters of an "averaged value" concept, advocating that the surplus be built into price in relation to prime costs; and supporters of the "supply price" concept, arguing that the surplus be built into price proportionately to the fixed assets and working capital tied up in production, i.e., in relation to the stock of capital in use.[7]

Massive administrative overhauling of the wholesale price structure took place in Eastern Europe, including the USSR, in the late 1960's. As in the past, the Soviet reform was to be guided by two "basic principles"; to make all processing industries profitable so as to allow accounting of full cost—i.e., fixed plus variable cost per unit—at each level; and to "stabilize" throughout the processing industries the rate of profit to the stock of capital so as to make prices comparable and more convenient for economic calculations. These elusive goals, however, had to be modified as soon as the process of price formulation got under way. By the end of 1967, the profit margins in the new Soviet price system varied from 30–35 per cent in the industries with high production outlays (viz., food processing and other light industries) to 10 per cent or less in the industries with low production outlays (viz., electric power industry). Under the uniformly fixed prices for each industry, variations among plants in their outlays for the manufacture of similar products continued to exist because of technological lags, inappropriate specialization, or poor organization. Therefore it was necessary again to resort to taxes or subsidies (e.g., fixed charges on enterprises with extremely high profitability rates, regionally variable rent payments in the oil and gas industry, etc.). The "guiding principles" had to be further circumvented when profitability of each item was being determined, when development of new techniques was being encouraged, when quality and standards were being upgraded, etc. As in all cases of central price fixing, the end result was a crazy quilt of patches and adjustments, only remotely related to the "principles" on which the price fixing was supposed to rest. These prices could hardly play the "new" roles intended for them in the NEM—namely, those of sensitive scarcity indicators and gyrocompasses guiding "profit-minded" operational managers of plants and enterprises.

## RELEVANCE OF PRE-EXISTING ECONOMIC LEVELS

As long as the Soviet Union was the only socialist country in existence its successes in achieving a high level of savings, in consistently attaining high rates of economic growth, in accelerating the process of industrialization, in incorporating some of the most advanced industrial techniques, and in "catching up," in terms of total outputs, with some of the most advanced countries of the world were all handily attributed to its "Stalinist system;" the contributions of its vast size, its endowments, and its already developed industrialization were scarcely credited by any Communist.

When a number of other countries started to emulate the Soviet system, it became cruelly obvious not only that size, endowments, and levels of development played their usual role in this as in any other economic system, but also that the "Stalinist" steering mechanism was in no way capable of delivering the results attributed to it. After the establishment of socialist regimes in the East European countries, the policy-makers and planners clearly viewed massive and thorough restructuring of each economy on the pattern set by the USSR during the late 1940's and intensified investment effort as the most appropriate means for accelerating industrialization and rapidly bridging the gaps which separated most of them from the more developed countries of the world. The underlying assumption in the concentrated drive of the 1950's was that differences in size, endowment, and development levels were inconsequential; each country could, by the will of its central committee and its planning arm, compress decades of industrialization into years, and years of development into months or days.

A loss in momentum by the beginning of the 1960's, particularly in the most-developed countries of the area, and the obvious difficulties encountered by all of them in their efforts to increase productivity and efficiency after the major industrialization drive and structural changes of the 1950's, engendered serious doubts about the capacity of a Soviet-type, edict-managed national corporation to propel any and all countries on the path of high growth rates, advanced technology and expanding industrialization. It was certainly true that the East European countries had significantly raised their rates of investment and made appreciable progress during the 1950's, as we shall see in more detail in Essay 9, but so did the capitalist countries which were not harnessed with centralistic planning and edict-management. Furthermore, during this period of rapid technological change, even within the socialist area itself, no country had been able to close the relative distance between itself and any other.

Data on income per capita, computed by Czech statisticians, reveal that the three general levels of income and development which existed in the early 1930's in Eastern Europe remained unchanged at the end of the 1950's: only East Germany and Czechoslovakia continued to rank as highly industrialized countries; Poland and Hungary followed as mixed industrial-agricultural economies; finally, Rumania, Yugoslavia, and Bulgaria ranked at a still lower level of development, with little Albania not even keeping up with that. If the per capita income of the USSR in 1958 is taken as 100, the East German per capita income in that year reached 164; the Czech, 159; the Hungarian, 133; the Polish, 125; the Rumanian, 82; the Bulgarian, 81; and the Albanian, 38. An alternative set of income data, also computed by the Czech statisticians, with other price weights gives a slightly different picture, but the ranking indicated above again clearly emerges. As these figures suggest, investment per capita was bound to remain relatively low in the least-developed countries, notwithstanding strenuous efforts to raise it. According to the same Czech source, for 1958, investment per capita in some of these countries, expressed in US dollars, reached the following levels: $133 in the USSR, $120 in East Germany, $127 in Czechoslovakia, $68 in Poland, $39 in Rumania, and $36 in Bulgaria. All other indicators concerning outputs, productivity, foreign trade per capita, and so forth, show that the intra-East European differences in development levels have not changed in any significant way.[8]

Moreover, accelerated development and technological advances on a large scale depend not only on investable resources per capita but also on the total investable "mass" of a country. Countries low in per capita income but vast in size and relatively well endowed—like the USSR or even China—can obtain a "critical mass" of total investments which may unlock technological paths—e.g., advanced military technology—that are completely closed to small countries even with high per capita incomes.[9] The small East European countries, in isolation, could hardly reach the "critical mass" of investment necessary for adopting some of the most-advanced developments of the last third of the twentieth century.

This failure to catch up, along with a number of similarly disappointing experiences, not only prompted the drive for the systemic reforms mentioned previously but also increased, in a number of ways, the scope and depth of inter-socialist conflicts. We shall return to this latter problem in Essay 8.


## EFFICACY OF THE POLICY CHANGES

The Yugoslav systemic changes of the 1950's—on which certain elements of the mid-1960's reforms in the other East European countries were patterned—were aimed at securing an investment distribution fully consonant with central decisions yet flexible at the level of the enterprises, and insuring the efficient utilization of the capital stock and new investments. These measures proved unsuccessful in Yugoslavia. Overcentralization of resources in the "investment funds" (both federal and republic) and abusive political controls over the operations of the banks led finally to overinvestment and dispersal of resources and to an exorbitant number of uncompleted projects. By the mid-1960's, the Yugoslavs felt forced to take further and much more decisive steps: they sharply reduced the role of the state bureaucracy in fiscal and monetary affairs and delegated most investment decision-making directly to the enterprises. Business organizations were left free thenceforth to determine their own development and to use the bulk of their profits along with loans from a reformed banking system over which they exercised control.[10]

As a number of economists suggested during Czechoslovakia's bid for "liberal socialism" (January–August 1968), all centrally determined *investment* policies are endowed with a kind of "inertia": complete reversals are not easily undertaken, since they entail abandonment of projects already initiated, a search for new and more appropriate investment opportunities, and, ultimately, a restructuring of the economy as a whole. Neither the Soviet nor most of the East European policy-makers can boldly discard the old investment policies. Even given the obvious retardation in modern, forward-thrusting industries—electrical engineering, plant instrumentation, computers, and chemistry—the Soviet and East European planners still incline toward production for production's sake in the traditional branches of producer goods, an inclination which literally gives rise to "useless consumption" of raw materials, of semi-finished products, machinery, equipment, and the like.[11]

The lessons of Yugoslavia's difficulties with its NEM have been lost on most policy-makers in the other socialist countries. A fuller break with the past would entail not only discarding some of the theories connected with the "law" of priority development of the means of production, not only shifting from one bureaucracy to another (from the budget to the bank), not only striving toward more rational price structures but also changing drastically the position of the producing enterprise within the socialist economy as a whole. In Essay 4, we shall examine the problems of managing the industrial enterprise under socialism. Let us note for the present that crucial change in investment decision-making directly affects the position of the enterprise vis-à-vis the state: is the enterprise to remain under the tutelary surveillance of some ad hoc supervisory state agency or is it to be free—though state owned—to chart its own course, guided by credits, prices, wages, and other market variables? In Yugoslavia since the mid-1960's (and limitedly in Czechoslovakia at the time of "liberal socialism"), the socialist enterprise has been left free to conduct its own financing, investment activity, pricing, and marketing of products, and to associate itself, as needed, with other enterprises, national or international. This solution, however, goes beyond "improvement" of the Soviet-type corporate system; rather it radically shifts the economy away from the goals and limitations which the policy-makers would want to set for it. It is an impression of such radical departure, *inter alia*, that the Soviets wanted to conjure up when their troops marched into Prague in August 1968 for the uninvited rescue of "Czech Socialism."

# [ CHAPTER 3 ]

## *"Catching Up" Strategies*

AN OFTEN-PROCLAIMED objective of socialist policy-makers is to re-organize their economies and expand their capacities so as to "catch up" with the most-developed capitalist economies and even surpass them, in the shortest possible time period. But even if the meaning of this objective were perfectly defined, a bewildering array of choices faces the decision-maker. How large a share of the national income should one earmark for development, military expenditures, and other governmental needs? How much should one allocate to each specific sector and branch? What factor combination should be aimed at in the various sectors, and what manpower uses should be envisaged throughout the economy? What kind of regional development should be stressed? What kind of monetary and fiscal policies, compatible with resources and institutional or other constraints, would maximize the flow of resources to the government? What kind of cooperation should be envisaged with other countries?[1]

The task of formulating the policies within and among these planning categories, of choosing appropriate economic instruments for each purpose, and of integrating these in a meaningful way into a fully consistent "catching up" strategy is extremely complex. First of all, the key objective itself is subject of a variety of interpretations; moreover, a number of proximate ends accompany the primary aim, each of which may be furthered or hindered according to the ways in which the primary and other aims are pursued. For instance, since the mid-1920's the leaders of the Soviet Union have set for their economy the objective of "catching up with and surpassing in the shortest historical period the highest indices of capitalism," i.e., the highest levels of labor productivity and of total and per-capita

36

product reached by capitalism. Simultaneously, these leaders have also proclaimed the goals of liquidating the rich peasants and eliminating market relations—objectives which in certain ways have impeded their main end of "catching up." Their economic strategy thus was shaped not only as a function of the ultimate goal but also as a function of a number of subsidiary goals, each of which reflected both objective possibilities and subjective interpretations of what was necessary and feasible for reaching the main goal.

Secondly, "data" considered at the inception of these policies as unlikely to change for a "reasonable" period of time may suddenly change radically. Finally, as the decision-makers increase their knowledge and experience, they may try to revise either certain of their proximate ends or certain of their instruments, or both—though, in many cases, doctrinaire attitudes may prevent such corrective "dialectical" processes from functioning properly.

When Mao's China committed itself, in the early 1950's, to rapid industrialization, it proclaimed, as Stalin's Russia had done almost thirty years earlier, its decision to aim high and boldly. If Russia had set as its goal to catch up with the "highest indices of capitalism"— i.e., with the performance of the United States—China set as its official goal first to surpass Great Britain's industrial development and then to "leave it and even the whole capitalist world behind" once a "socialist industrial China, mighty, prosperous and unshakeable" had been established.[2] While taking Britain's outputs as their apparent target, the Chinese naturally and continuously compared their own problems, solutions and achievements with those of the USSR during its own industrialization drive, since the USSR is a country of roughly comparable size, had started from a low level of development, and was guided in its drive by a single-mindedness extremely appealing to Mao's China. The Chinese Communists hoped, up to the late 1950's, even to better the Russians not only by continuously stepping up their "tempos" of industrialization, as Stalin had done during the Soviet First Five-Year Plan, but also by relying heavily on the other socialist countries, especially the Soviet Union, for assistance in a variety of forms (machinery, technical aid, markets for certain products under favorable trade conditions, etc.).

Paradoxically, the Sino-Soviet break at the end of the 1950's, severe crises in the implementation of some targets of the Chinese Second Five-Year Plan, and increasing domestic difficulties of all sorts finally placed China, in the early 1960's, in a situation even more like that of the Soviet Union in its all-out industrialization drive some thirty years earlier. Like Stalin's Russia in the early 1930's, Mao's China of the early 1960's was reeling after a short and intense period of whole-sale collectivization and accelerated industrialization, which had left in their wake unbearable socio-economic strains. Like Stalin's Russia, Mao's China had to resort now to increasingly extensive and bloody purges—though in China these were to be carried out by the "masses" rather than by the secret police—in order to liquidate bureaucrats, dissenters, doubters, and critics, and shift the onus for official failures onto them. Finally, like Stalin's Russia, Mao's China could now pro-claim itself "alone and encircled"—ironically, this time, because of an "unholy" Soviet-American alliance—forced to build alone a "heavy industrial base" capable of sustaining both rapid economic growth and an advanced (nucleonic) military establishment. But if the ulti-mate goals and the general setting in which the two great communist powers operated at some thirty years of distance tend to be strikingly similar, their strategies differed considerably. The difference stemmed not only from crucial objective dissimilarities in the underlying factor endowments but also from subjective interpretations concerning utili-zation of peasant manpower in the process of industrialization, "opti-mal" correlation between the growth rates of industrial and agricul-tural outputs, "best" ways of spreading modern technology in a vast and extremely backward economy, and most "effective" planning principles and methods. The rationale of the two strategies is of in-terest, I believe, for those who follow not only developments in the communist camp but also the efforts toward industrialization of all newly emerging nations.

This essay recalls briefly the main characteristics of the Soviet strategy of economic development and the ways in which they were shaped during the 1920's; examines China's basic resource problems in launching an all-out industrialization drive during the 1950's; un-derscores both Mao's basic approach to the "peasant question" and its influence on China's strategy of industrialization as formulated in the mid-1950's; presents a balance sheet of the "leap forward" policy, underlines its fundamental choices concerning labor utilization, size, technology, and locational pattern of industries, examines the basic changes made after 1960 in planning and management, and points out their impact on strategy; and concludes with an assessment of the strategy's options and an analysis of performance and perspectives.


## SOVIET STRATEGY FOR ECONOMIC DEVELOPMENT

When the USSR launched itself on the path of all-out industrialization in 1928, the US was producing 16.9 times the USSR's coal output, 11.8 times its pig-iron output, 12.2 times its steel, and 20.0 times its electricity. In agriculture the US produced 1.4 times the Soviet output of wheat, 1.1 times the rye, 1.8 times the barley, and 1.3 times the output of oats. The US outputs per capita ranked still higher because the USSR had a population of over 150 million as against less than 120 million in the US. The per capita income was probably 5.3 times higher in the US than in the USSR.[3]

Not being plagued by a deficit of natural resources—only locational problems—the Soviet Union could erect at a rapid tempo a new, modern industrial and military structure on a rather limited domestic foundation. In 1928 its industrial plant consisted of 9,190 "large" enterprises with an installed power capacity of 2.5 million horsepower and employment of some 2.2 million people. Within these totals, the producer-goods industries—fuel and power, iron and steel, machine construction, chemicals, and building materials—comprised only 3,019 plants with 1.4 million horsepower and 1.2 million workers. Small industry, including handicrafts, employed some 3.9 million workers, 76.2 per cent of whom were in rural areas.[4] On this foundation alone, and for a long time with very limited imports of machinery and equipment from abroad, the Soviet leadership built a respectable industrial and military base in nine years (1928–37).

Although the rural population was 4.4 times as large as the urban population, the Soviet leaders placed the former, from the early 1930's on, within the tight organizational framework of peasant collectives, a framework which made the peasant a residual claimant to his own output and allowed both a sharp step-up in the rate of savings in agriculture and the channeling of most of these savings by the state into the planned expansion of heavy industry. The Soviet leaders regarded the peasants as a passive element to be dragged along while the process of industrialization gathered full speed. After the development of industry on a large scale, peasant agriculture and the villages would reap the benefits: the expanding domestic producer-goods industry would fully mechanize all agricultural work, while cheaply re-equipped consumer-goods industries would fill all mass-consumption needs.

Notwithstanding the general acceptance of the idea that the peasantry could not change in any significant way through its own efforts, divergent views arose as to what was both feasible and appropriate in order to accelerate the industrialization of the country. Three main positions emerged during the Soviet debates of the mid-1920's regarding the rate of growth, the intensity of industrialization, the strategy of development, and the principles and methods of planning.

Economists such as Lev Shanin averred that, in a backward country like the USSR, the swiftest industrialization would be achieved through a rapid rise in agricultural productivity. Massive investment in agriculture, and the ensuing expansion of output, would guarantee quickly increasing savings which could subsequently be channeled into industry. The growth of agricultural output would furnish the means for importation of equipment from abroad and would at the same time assure adequate raw materials for domestic light industry. All this, added Shanin, would prevent disruption of trade between town and countryside, would further urbanization and industrial growth, would in time allow the development of a domestic heavy industry, and would generally provide for uninterrupted and harmonious overall progress.

A second position on the best method to achieve industrialization was formulated by N. Bukharin, leader of what later became the Right wing of the party. Bukharin stressed the need of simultaneously developing industry (light as well as heavy) and agriculture. According to him, industry and the towns depended on agriculturally-needed producer goods as well as consumer goods; hence Bukharin rejected the postponement, implicit in Shanin's reasoning, of the development of domestic producer-goods industries.

A third position in the debate was propounded by the so-called Left wing of the party. The Left emphasized, for both political and economic reasons, what it called "the dictatorship of industry" and the absolute primacy of heavy industry in any rapid, autarkic economic development. In a crucial document of the 1920's, E. A. Preobraz-henski, the economic spokesman of the Left, maintained that the rapid industrialization of the country and the mechanization of its agriculture—in Soviet parlance, the shifting of the national economy as a whole onto a higher technological level—could be achieved only if a massive and sustained effort was made to develop the domestic producer-goods industries. Asserting that the existing underdevelopment forced a skewed type of growth—with industry expanding faster than agriculture, and heavy industry expanding faster than light industry—Preobrazhenski affirmed that for a long period agriculture would have to pay a "tribute" to industry as the lever for the rapid economic transformation of the country as a whole.

After hesitating between the Right and the Left position, Stalin finally chose to implement the Left, while smashing both factions politically. The overall pace of development was sharply speeded up in face of unprecedented disruptions and disproportions generated in the economy as a whole. To compel peasant cooperation with the bureaucracy and the industrial workers, that is, to compel agriculture "to feed them gratis while building up Soviet industry" (in the apt expression of L. E. Hubbard[5]), Stalin's party-state machine forcibly collectivized the peasants within a few years. At the height of the drive, during the first three months of 1930, millions of peasants were herded into collectives, and in the process an enormous amount of rural capital was annihilated. By 1932 Trotsky himself, from his exile, warned against "adventurism," but this first socialist exercise in leaping forward was not slowed down. The leading bureaucrats were not at all ready to accept any suggestion that a pause was needed in the development of key industrial branches.

The basic characteristics of Soviet development strategy are by now quite familiar.[6] Throughout the era of comprehensive planning that opened in 1928, the Russians consistently allocated from 40 to 50 per cent of all their investable resources to industry, and of this, 80 per cent was concentrated in heavy industry, particularly the essential group of electricity, coal, iron and steel, and machinery construction. The most advanced technological processes known at the time were introduced on a grand scale into this group. The lowest priorities in investment were assigned to light industry and agriculture. Although Russians introduced tractors into agriculture when they collectivized it—partly to offset the losses in production potential from the slaughter of draft animals by the peasants during the forced drive—many aspects of agricultural work and of livestock husbandry remained highly labor-intensive, and farming continued to absorb close to half of the total labor force.

Since 1928, no debates on this chosen path of development have taken place in the USSR. While, as we saw, the underlying assumptions have begun to be questioned, the basic investment pattern, determined in the late 1920's, has never been modified. The Soviet literature on growth continues to portray this pattern of allocation as the embodiment of universal "laws" of economic development and to tout the Soviet economic strategy and planning procedure as a model valid for any underdeveloped area—*a fortiori* for Communist-led backward countries.

## INDUSTRIALIZATION AND RESOURCE PROBLEMS IN CHINA

Compared with China at the beginning of its industrialization drive in 1952, the USSR at the inception of its accelerated industrialization process in 1928 produced 1.7 times China's pig-iron output, 3.3 times its steel, 1.5 times its coke, and 29.0 times its oil. In relation to the production levels of the industrial giants, China's industrial posture was even more precarious than that of Russia in the 1920's. In 1952, Great Britain, the USSR itself, and the US produced 5.7, 6.3, and 30.2 times, respectively, China's pig-iron output; 12.8, 16.8, and 65.0 times its steel; 6.2, 5.6, and 22.1 times its coke; and 8.8, 11.4, and 64.5 times its electricity. The USSR and the US produced 65.2 and 784.5 times China's oil output.[7]

In the early 1950's China had an apparently larger industrial and handicraft plant than that of Russia in 1928. China counted, in 1952, about 27,000 "large" and 140,000 small plants with a combined labor force of some 12.0 million people, of whom 5.1 million were gainfully employed in industry and 6.9 million in handicraft production. China had, moreover, significant help from the USSR and the other bloc countries in the form of plant construction and equipping and technical assistance; hence, it took China only three years to reach, in the mid-1950's, some of the outputs obtained in the USSR at the beginning of its all-out industrialization. But the Chinese achieved their results with an industry heavily concentrated in the country's costal area, burdened with a poor transport system, handicapped by the lack of some key raw materials—such as oil—and hampered by the absence of a diversified machine-building industry. Even though China caught up rapidly with the Soviet industrial output of the 1920's, it ranked far lower than did Russia in the 1920's in relation to contemporaneous levels of the main industrial countries.

In the early 1950's, China had a total population and an agricultural labor force four times larger than that of the USSR in the late 1920's, yet China's total grain output in the early 1950's was only twice as large as that of the USSR in 1928—some 142 million tons (1953-54) as against 73 million in the USSR (1928). In 1958, its best harvest year of the 1950's, China allegedly produced 250 million tons compared with 141 million in the same year for the USSR.[8] Thus China's overpopulated, poverty-stricken countryside yielded a lower capital accumulation for sustained industrial growth than had Russia thirty years earlier.

Only a small part of China's land is under cultivation. In the vast expanses of Sinkiang, Kansu, Tsinghai, Inner Mongolia, and Tibet, a mere 2 per cent of the land is cultivated, and in northeast, north, east, and central-south China, only 20 per cent. A vast tract of fertile wasteland could be reclaimed—in China just as in the USSR—but China has lacked the necessary machinery and oil, and its transport facilities have been very limited. Now as in the past in Chinese agriculture, "manual labor is the main factor in operation, animal power is the main factor in cultivation and natural fertilizer is the main factor in fertilization."[9]

In launching both industrialization and collectivization simultaneously, the Soviet leaders had planned to gain from the collectives an increased marketed share of grains and the additional manpower needed to sustain industry. When, in 1952, the Chinese started to industrialize and prepare the conditions of "cooperativization" of agriculture, they had the same aims in view; but there were significant differences between the two countries with respect to the initial and projected magnitudes of the marketed share of grains and the manpower freed from agriculture.

In most of the late 1920's and early 1930's, the marketed share of grains rose in the USSR both relatively and absolutely, even in the face of a falling output. The state's grain procurements rose from 16.9 per cent of the total grain output in 1928 to 22.7 per cent in 1929, 27.0 per cent in 1930, 32.7 per cent in 1931; although it fell to 27.5 per cent in 1932—a very bad harvest year—it reached 28.9 per cent in 1933 and climbed to 34.1 percent in 1934, where it remained throughout the rest of the 1930's.[10] China's enormous and growing population has rendered such a performance impossible; in the 1950's, the state collection and purchase of grain fluctuated between 25 and 38 per cent of the total output, but a large part of this grain had to be sold back to the farmers. The share secured for urban consumption and exports actually fell, despite a rising grain output, from 17.1 per cent in the year 1953–54 to 15.7 per cent in 1954–55, 15.8 per cent in 1955–56, and 11.29 per cent in 1956–57.[11]

Even if the Chinese leaders had wanted to follow the Soviet strategy of development blindly—a presumption which I doubt for reasons that will become clearer below—they could not fail to notice that, under the given conditions, their peculiar problem was to find ways of massively employing rural manpower in capital construction both inside and outside agriculture. Although China's agriculture continued to use the most primitive techniques—the sickle, hoe, pick, and shovel were the basic tools in the countryside—the accelerated cooperativization of the peasants, carried out during the mid-1950's (after a short period of widespread private ownership of land), was bound to release appreciable manpower. The Chinese leaders did not stop with the formation of agricultural producers' cooperatives, corresponding to the Soviet collective farms (*kolkhozy*); they rapidly pressed farther than had the Russians with the formation of the so-called *communes*—an equalitarian form of social organization of the peasantry merging the administration of production with the basic unit of state power in the countryside—a form intended not only to increase the marketed share of grains and to release more manpower for labor other than field work, but also to integrate fully all aspects of production and state administration in the countryside. No matter how much labor was forthcoming, China's leaders always seemed to need more: indeed, the Chinese viewed mass mobilizations of their manpower into all levels of work as one of their constant factors for industrialization and economic progress.

## THE STATUS OF THE PEASANT IN MAOIST CHINA

At the start of its first long-term plan in 1953, China seemed to follow the Soviet strategy of investment. It allocated four-fifths of its industrial investment to heavy industry to create "the material basis on which to strengthen our national defense, meet the needs of the people and bring about the Socialist transformation of our national economy."[12] Light industry and agriculture received low shares of investment. But the Chinese planners, unlike the Russians at the end of the 1920's, asserted that substantial unused potential remained in light industry and in its auxiliary handicraft industry and that the latter could be expanded "especially for meeting peasants' demand for farm tools and daily necessities";[13] and that appropriate measures for the development of agriculture had to be taken immediately to preclude "a gap between industrial and agricultural production." For this purpose the planners stressed the need of improving farm techniques (particularly through the "widespread use of two-wheeled . . . and other improved animal-drawn plows"[14]) and organizing the "peasant masses on a wide scale" for irrigation, drainage, water and soil conservation, and afforestation projects.[15]

During the Chinese civil war, Mao had emphasized unison of the "bloc of the working class, the peasantry, the urban small bourgeoisie, and the national bourgeoisie"; unlike the Russian Bolsheviks, he relied in fact and not in words on the organization of the peasants rather than on the urban workers for conquering the towns and placing the party in power. In carrying out the first and most arduous phase of China's industrialization, Mao and the Chinese Communists again assigned an active role to the peasants.[16] In June 1950, Mao declared: "The majority of China's population are peasants. The revolution was won with the help of the peasants, and the industrialization of the country must again depend on their assistance for its success." In July 1955, he affirmed that industry and agriculture could not be separated and that "there must be no attempt to put emphasis on one only and underrate the other." Finally, in April 1956, he set forth the policy of "walking on two legs," stressing the need of a "correct balance" between the development of industry and agriculture and the development of heavy and light industry.[17] Again and again Chinese documents dwelt on the immediate importance of the country's peasant masses as suppliers to industry and as buyers of its products —aspects seldom pressed by the Russians after the rejection of Bukharin's approach to industrialization.

From the beginning of the Chinese First Five-Year Plan, the organization of the peasantry and the mechanization of agriculture were viewed as sequential, with each consisting of two stages: co-operativization of the peasantry could grow into collectivization, and widespread semi-mechanization (horse-drawn or ox-drawn double-wheeled, twin-bladed plows) could lead to large-scale mechanization.[18]

The form and scope of collectivization, however, took on new characteristics as the population pressure started to mount. Between 1952 and 1957 China's urban population grew from 70 to 90 million people, 8 million of whom had come from the countryside. After 1957 the growth of the urban labor force exceeded one million per year, more than adequate to fulfill planned needs. To cut off the influx of rural labor to the cities and sustain the growth of all sectors, the Chinese leadership decided to expand the use of rural labor in an unprecedented way. With the launching of the Second Five-Year Plan, the Chinese used a new slogan: the country was invited to achieve a "Great Leap Forward" in all the economic sectors, primarily in all forms of capital construction. The "big leap" policy of stepped-up capacity expansion based on the massive use of peasant muscle was to lead to the simultaneously building of large-scale, medium-scale, and small-scale enterprise, to erect a widespread national iron and steel industry, to stimulate the spread of technological change from the developed coastal areas to the backward interior, and to provide for agriculture "with meticulous care as one would a garden." The peasants were organized into communes, whose role was to coordinate their work simultaneously in agriculture, forestry, animal husbandry, fisheries, and subsidiary occupations, including factories for making and repairing their machines and for processing farm and related products.[19]

By the beginning of the Second Five-Year Plan, China's rural labor force was estimated at 260 million and was increasing by 4 million a year. Balancing human resources against planned needs on a wide front encompassing a variety of capital-construction works in agriculture, the planners foresaw in 1957—before the launching of the "leap forward"—increasing shortages of labor in the countryside.[20] As we shall see, the ambitious "leap forward" and the consequent taxing of the available human resources, grave miscalculations in planning, poor incentives in the communes, and a succession of poor harvest years forced the Chinese leadership to readjust their plans substantially by the end of the 1950's; but they made the readjustment, for the most part, without abandoning their basic strategy, predicated on the overwhelming utilization of rural manpower in capital construction.

## CHINA'S "LEAP-FORWARD" POLICY

The Second Five-Year Plan, scheduled to be completed in 1962, was proclaimed fulfilled at the end of 1959. After two years of "leap forward," China had significantly expanded its industrial complex. A widespread network of small- and middle-sized plants had been established in a number of industries ranging from metallurgy to chemicals, machinery, instruments, and farm tools. Further, an integrated industrial system based on the production of iron, steel, and machinery, and combining large, medium, and small enterprises with a broad geographical distribution, had taken shape by the end of the 1950's. Western estimates place the average annual rate of growth of industrial output at an impressive 11 per cent between 1949 and 1965. The peak year of industrial output—88 per cent above that of 1956— was 1960, followed by two successive years of backsliding.[21]

Before 1958 capital construction in the steel industry had centered on the expansion of capacities at Anshan, Chungking, Tashai, and Taiyuan and on the establishment of two new giant centers at Wuhan and Paotou. After the "leap forward," by the end of 1959 some 1,400 iron and steel enterprises of varying sizes and another 3,000 small iron and steel units, employing indigenous processing methods, had sprung up in all the provinces, municipalities, and autonomous regions (except Tibet), enabling many areas of the country to produce their own iron and steel.[22] A considerable number of chemical plants utilizing local resources and operating for local needs started to produce fertilizers, paints, and drugs, giving a substantial boost to the country's chemical production. Some 20,000 factories produced tools, building materials, and processed foods in the vast rural areas. The simultaneous development from east to west of the links of a chain of large, medium, and small enterprises allowed the rapid introduction of new techniques and their integration with various indigenous methods. Products manufactured by modern plants were reproduced by both new and old techniques in small plants operating with old-line or indigenous machines.

Before the "leap forward" China had been confronted with the following choices: (1) expanding the traditional industrial centers or creating new centers—big as well as small—according to resources and possibilities in various areas; (2) expanding the capacity of the large plants—mainly in the east—or forging a wide network into the interior, of primarily medium and small plants, with the smaller plants depending heavily on local resources and servicing local needs; (3) relying systematically on modern technology (in the major branches) or using both modern and artisan techniques, even in the top priority branches. From the inception of the Soviet industrialization drive, the Soviet leaders concentrated a large share of their investable resources in a limited number of mammoth industrial centers and giant plants, particularly those involved in electricity, metallurgy, and machinery, and introduced the most advanced techniques in the key production processes.[23] The Chinese leaders chose instead to create some big and some small new centers, to develop medium as well as small local plants or artisan workshops, and to combine, even within the priority sectors, old craft techniques with modern techniques and equipment in the production processes. The Chinese fitted their choices to the facts that some local resources and labor (in the form of part-time or even at-home work) available for local small-scale industries were not available for large-scale enterprises; that small industries would not require supporting capital-intensive services; and that, particularly for alleviating the pressing needs of the peasant market, more output could be obtained immediately with relatively little investment of capital if the capital was spread over a large number of small-scale, labor-intensive industries.[24]

In the process of mass mobilizations to expand capital construction in several competing directions, the Chinese leadership overextended itself. On the basis of scattered official data, it is estimated that, in the late 1950's, from 20 to 90 million peasants worked each day in the campaign for building "back-yard" iron and steel plants. Some 55 million women were drawn into the kitchens, nurseries, and laundries of the communes. In agriculture, collecting manure engaged some 90 million peasants a day in 1959; the small irrigation projects begun in the winter of the same year occupied daily 75 to 80 million peasants; the deep-plowing movement launched in the autumn employed some 100 million peasants.[25]

In 1959, however, agricultural output fell far below the level required for sustaining vast mobilizations of labor outside the agricultural sector. Because 1958 had been an excellent harvest year, the best since the Communist conquest of the mainland, the Chinese planners overestimated the results and, believing that high yields were henceforth definitely assured, they reduced the grain acreage. Then severe natural calamities struck in 1959, 1960, and 1961, sending the output of grain below the 1957 level. The fall in agricultural production, coupled with a population expansion in the multimillions and the stepped-up investment efforts, forced substantial reductions in per capita consumption levels after 1958.[26] Industry was affected by the dwindling supplies of agricultural raw materials; mass mobilizations in all directions led to an enormous waste of resources and sometimes to patently poor results. For example, the 1958 iron and steel campaign led to rapid expansion in both capacity and output, but in many instances the products obtained were of extremely low quality and limited usefulness, hardly justifying the immense, nation-wide concentration of human resources into this mass campaign.[27]

Faced by a crisis of enormous magnitude, the Chinese leadership organized a vast retreat from 1961 on, more widespread than the retreat called the "New Course" attempted in Eastern Europe be-tween 1953 and 1954, following the first round of long-term plans in that region. The Chinese leadership cut back the scope of capital con-struction, lowered the planned rate of industrial development, and started to divert a far larger share of the output of so-called sector I (producer-goods industries) to light industries and agriculture, in the form of more tractors, drainage and irrigation equipment, chemical fertilizers, insecticides, and transport vehicles. The commune system was readjusted to permit a larger play of incentives in agriculture: members of the communes were allowed to grow vegetables and other crops on their personal plots, to raise pigs and poultry, and to produce handicrafts for personal use; rural trade fairs were re-insti-tuted to provide additional supplies and a better circulation of goods in the countryside. Furthermore, the basis of agricultural levies was changed from predetermined, invariant quotas, to shares of actual production; and in December 1960, notwithstanding shortages of for-eign exchange, China shifted from imports of machinery and raw materials to imports of grain.[28]

Until the end of the 1950's, the Chinese leadership interpreted its slogan that "agriculture is the foundation of the national economy and industry the dominant factor in the national economy" as con-noting essentially "the mobilization of the world's hugest army of labor to develop the production of the basic means of livelihood . . . to promote the production of heavy and light industrial goods . . . to high-speed construction of a great, modern, socialist society."[29] By January 1961, when the Chinese "New Course" was launched, this slogan was reinterpreted as meaning "to concentrate our strength in making readjustments—working hard to restore and develop agricul-tural production . . . and so create good conditions for the further expansion of the national economy in the forthcoming Third Five-Year Plan."[30] But the party's spokesmen still stressed that the policy of simultaneous development of all sectors—agriculture, heavy and light industry, and enterprises of all sizes—had not been abandoned.[31]

It became imperative, however, to retreat farther than was first anticipated. By 1962 the party's spokesmen had to affirm that the "general policy of developing the national economy with agriculture as the foundation and industry as the leading factor" henceforth implied specifically that top priority would be given to the restoration and development of agriculture, because agricultural production "still cannot meet the demands of national construction and the people's livelihood."[32] All references to the launching of a Third Five-Year Plan were dropped until 1966, and no yearly plan data was released.

The Chinese leadership marked time in its effort to push the rapid expansion of certain heavy industry branches. It was forced to come to the aid of agriculture, more than it had counted on. But it neither abandoned its basic strategy of industrializing through mass mobilization of rural labor nor revised its commitment to expand heavy industry. The Chinese "New Course" did not imply a new strategy, but only a temporary shift in priorities.

## AN ASSESSMENT OF CHINESE STRATEGY, PERFORMANCE, AND PROSPECTS

The Chinese Communists shaped their strategy of industrialization, not in open debates as did the Russians in the mid-1920's, but in closed meetings of their top leadership. However, the bitter attacks against Mao's "opponents" before and during the "great leap," and before and during the purges of the subsequent "cultural revolution" (started at the end of 1965), show clearly that wide policy divergencies existed, though there is as yet no direct way of examining the specific proposals and the exact views of the defeated.[33]

In terms of the three Soviet strategy proposals noted previously, the Chinese approach comes closest to Bukharin's preoccupation with both agricultural supply and peasant demand, his insistence that the countryside needs the products of both heavy and light industry— both agricultural machinery and manufactured goods for mass consumption—and his understanding that industry's growth is limited directly by the growth in output of grain, cotton, hides, wool, and flax.[34] But the Chinese rejected Bukharin's idea of "peaceful competition" between different forms of ownership in agriculture, and have acted to further industrial and agricultural output simultaneously in a way not clearly perceived in the 1920's. They understood, as Professor Nurkse has stated, "that the state of disguised unemployment implies at least to some extent a disguised saving potential as well" and that the use of rural "unproductive" laborers would transform this savings potential into "effective" savings.[35] They opted for technological dualism, i.e., for the simultaneous development of two industrial sectors, a modern, capital-intensive one based on fixed-factor proportions and a small-scale, labor-intensive one based on variable factor proportions. Conditions for implementing this "Nurkse cum Eckaus model of economic development," as Professor Eckstein has called it, were being established in the early 1950's.[36]

Throughout the 1950's the Chinese hoped that the small-scale sector would be able to cope with the needs of agriculture for both implements and consumer goods, so that the larger part of the centralized investment could be poured into the modern sector. For a while the emphasis on heavy industry and the emphasis on multi-purpose developments in agriculture did not conflict, since the scarce inputs they demanded were dissimilar in many respects. But the Chinese could not seriously hope either for a continuous "orderly advance" on all sectors, since the planners and organizers were dealing with numerous unknowns in this phase of the economy's development,[37] or for a lasting separation between the modern sector and the rest of the economy, since small-scale industry could not be expected to provide the machinery with which to mechanize agriculture.[38] The advance in all directions proceeded often blindly and wastefully; on the other hand, the need to shift much of the modern sector's output from heavy investment goods toward other goods needed by the rest of the economy soon became pressing and unavoidable.

Mao's tenet that socialism means "incessant struggle" seems to reflect faithfully Stalin's idea, later rejected by Khrushchev, that a nationally-bound socialism is a system of permanent purges, if an industrialization steamroller is to be kept going. Wishing to push industry ahead at top speed, Stalin was impatient with constraints, economic equilibria, or objective laws and limitations. Since he could not, of course, remove all constraints, he tried simply to ignore them while shooting toward his primary targets regardless of the consequences and the "disproportions" engendered. He disregarded the economists and their warnings concerning economic balance, economic regularities, and the "law of value" (i.e., cost-price considerations). He introduced what the Russians call a "voluntarist," subjectivist attitude toward industrialization, rather than an "objectivist" attitude toward its inherent limitations and drawbacks. Like Stalin, Mao advocated a voluntarist policy, in its Chinese version called "Politics in Command," based on the concept that the will of the leadership can overwhelm any constraints, whatever their nature. The anti-Maoists, like the Russian economists and so-called geneticists (advocates of the significance of past trends and relationships and of properly projected forecasts) of yesteryear, rightly pointed out that constraints exist which no subjective will can break. But beyond this point the analogy of Stalinism and Maoism ceases. Stalin relied on secret police purges, along with powerful wage incentives and various privileges, to achieve his goals. In China, Mao's enemies stressed the need for proper wage incentives and rewards to build up the economy successfully. The Maoists, on the contrary, in their incessant campaigns against the "right-wingers," the "anti-party revisionists" of Liu Shao-chi, and the "partisans of economism," fostered a sort of evangelical equalitarianism and rejected virtually all material incentives. They propounded instead the need of reducing everybody's material desires, including those of the Communist bureaucrats. Stalin's bureaucrats glittered in shiny uniforms and trembled only at the call of the GPU. Mao's regime, on the other hand, is symbolized by obligatory blue overalls; his hierarchy trembles before legions of the masses righteously enforcing "equalitarianism." This Spartan version of Stalinism is undoubtedly meant to suppress consumption to incredibly low levels within a population which will reach 1.0–1.2 billion in 1985.[39]

Notwithstanding their overambitious goals, their ruthlessness, their uncoordinated advance in several competing directions, and their gross miscalculations in planning, the Chinese leaders' approach to economic development has had an unmistakable international impact, particularly in the densely populated, very backward Asian and African areas. The approach may be summarized as threefold: reliance on the mobilization of vast masses of labor for capital construction work in heavy industry, light industry, and multi-purpose projects in agriculture; simultaneous expansion of a modern, large-scale industrial sector and a traditional industrial sector; and postponement of the mechanization of agriculture until domestic industry is able to supply a substantial quantity of tractors and fuel. In fact, as a result of Maoism, some of the tenets of the Soviet method of industrialization—the unstinting concentration on certain branches and on a certain output mix, the overarching preference for the most advanced production techniques in the top priority branches and the downgrading of small plants and handicraft production, the doctrinaire approach to the role of the peasantry in furthering economic growth—have been brought under critical scrutiny throughout the socialist camp.

Notwithstanding their tight organizational establishment, the Chinese have probably not reached the rates of savings attained by the Russians—or for that matter, more recently, by other Asiatic countries with special advantages, such as Japan or Burma. The Chinese yearly rate of savings from current output has been only about 16.8 per cent for the period 1950–59 as compared to 19.5 per cent for Burma and 28.9 per cent for Japan. These figures, however, exclude the contributions to savings made by unremunerated labor in the mass mobilizations—a contribution difficult to evaluate.[40] The reason for the paucity of savings is the population growth together with the planners' apparent, persistent belief that, on balance, an expanding population is an asset for a country relying on the services of its underemployed populus. The failure of agricultural output to increase rapidly may jar the planners into realizing that population growth puts mounting pressures on the country's slim savings from current outputs.[41]

In spite of very significant strides, China is still far removed from its goal and is still far behind the main industrial countries. While pushing vigorously ahead in the development of certain basic intermediate products, China has yet to catch up with Great Britain, not to mention the USSR even at the Soviet level of 1940. In 1960, Great

Britain, the USSR, and the US exceeded China's steel output by factors of 1.3, 3.5, and 4.8; moreover, China is far behind in some crucial modern industries, such as electronics and plastics. In agriculture, despite strenuous efforts, tractorization had to be relegated to a second place, while emphasis was shifted to mechanized irrigation, drainage, and overall "semi-mechanization"; by the beginning of the 1960's China possessed only as many tractors as Russia did in the early 1930's. But the Chinese leadership has exploded a hydrogen bomb, and does have the ruthlessness and power to call up quantities of manpower for carrying out the further industrialization of the country.

The Chinese profited from the Soviet errors, but they committed errors of their own, no less disastrous than those of the Russians. The Chinese avoided herding the peasants into collective farms before an active psychological and organizational campaign had been conducted. But once the organizational coercion began, they pushed the peasants farther than the Russians had, into "communes" wherein all personal ownership was abrogated. The failure of the experiment, manifested in falling output and productivity, forced the Chinese in the early 1960's, to revert to certain concepts typical for the Soviet collective farms, with personal ownership recognized within certain limits. Unlike the Russians, who relied heavily on a system of *forced labor camps* for carrying out certain large-scale public works (e.g., canals, railways, and roads), the Chinese resorted to truly sweeping mobilizations of *peasant* labor—a traditional Chinese method—for achieving a variety of construction projects both inside and outside agriculture. But they finally overstrained their human resources, jeopardized agricultural output, blunted incentives, overestimated the results achieved, and drew erroneous plans. Again unlike the Russians, the Chinese did not resort to the Stalin-type police terrorization and purges for keeping the society and its managers on the course set by the top decision-makers of the party-state. Instead, they mobilized the rural and urban youth against the bureaucracy; the vast movement initiated in the mid-1960's under the name "Cultural Revolution" led *inter alia* to an enormous purge and replacement of the party-state bureaucracy. The bloodletting was as severe as that in Russia for a number of years.

All these errors and barbarisms, however, are not likely to check the Chinese advance indefinitely. Growth will continue because the system manipulators of a centrally managed economy can maintain a high rate of investment, can continuously expand its productive capacity, can achieve its transformation from an organism producing only agricultural raw materials into one producing capital goods for industrial expansion. Nonetheless, growth will continue to be both unstable and subject to periodic setbacks, because the Chinese economy now depends almost exclusively on its own resources, and is still strongly tied to a very backward agriculture.

# II

## SYSTEMIC CHANGES
## AND DILEMMAS IN
## SECTORIAL
## MANAGEMENT

INTRODUCTORY NOTE

THE VARIOUS effects on growth and development of different methods of management in a socialized economy—notably alternative structures and distributions of decision-making power—did not seriously concern the Communists until the mid-1950's. From the inception of the USSR, the Communists assumed that, with respect to both management and planning, the socialist state simply picks up where capitalistic monopolies leave off: the "mature" phase of capitalism is characterized by the "monopolization of whole industries," the corporate sections being "islands" of purposefully integrated activities within the "chaos" of the market; finally the socialist state organizes the entire economy into a "single corporation" and directs it according to a unified national plan, thus taking over from capitalism its corporate managerial structure, *mutatis mutandis*.

Quite simplistic views have been entertained—in the East and, incidentally, also in the West—concerning the formation, transmission, and implementation of decisions within the business firm. Stemming from pre-corporate times, public notions about these complex processes would more nearly fit the conduct of the patriarch-dominated, single-family firm, obeying rigid rules on inputs, prices, and outputs, and enforcing them through disciplinary power within a hierarchical organization. Within expanding corporate structures in the West, however, increasing experience in decision-making has led to the abandonment of these old ideas, and, indeed, the study and analysis of decision-making processes within the business firm have given rise to new disciplines: general management, finance, marketing; systems theory; and information theory. In the East, increasingly evident malfunctions and failures of the Soviet corporate analogue, in which economic and political fusion and the universal enforcement of central edicts have maximized the concentration of power, have stimulated progressively more searches for and experiments with alternative methods of management.

The three essays which follow examine three sectoral aspects of these managerial changes. The first essay considers the decision-making processes within the Soviet corporate-type industrial organization and contrasts them with the decision-making methods of a decentralized management within a market-guided socialist economy such as Yugoslavia's. The second essay focuses on land-tenancy dilemmas in Eastern Europe pursuant to the interaction between the economic-technological development of agriculture and the socio-economic motivations and reactions of the peasantry. The third essay examines the conflicts between policy-makers' tendencies to insulate their planned economy from the world market, via governmental monopoly of foreign trade and exchange, and the economic advisers' pressures to cast away such monopoly to incite producing enterprises toward marketing what they produce and correcting their isolation-induced technical retardation.

# [ CHAPTER 4 ]

## Patterns in Industrial Management

MODERN SOCIALIST controversies on industrial management, specifically concerning the relations of the enterprise with the state, with
other enterprises, and with its own personnel, are not always com-
prehensible outside the Marxian frame of reference. Socialization of
the means of production was viewed by Engels, for instance, not only
as the way to abolish "exploitation and alienation" of the proletariat
by those in power but also as "the last independent act of the state."
After socialization, the "government of persons," affirmed Engels, becomes superfluous: the state starts to wither away of itself in one domain or another and is replaced "by the administration of things, and
by the conduct of processes of production."[1]

The forecasted Hegelian grand finale of "the state as a state"—once
the workers had used their organized force to crush enemies of the
revolution—was the Marxian answer to the anarchists' contention that
Marxist socialism is authoritarian since it advocates the passage of
the means of production into the hands of the state. The anarchists—
Stirner, Proudhon, Bakunin—took as their goal the outright abolition
of the state and accordingly proclaimed themselves *anti-authoritarian*
or *libertarian.* In lieu of public ownership, the anarchists suggested
curious post-revolution organizations to control production: Stirner
proposed "free organizations of the selfish"; Proudhon advocated mu-
tualist, voluntarist, federated, communal organizations; and Bakunin
promoted various forms of "workers' associations." Interestingly
enough, anti-authoritarian schemas have now been revitalized among
the Yugolsavs turned critics of Soviet statism. Since some of these
old suggestions are applicable only for small-scale industry and handicrafts, however, some neo-anarchists are claiming that the "future

belongs at least in large sectors of the economy to small scale production units" and that therefore "the future belongs, without any doubt, to the autonomous management of enterprises by associations of workers."[2]

The management problems created by the potential passage of the means of production into the control of workers' states have not been regarded with equanimity by all Marxists. Marx himself had carefully distinguished between the "leader of industry," whom he described as an idle capitalist, and the "coordinator" of the specific tasks within the factory arising from division of labor, i.e., the operational manager hired by the capitalist to carry out some of his own functions. According to Marx, the capitalist then reaps large (and illegitimate) profits while the manager receives only modest wages of superintendence (as in workers' cooperatives and joint-stock companies). As M. M. Bober has noted, aside from the ordinary work of factory management, Marx saw no place for the entrepreneur in his scheme. He was unconcerned with the risks of introducing innovations, the uncertainties of shifting costs and demands, or the other unknowns facing the entrepreneur in a dynamic world. Rather, under communism, production would finally be brought into the conscious and prearranged control of society, and the associated producers, able rationally, to regulate their interchange with "nature," would no longer be "ruled by it as by some blind power."[3]

The early revisionists, such as Eduard Bernstein, were dissatisfied with these generalities. Bernstein considered the organizational problems of socialization to be much more complex than the founders of Marxism had apparently assumed them to be. In practice, how could a socialist state cope with a task of such magnitude? wondered Bernstein: "What abundance of judgment, practical knowledge, talent for administration must a government or a national assembly have at its disposal to be even equal to the supreme management or managing control of such a gigantic organism."[4]

Lenin never doubted that the organization of industry was as simple as Marx and Engels had posited. Good socialist administration and an overwhelming but temporary application of authoritarianism could easily solve any managerial problem regardless of apparent complexity, simplify accounting and control in production and distribution, and solve the old and seemingly intractable problem of workers alienation. Writing on the eve of the Soviet revolution, Lenin explained how, in his view, the "administration of things . . . and conduct of processes of production" would arise in practice. Like Engels, Lenin believed that a "mechanism of social management is here at hand," and that once the workers had overthrown the capitalist political power and broken the old state machine, they would be left with an economic mechanism of the highest technical order which they could run in a simple and direct fashion. He then added that the whole economy would become a single factory and a single office organized "on the basis of the postal system, so that the technicians, managers, bookkeepers, as well as *all* officials, shall receive salaries no higher than 'workmen's wages,' all under the *control* of the armed proletariat."[5] At first the armed workers would hire their own technicians, managers, and bookkeepers. But then a new order would start to emerge: as accounting and control—operations so simplified "that anyone who can read and write and who knows the first rules of arithmetic can perform them"—would become universal, the state (i.e., organized coercion) would start to wither away. The functions of accounting and control, performed by each individual in turn, would become a habit and finally "die out as the *special* function of a special stratum of the population."[6] Thus, just as in Marx's vision of the capitalist firm, the technicians, managers, and bookkeepers would be hired at modest wages of superintendence, and, in the comforting shadow of the state power of armed workers, these specialists would perform with enthusiasm and efficiency in the new *sui generis* "postal system" until experience and arithmetic proficiency would permit the workers themselves to account and control.

If the Soviets implemented Lenin's (and, in fact, Marx's) idea of organizing the national economy as a single corporation, experience nevertheless has made them see and correct the innumerable pitfalls and illusions in Lenin's blueprint on "bookkeeping and management." The single corporation has proved to be simultaneously similar to and substantially different from the corporations which it integrated into a single pyramid. Management turned out to be at least as complicated a function as Bernstein had surmised, rather than the simple task Lenin had foreseen. The universal teaching of fundamental arithmetic helped fight illiteracy but hardly simplified the problems of accounting and control or planning in an increasingly complex industrialized society. In the pages that follow we view again, but with a different vantage point from that of our first essay, the evolving Soviet solutions to the problems of economic management and control in a single, all-embracing corporation and the Yugoslav solutions to those problems through decentralization of economic management in a socialist guided-market setting. We may then examine various criticisms of these two models and the problems raised by diverse managerial reforms in the 1960's, and finally assess the role of management under socialism and consider what should be the relationship of information, data processing, and decision-making in a socialist environment.

## SOVIET SOLUTIONS IN MANAGEMENT PROBLEMS

The basic functions of steering the entire economy, supervising its branches and plants, and managing the day-to-day operations of each enterprise are discharged in a Soviet-type economy, as in any large Western corporation, by the following managerial layers:[7] At the apex of the USSR, the *trusteeship management,* or board of directors, is represented by the party's top organs, the *politburo* and the central committee; these determine basic policies, production lines, key targets, and the course of development of the economy as a whole. Immediately below is the *general management,* or executive power, delegated to the Council of Ministers and some high-level state agencies, such as the Central Planning Committee; these plan, direct, and coordinate the operation of the economy as a whole and establish its specific objectives, costs and prices, levels of technology, manpower needs, overall operating policies, and identifiers of its performance. The *divisional management* is entrusted to lesser state committees (e.g., labor and wages, procurement, etc.) and to the heads of economic ministries or other *ad hoc* supervisory agencies; they are in charge of product determination and distribution for their sector, industry, division, or department. *Subdivisional management* and enterprise *operational management,* in short, the management of the

everyday aspects of business, is entrusted to various ministerial administrations and the controlling bodies of trust, conglomerates, and
plants.[8] Alternatively, recalling Essay 1, we may think of the first and
second layers and part of the third layer as forming the top management of the Soviet corporation; the other part of the third layer and
the fourth layer as representing the actuators of the enterprises, i.e.,
their tutelary organs; and finally the fifth as representing the operative management, i.e., the enterprises' directors.

As in any corporation of great size and diversity, binding forms
and rules of unity need to be devised: specifically, the top management must be allowed to make the most critical decisions, integrate
the various divisional plans into a unified scheme, and have the final
say in interdivisional conflicts; and the top management must have
the final say on the goals of the corporation, since it alone embraces
the interests of the corporation as a whole. Furthermore, as in any
corporation, some central plan must be drawn up, a plan which represents both a guide to action (i.e., a set of goals to be reached) and
a management process (i.e., a way of unifying and reconciling divergent tendencies). Since plans that designate targets necessarily
become measures of performance, and since management, from the
divisional stratum on down, is judged on performance, the plans of
any corporation may tend to become—as a Western author once remarked—"havens of conservatism and of insufficient achievement."[9]
Operational managers are inclined to set the lowest goals acceptable
to their superiors, and therefore comprehensive planning may, as the
same author remarks, lead to "the lowest common denominator of
individual experiences rather than the true potential of improvement
for growth." Last but not least, in any big corporation, a danger con-
tinually exists that operational responsibilities will tend to drift
toward the top instead of being taken at the appropriate operational
levels.

There are enormous differences in problems, processes, and solutions between the single Soviet "corporate" analogue and the capitalist corporation. For instance, in establishing tasks, planning, and criteria of performance, a multi-product or a single-product commercial
corporation has an obviously simpler job than does a state "corporation" embracing *all* types of necessarily interrelated industrial activi-

ties. General Motors, say, focuses on one final commodity, the auto-mobile, and its divisions are all geared toward the same market. Complexity within a single all-embracing corporation necessitates, first of all, a determination of the pace at which the overall objectives are to be pursued (e.g., "catching up and surpassing" more advanced economies), an allocation of resources among sectors and branches, and a priority scale for all the goals involved.

Secondly, in a capitalist corporation, short-term or intermediate planning may truly start from below. According to P. F. Drucker at General Motors, for instance, each division submits its estimates of sales, costs, and capital requirements for the year ahead, under the assumptions of a good, an average, and a bad year for the industry as a whole. The central management correlates these estimates, checks them against the analyses of the company's economics re-search staff, and then establishes a broad "objective frame for the work of the members both of central and divisional management."[10] In the Soviet system of edict management, plan formulation starts from both the top and the bottom. It is based first of all on produc-tion possibilities and their corresponding input requirements—par-ticularly for expanding capital goods and military production ac-cording to the policy-makers' priorities—and subsidiarily only, on consumers' demand. The final plan essentially consists of centrally determined, obligatory indices and methodological instructions di-rected to the system's actuators—i.e., the divisional and subdivisional management—and through them to the enterprises. The targets es-tablished by the central planners, in both physical and value terms, are theoretically equal to the sum of the targets set for the individual enterprises.

Finally, the capitalist corporation makes use of a number of market-determined criteria, which are independent of its own plans, for mea-suring performance as a producer or seller. Its first gauge as a pro-ducer is base pricing: its core is the analysis of all cost factors that enter into production—return on capital invested, efficiency of opera-tion, lifetime of production equipment, etc.—at various rates of ca-pacity. This "norm" shows whether a good or bad result is attributable to the management or to market changes (viz. demand shifts). The second gauge, which measures the performance of the division (and of the company) as a seller, is the analysis of the competitive standing of the company's products, in terms of their percentage of total market sales in the given price range.[11] In contrast to these two gauges, the Soviet "norms"—in either physical terms or administered cost-price relationships—are of dubious value in ascertaining performance either as a producer or as a seller. The enterprises's complex connections to its tutelary organs—e.g., supervisory managerial agency (such as a ministry), planning board, state budget, state bank—are tailored to its specific needs according to the planned goals. The unification of all economic activities under a single, all-absorbing, edict-managed corporation operating with compulsory instructions for each division, subdivision, or plant, creates a business environment extremely unfavorable for manifestation of initiatives from lower levels.

To remedy the problems of increasing divergences between decisions made above and results achieved below, lack of progress in output techniques, unrealistic prices, poor quality, various decentralization schemes for the redistribution of decision-making power within the Soviet-type corporate analogue have been initiated. Keeping intact the interlocking party-state relationship at the apex of the Soviet corporation and the authority of the trusteeship and general management over any aspects of the activity of the corporation, policy-makers and planners have reshuffled the "actuators" of the enterprises, asked the top divisional management to share in the formulation of production preferences, and invited divisional management to display more initiative within the directive framework. Yet the Soviet mechanism for establishing priorities remains geared basically toward subordination of public or operational management preferences—though in practice the demands of the operational management may sometimes gain ascendency.[12] In other East European countries (for instance, East Germany), decision-making powers at the divisional and subdivisional management levels have been increased significantly. Thus *ad hoc* industrial "amalgamations," integrating various enterprises either horizontally or vertically, were established in East Germany, as we already noted, with wide managerial decision-making powers over outputs, prices, and sales. But decentralization has not been pushed to the point where these amalgamations could function as independent companies loosely controlled by the center acting as a holding company.

In the Soviet corporate analogue, supply and distribution of capital goods remain highly centralized within the "material-technical supply system," nor is freer choice of suppliers and customers at the divisional and subdivisional levels envisaged. Efforts to foster meaningful business relationships among either "competitive" producing firms or retailers therefore remain futile. Finally, no true business relations have been developed between the enterprises and the banking system. Even though, as we saw in the second essay, the central bank (or its subsidiaries) rather than the budget bureau may become more active in pooling and disbursing investable resources, the criteria for allocating those resources are still predetermined by the physical plan. No matter what redistribution of decision-making power has occurred, decentralization is not being pushed to the point where a difference arises between the central goals and the explicit goals of the divisional or subdivisional management; the lower ranges of management cannot overturn decisions of the general management. In contrast, such a situation is possible in a capitalist corporation, both because the decisions of the subdivisional management may be based on market criteria and because alternative sources of supply are usually open to any customer, including the government itself.

Finally, while the Soviet centrally directed system lacks central labor planning and leaves the individual free to move from job to job, it does, however, attempt to set rigid rules for employment policies and for manpower requirements. Binding regulations concerning costs and prices narrow sharply the sphere of decentralization and individual responsibility in the Soviet corporate analogue. The trade unions themselves have been reduced to the role of company unions, and Lenin's vision of "workers' control" over managerial decisions at any level has, in fact, vanished without a trace.

## YUGOSLAV SOLUTIONS IN MANAGEMENT PROBLEMS

Having experimented with the Soviet system of the all-embracing corporation and discerned its strengths as well as its weaknesses,

Yugoslavia gradually shifted to decentralized guided-market social-ism through a number of reforms in the 1950's. However, Czecho-slovakia's short, rapid preparation for decentralization during the first eight months of 1968, cut short by the Soviet intervention, shows that in principle, given the Yugoslav model, changes can probably be effected much faster when sufficiently strong socio-economic and political pressures accumulate within the socialist society. Pivotal in the Yugoslav reforms were the weakening and final dissolution of the interlocking relationship between political and economic power, characteristic of the Soviet-type corporate organization. The enter-prises—state, collectively owned, and privately owned but authorized to develop within narrow ranges—were released from the multiple bonds which held them together inside the "single corporation." Within general limits set for all by the law concerning overall market environment, the enterprises have been freed from the tutelage of central controlling bodies: specifically, the central planning board, whose responsibilities henceforth relate only to the economic policies of the government, and whose targets may differ from the targets of the enterprises or from their sum (except in a highly aggregated sense, such as the rate of growth of the gross national product); state supervisory agencies (e.g., ministries, administrations, etc.) and their orders concerning inputs, outputs, prices, suppliers, distributors, etc.; the state budget bureau divested of overall control of investments; the state bank, reduced to a bank of issue and relieved of its previous position of a hybrid acting both as a quasi-commercial bank and a central accounting unit of the entire economy. Accordingly, this kind of decentralization in economic decision-making has meant freedom from "vertical" orders, direct "horizontal" relations among all enter-prises through a market-like arrangement, freedom of association among any enterprises in any economically expedient or efficient manner, and freedom to establish true business relations with *ad hoc* commercial banks spawned by the state-owned enterprises them-selves.

Decentralization along these lines in a socialist state, in which an overwhelming share of the industrial output is produced by state-owned enterprises, raises a number of fundamental questions: By whom should these enterprises be managed? How should the managers be selected? By whom and how should the managers be controlled? The Yugoslav answer to these questions since the early 1950's has been embodied in the system of "workers' self-management." This system rests on the principles of separation between ownership and management, "equal rights" for all members of a working organization to participate proportionally in all decision-making, and progressive elimination "of any intermediary between the worker, free and associated, and his product."[13] The Yugoslavs have stated that they have aimed at more than the simple replacement of edict management in an all-embracing Soviet-like single corporation by an expedient form of management. They have attempted to democratize decision-making both by stressing the right of each worker to participate directly in management and by stimulating the will to eliminate any middle agent between workers and their product. "When we refer to statism and to keeping investment within reasonable bounds and patterns," notes a Yugoslav writer, "we are introducing an intermediary between the worker, free and associated, and his product. It matters little whether the intermediary is the absolute monarch of pre-capitalist days, the bourgeoisie in the capitalist system, or the state, or whether it is a revolutionary government or party, in socialism."[14] The whole issue of self-management, it is worth emphasizing, is basically a political one, since the decisions about the "workers' product" evidently raise the key questions about the saving rate and the control over the composition of final demand.

The Yugoslavs decided that each enterprise, created by socio-political communities or organizations, by other enterprises, or by the citizens, will be managed by those gainfully employed in it (its "labor collective"). In small enterprises (up to thirty workers), the collective exercises it sovereignty directly. In larger enterprises, the collective elects a "workers' council" which in turn elects a smaller "management committee" and, with the agreement of the administrative units under whose jurisdiction the plant falls, the committee appoints a director. The director, his assistant manager, engineers, and technicians, carry out the operational managing, subject to the control of the committee and ultimately of the full council.

During the early years of the system's operation, two elements severely hampered the attainment of these objectives: the Communist

League tended to dictate its will through its members in such matters as the selection of the director. Second, the government took away a large share of the factories' "income" (net income after material cost and overhead but before payment of wages), thereby appreciably restricting the latitude of the producers in regard to income distribution and capital formation. Since the mid-1960's, however, the weakening role of the party (and of its satellite organizations) and a sharp reduction in the state's direct share of the "social product" have substantially increased the freedom of the managerial organs of the enterprises to allocate their income as they see fit.

The virtual withdrawal of the party-state organs from the selection of top management has, up to a point, curtailed the abuses of power, nepotism, and arbitrariness that were rampant during the 1950's. However, the conflict within the enterprise between the technical-managerial staff and the worker, which was supposed to be eradicated by the system of "self-management," has not subsided. The managing groups feel that they have their hands tied, while the workers feel unable actually to hire and fire the managers in conformance with their own interpretation of the enterprise's interest and efficiency. According to Yugoslav writers, the alleged equal rights in management have become "a screen to cover the power and domination of the technical managerial staff and their assistants."[15] The workers' councils themselves are "not immune to the weaknesses usually attributed to employers," namely, overlooking "the interests of the workers and their position in production."[16] "Experience has shown," notes a disenchanted Yugoslav commentator, "that attempts to have all workers in an enterprise participate in decision making on all problems, even on those of a professional nature, have failed."[17]

Curtailment of the state's role in the investment field, in general, and reduction of its investment in "political factories" (e.g., in the less-developed regions), in particular, have substantially reduced misallocations and scattering of public funds, and reinforced the idea that "statist" forms of investment and expanded production are not necessarily indispensable for planned guidance of economic development. However, the systematic withdrawal of the state from the investment field, allegedly to eliminate any "intermediary" between the worker and his product and to further the "self-organization of the economy," has had some other interesting consequences. It is not the "worker-producer" but the executive management who decides on the distribution of income and has "the last word on investments"[18]— and this in *vastly different types of enterprises*. The capacity for capital formation, whether among enterprises and branches or among other types of collective organization, regional or local, will tend to vary enormously; however, now no Yugoslav "statist" mechanism may interfere in the process. As a Yugoslav commentator has expressed it, "When most of the funds are left to the direct producers, then their working organization . . . will see to it that it is used in the most rational manner,"[19]—a sententious tautology, since "most rational" means simply "according to the collectives' preferences." In a curious way Stalinism and Titoism converge: at its inception, Stalinism formulated the theory of "socialism in one country," and stressed the idea that, when a number of other "socialist" countries emerged in the world, they would rely autonomously on their own resources whatever their size or endowments might be; Titoism apparently emphasizes "socialism in each [autonomous] collective" whatever its size or resources may be. However, as Edward Kardelj noted, the Yugoslavs certainly do not regard the increasing differences of income and growth potential among socialist enterprises as a "static ideal."[20] There is little idealization of what are alleged to be only inevitable transitional steps toward communism. A number of proposals have already been advanced for both placing management-labor relations on a new footing and counter-balancing at least some of the tensions generated by the exclusive reliance on the economy's own "self-organization" drives. We shall discuss some of these problems further below.

## EDICT MANAGEMENT *VS.* "ASSOCIATIONIST" SOCIALISM

The policy-makers of China, the Soviet Union, and some of the Soviet Union's closest East European allies, on the one hand, and the policy-makers of Yugoslavia and Czechoslovakia, on the other, have tried to improve their respective economic models in significantly different ways. The first experimented with variations of edict-management either within a strongly centralized, single corporation or within a sort of "holding company" of a number of corporations rendered more or less "autonomous." Yugoslavia's changes have centered around market-determined relations within a loosely defined aggregation of fully "autonomous workmen's associations" or collectives—a model which the Yugoslav economist Branko Horvat, following Schumpeter, calls *associationist socialism*.[21] The arguments in the debate and the directions in which the policy-makers of these economies are actually moving can be brought into relief by contrasting the criticisms of associationist socialism by the partisans of edict-management, and vice versa.

The primary criticism lodged by the USSR and its allies against the intended Czech reforms of January–August 1968 concerned the Czech plan to separate the political and economic leadership of the country and to free all enterprises from political tutelage. The Russians accurately recognized in such attempts a shift in effective preferences, along with possible improvements in economic performance—that is, changes on the demand side of a political nature, as well as changes on the supply side influencing the economy's efficiency in the provision of goods and services. The so-called Five-Party Letter, addressed to the Czechs by the leadership of the Bulgarian, East German, Hungarian, Polish, and Soviet Communist parties in July 1968, stated: "We are not interfering in the methods of planning and management of the Socialist national economy of Czechoslovakia and in your actions aiming at improving the structure of the economy and developing Socialist democracy. . . . The might and firmness of our alliance depends on the inner strength of the Socialist system in each of our countries. . . . Hamstringing of the leading role of the Communist Party leads to liquidation of Socialist democracy and the Socialist system. Flouting of any aspect of this principle [of democratic centralism], democracy or centralism serves to weaken the party and its guiding role by transforming the party into either a bureaucratic organization or debating club."[22]

If for the Russians the crux of the matter is maintaining the "centralized" influence of the party "on the course of the basic processes of development of the national economy"[23] without precluding eventual changes in planning and management methods, for the Chinese any departure from edict-management is "harmful." They reject *in toto* any intended Soviet changes in the original model of management. In their criticism of Yugoslavia's socialism, which they call "a state capitalist economy of a peculiar type," the Chinese assert that systemic "degeneration" has occurred there because of the "dissolution of the unified system of planned economy, the locking in fierce competition of all the economic departments and enterprises . . . under the signboard 'workers' self-government,' " the stressing of production "for profits instead of the needs of all members of the society," the determination of the product mix in accord with "market and not on the basis of the unified state plan of production," etc.[24] Furthermore, bent on "scoring points" against the Soviets, the Chinese add that the Soviet leaders have made up their minds "to learn from the renegade Tito clique," and that the Soviet's reformed system of management of 1965 is but a means "to enforce the capitalist principle of profit and to make profit-seeking the basic motivating force of production,"[25]—an affirmation only partly true.

The Czech, Hungarian, and some Polish reformers reject the notion that disentangling the political leadership from the economic leadership of a socialist country necessarily means "hamstringing" the role of the Communist party. "Disentangling" certainly entails shifts of effective preferences, but the party may nevertheless continue to predominate in determining the broad directions of the country's development. No reformer yet has advocated ending the party's "leadership." Some critics of the Soviet system add further that refusal to transform the system of edict-management is ultimately harmful, costly, and hence totally unwarranted. In their answer to the Five-Party Letter, for instance, the Czech liberal leaders noted: "On the outside it seemed that everything was in order in Czechoslovakia. . . . In actual fact the decline in the confidence in the party was masked by exterior forms of directive party control. Although this regime was given out as being the firm guarantee of the interests of the entire Socialist camp, inside problems were growing within, the real solution of which was suppressed by forceful means against those advocates of new and creative approaches."[26] Improvement in management by edict along the lines discussed in Essay 1—namely reorganization of the various actuators, devolution of certain decision-making upon some managerial strata, reduction in the volume of instructions, and changing of the "key" indicators as well as checking for plan fulfillment through certain market mechanisms—has therefore been rejected by the associationist socialists as totally insufficient, for reasons based on economic experience and modern management, information, and control theory.[27] Even the Soviet "new system"—as amended by what usually goes under the name of "Libermanism"—with its emphasis on the "profit motive" has been criticized by the associationists for its retention of centrally determined quotas, avoidance of price competition by enterprises for productive factors, prevention of meaningful business accounting, and, above all, failure to solve the problems of efficient allocation of resources for the economy as a whole.[28]

The systemic improvements envisaged in Yugoslavia are of a completely different nature from those in the USSR. Their focus is how to create a meaningful countervailing force to the inevitable rising power of the management of the associations—free now to handle the bulk of the investable resources of the country—without imperiling their efficient functioning or resorting to statist controls. Among the solutions suggested have been the election of the managers within each enterprise by the workers only, rather than by all the gainfully employed, and the strengthening of the trade unions.

The partisans of a system of self-management by the workers only wish to replace the present order of management, since they believe that effective democratization could obtain only if the workers alone were empowered to act "as independent entrepreneurs and employers of the technical managerial staff and their auxiliary services,"[29] in somewhat the fashion suggested by Lenin before and immediately after the Russian revolution. On the other hand, those who advocate strengthening the trade unions wish to maintain the prevailing system of management by all "associated producers," provided that an already-existing countervailing force within the enterprises namely, the trade union, is set free from the bonds of party and state tutelage, to interpret as it sees fit the "principles of self management and socialist distribution of income."[30]

Actually, regardless of the fact, that in the present system, management is alleged to be "their own," the Yugoslav workers have already gone on strike repeatedly in support of their wage demands or related causes. The general conclusion which seems to emerge from the experiment with "self-management by all producers" is that this or any similar "self-management" system which does not generate solidarity between management and the workers cannot both insure efficiency and avoid alienation. Only a broad and genuine democratization, achievable through the recognition of the "pluralist" character of modern society and the rights of all its interest groups to organize freely and assert their interests, would seem able to reconcile and approach those apparently conflicting, elusive goals.

## ASSESSMENT OF SOCIALIST MANAGEMENT AND ITS FUTURE

Engels' forecasted withering away of the "government of persons" and its replacement by "the administration of things" have not come into sight anywhere in the socialist camp. The Soviet writers confidently assert now that the idea of noninterference of the communist or workers' parties in the state, economic, or ideological life of a socialist country is simply bourgeois ideology. Communist construction gives rise to such an "upsurge of creative activity," writes an official Soviet commentator, that "the constant growth of the guiding role of the proletarian party is one of the most important social laws."[31] Lenin's prediction about the demise of management "as the special function of a special stratum of the population" has also come to a sore pass. According to the Soviet mathematical economist Iu. I. Cherniak, management in the industrially developed countries has become "the largest industry, employing, as a rule, more than 10 per cent of the entire working population." And Cherniak correctly adds "that the raw material processed by this industry is information; that the product it turns out is decisions; and that its technological process is reduced to obtaining, conveying and processing information."[32] Cherniak's round figure for the specialized managerial stratum in the Soviet Union exceeds twelve million people in the mid-1960's. Only the Chinese continue to contend that management is not a specialized function and that their managers must take part "not only in mental labor, but also in physical labor with workers"; China's unchanging policy is "to turn intellectuals into people capable of manual labor, and laboring people into cultured people."[33] All this helps to justify not only theoretical constancy, but the application of tremendous pressures against wage differentials to keep up the share of investment in the material product.

If the Soviet all-inclusive "corporation" did not turn out to be the automated "single factory" envisaged by Lenin, neither has the Proudhonesque "workers' self-management" in Yugoslavia become a libertarian democracy for all—except perhaps in the enterprises where the workers' council has coincided with the whole body of the employed. In all other situations, the workers have soon felt alienated from their elected representatives; innumerable conflicts have arisen concerning conditions of production, labor relations among workers (including hiring, firing, and job assignments), planning of production, and income distribution. Moreover, the workers' councils consist in fact of foremen, managers, and other executives. Since the early elections in the 1950's through the 1960's the vocational characteristics of elected members of workers' councils have not changed at all: highly-skilled and skilled workers and office staff with higher education or secondary school certifications "account for nearly two-thirds of the total number," states a Yugoslav source. Out of some 2.1 million gainfully employed in the early 1960's, the same source points out, over 212 thousand persons—roughly 10 per cent—were elected to workers' councils, and a third of them manned the higher managing boards.[34] On the other hand, as was probably unavoidable after the closing down of inefficient plants and the policy-makers' efforts to integrate Yugoslavia into the world-wide division of labor, thousands of unskilled workers who had migrated toward the cities in the era of "political factories" had to be dismissed in the mid-1960's and were forced either to return against their wishes to their villages to try to earn a living off the land or to go abroad to work—an important Yugoslav safety valve.

The Chinese and some Cuban revolutionaries have tried to avoid these dilemmas by basing their socialism on a curious idealization of the economic significance of poor and unskilled labor. They affirm that the "law of value," which is an euphemism for the utilization of rational cost-price calculations, kills socialism and drives the economy back to capitalism. "Is politics or welfare in command?" rhetorically ask the Chinese, who constantly reiterate that the revisionists alone have "welfare" at heart. The late Che Guevara affirmed for his part that "work . . . differs and is independent of labor productivity, because productivity primarily depends on production means," and that accordingly, "a person who cuts sugarcane must be paid higher wages than highly qualified industrial workers, since the former performs physically harder work and since his work productivity is not important."[35] Neither the Yugoslavs nor the Russians brook such "romanticism," though the Russians exploit the fear of unemployment of the unskilled when they attack the partisans of liberal socialism. Thus, when criticizing the January–August 1968 Czech regime, the Russians noted that planned (administrative) socialism indeed gave employment to all and absorbed vast pools of unskilled labor, whereas guided-market socialism may breed unemployment, highly reward the managers, and subvert socialism. To this declaration, of course, the reformers answered that edict-management, improved or not, does not eliminate "negative phenomena," such as disproportions in the economy, obstacles to efficient output, disguised unemployment, etc.; it only hides them behind new orders and liquidates dissenters.

Dilemmas in socialist industrial management thus run a very wide gamut. Neither the search for an "optimally functioning economic system" or for "optimal planning" nor the experiments with countervailing forces within "self-managed" enterprises have yielded satisfactory and stable operational results. The idea that a unified single-corporation form would automatically solve all the problems of a socialist state is ailing if not dead, notwithstanding Chinese efforts to keep it alive and healthy. What can replace it are pragmatic experiments which will tend to vary from country to country and from period to period even more than they do now. As C. Bobrowsky once stated with reference to the Polish debates on the socialist economic model, "These discussions have demonstrated that a search for proper forms of planning and management is not merely a question of correcting past mistakes. On the contrary, in a socialist economy, such changes must have a character of a continuous process if only because of the fact that forms of economic management must correspond to each successive phase of development."[36] The socialist camp, once proud of its industrial achievements through Stalinist edict-management, now wades through the disproportions and tensions it engendered, with increasing doubts and uncertainties, toward heterogeneity —toward divergence rather than convergence on some pre-established model.

# [ CHAPTER 5 ]

## Uneasy Symbiosis in Land Tenancy

THE CRUCIAL importance for economic growth of the patterns of output, consumption, and savings in agriculture, and the system of land tenure underlying them, has long since been obvious to policy-makers in underdeveloped countries. What has been perhaps less obvious is that the economic-technological problem of advancing agricultural production by modern techniques and the socio-economic problem of the peasantry—its traditionalist values and motivation, low productivity, low standard of living and so on—are distinct problems which may require different though interrelated, approaches and solutions. Edward Kardelj perceptively noted with reference to Yugoslavia, tha' the question of the peasantry "cannot be solved automatically merely by advocating new technology." It involves the "whole economic and social development of the village,"[1] which is, in turn, dependent on a number of factors. Among these, of crucial significance is the availability of employment opportunities outside agriculture.

With its wide diversity in levels of development among countries and regions, with its wide disparities in growth rates between industry and agriculture, with its marked differences between the towns and the countryside, East-Central Europe is a unique meeting-ground of the crucial dilemmas in land tenancy which face most of the less-developed countries of the world. In the interwar years, the area suffered in varying degrees the perennial problems of agrarian countries: unequal distribution of landownership, widespread small-scale subsistence holdings, high population pressures in the villages, disguised and overt rural unemployment, and low absorptive capacity in industry for rural labor. Technological advances were limited to the up-to-date agrotechnical methods adopted in only a few privately-owned, large-scale "model" farms and certain smaller farms, ranging from about 30 to 50 hectares (1 hectare = 2.47 acres), that contributed a significant part of their output to the market. On smaller units hardly any advances were introduced. In most of the area, the policy-makers fought an unending battle against continuous fragmentation of land into uneconomical "dwarf" units—too small for application of any but the most backward agricultural techniques, insufficient to support a family, and, *a fortiori,* unable to supply the market with any produce. In many of the countries of the area—notably Poland, Rumania, Yugoslavia, and Bulgaria—population pressures and lack of urban employment opportuniites accelerated land fragmentation in spite of various prohibitive provisions in the post-World War I land reforms. In these latter countries particularly, a shifting landownership structure in the countryside was constantly inflating the already oversized group of inefficient, backward, highly indebted dwarf holdings, and continuously depressing further the notoriously poor performance of this sector.[2]

The structure of land tenure and ownership presented a substantial diversity from one region or country to the next. In three countries—Czechoslovakia, Poland, and Hungary—domains of over 100 hectares made up only 0.5–0.6 per cent of the total number of agricultural holdings but accounted for 41–45 per cent of the farmland acreage. Territorial displacements after World War II partially changed these basic data only in Poland, which lost its regions with predominant latifundia and forests to the Soviet Union, but acquired formerly German regions where estates of over 100 hectares still covered one-third of the farmland area. In tiny, isolated Albania, the structure of ownership was far less lopsided toward latifundia: large landowners and the state held jointly only some 16 per cent of the cultivable land in 1938. However, the relations in the countryside and in the country at large were extremely primitive, a pastoral pre-market economy prevailing in the villages. By contrast, in Bulgaria and Yugoslavia, holdings of over 50 hectares—0.1 per cent of the total number of holdings in Bulgaria and 0.5 per cent in Yugoslavia—covered, respectively, only 1.6 per cent and 9.7 per cent of the total cultivable land. In those two countries the process of expropriation of big landholdings and their "parcelization" to landless peasants and small landowners had already been carried to extremes: in certain regions the process had been underway for more than a century and had entered into its last phases before the end of the pre-World War II period. Finally, the landownership structure in Rumania held a somewhat intermediary position between that in Poland and that in Yugoslavia and Bulgaria: properties of over 100 hectares covered over 27.7 per cent of the cultivable acreage within the prewar boundaries and 21.6 per cent in the postwar boundaries. However, in Rumania, too, successive land reforms had dissolved most of the large estates and the traditional socio-economic relations in the countryside.

Notwithstanding these differences from one country or region to the next, the Communists claimed that the "liquidation of feudalistic remnants" in all landownership throughout Eastern Europe required sweeping reforms along substantially the same lines in all the countries. If one equates "feudal remnants" to the concentration of a considerable part of the cultivable land within a relatively small number of large estates—"large" being also a relative magnitude within different countries—then one may speak of "feudal remnants" in the agricultural land tenures of Czechoslovakia, Poland, and Hungary—though one should also note that these remnants have, in some cases, facilitated the introduction of modern agricultural methods, particularly in Czechoslovakia and Hungary. However, one cannot say, under the same definition, that "feudal remnants" had any real significance amidst the fragmented farmlands of most of Yugoslavia and all of Bulgaria. In those two countries, and up to a point in Rumania, land reforms and parceling could only perpetuate the fractionation of an already subdivided landownership. On the other hand, if one uses the term "feudal remants" to refer broadly to "pre-market"-determined relationships in the countryside—relationships based on non-market customs, traditions, and sometimes specific obligations toward the landowners, along with weak and sporadic economic encounters between the peasants and the towns—then, such "feudal remnants" were certainly strong not only in countries with large landowner-ships like Poland and Hungary, but also in the least-developed countries of the area, including Albania, Rumania, Yugoslavia, and, up to a point, Bulgaria.

The Communists attacked the intertwined economic-technological and socio-economic problems of the area in a roundabout way. They deliberately postponed economic-technological advances and dealt first and foremost with the size-structure of private holdings, re-lationships among various nationality groups in the countryside, and ratios of private to public holdings. Under the appealing slogan, "Land to the Tillers," they aimed not only at parceling some lands and "winning over the peasants" but also at substituting "social ownership" for private-estate ownership whenever possible, thus setting the stage for a later, more complex round of reforms of socio-economic and economic-technological conditions.

In this essay I propose to examine the Communist economic policies in Eastern Europe during the land reforms (1945–49), during the col-lectivization drive (1950–60), and after the virtual completion of collectivization in most of these countries, with continuous attention to the evolving relationships between large-scale and small-scale (peasant) farming and to their prospects. In the first three sections of the essay I shall deal with the different emphases which the land re-forms have had: those which aimed primarily at the mass coloniza-tion of former German lands—in Czechoslovakia and Poland; those which aimed primarily at liquidating "feudal remnants" of all types—in Hungary and Albania; and those which had to deal with relatively little remaining land for either colonization (as in Czechoslovakia and Poland) or latifundia liquidation (as in Hungary, in particular)—in Rumania, Yugoslavia, and Bulgaria. In the fourth section, I shall sum-marize the consequences of all these reforms as far as the structure of landownership is concerned and indicate the common characteristics of the reforms, notwithstanding their differences in emphasis. In the fifth section, I shall examine the processes of collectivization and the rationale behind the differences in implementation which arose, notably in Yugoslavia and Poland, on the one hand, and the rest of the area, on the other. Finally in the last section, I shall describe the uneasy symbiosis between large-scale farming and household plots and the dilemmas facing the socialist organizers of the agricultural sector in their efforts to cope both with the requisites of economic technological changes in large-scale farming and with the intricate socio-economic problems of the peasantry with its individual small-scale plots.

## MASS COLONIZATION

Mass colonization of former German and Hungarian areas—the Sudeten lands of western Czechoslovakia, southern Slovakia, and formerly German-settled areas in the newly acquired western territories of Poland—played an overwhelming role in the Czechoslovakian and Polish land reforms after World War II.

Prior to the liberation of Czechoslovakia from the Nazis, the "radical solution" of minority problems in the border regions was embodied in the "Košice Program," which called for confiscation of all the land belonging to the enemy "minority groups," both German and Hungarian. As the liberation was effected, all agricultural property belonging to persons of German and Hungarian nationality, as well as that of traitors and enemies of the Czechoslovak Republic, was seized and, except for the forests which were taken over by the state, the land thus acquired was allotted to "persons of Slav nationality."[3] This so-called national purge of the Czech lands left, on the one hand, large-scale ownership of land by Czech and Slovak nationals untouched, and on the other hand, completely liquidated not only German-owned estates but also medium and small peasant holdings owned by Germans.[4] Subsequently, a second reform, adopted in 1947,[5] extended the revision of landownership to include any landed property of over 150 hectares of agricultural land (or over 250 hectares of land exempt from sequestration during the prewar land reforms). Later still, in 1948, a bill, called the "New Land Reform Act," fixed the maximum amount of land to be owned by a "working farmer and his family" at 50 hectares, the rest to be purchased by the state.[6]

These three phases of the Czechoslovak land reforms involved 3,050,000 hectares, 940,000 hectares, and about 130,000 hectares, respectively. In the first phase alone—the colonization phase—ownership of over 2,500,000 hectares in the Czech lands and over 550,000 hectares in Slovakia was transferred, representing 36.5 per cent and 11.4 per cent of the total agricultural and forest areas of these regions. During this phase, over one million hectares were transferred in the border regions to 122,000 families of Slav settlers. In the other two phases only 105,000 hectares were parceled out to some 100,000 beneficiaries. Concomitantly with colonization and parcelization, the state substantially expanded its own holdings of both arable land and forests (Table 5.1).

TABLE 5.1. LAND CONFISCATED AND PARCELED OUT IN THE 1945–49
LAND REFORMS IN SOME EAST EUROPEAN COUNTRIES[a]

| COUNTRIES | CULTIVATED LAND[b] AND FORESTS AND WOODLANDS (*in* 1000 *hectares*) | | | RATIOS | | BENEFICIARIES |
|---|---|---|---|---|---|---|
| | (1) Total | (2) Con-fiscated | (3) Parcel-ized | (2):(1) × 100 | (3):(2) × 100 | |
| Czechoslovakia | 17.098 | 4.120 | 1.105 | 24.09 | 26.80 | 222.000 |
| Poland | | | | | | |
| West. ter. | 9.242 | 7.166 | 3.685 | 77.50 | 51.40 | 601.500 |
| Old ter. | 18.222 | 3.089 | 2.384 | 16.95 | 77.10 | 466.900 |
| Hungary | 8.602 | 3.225 | 1.900 | 37.40 | 58.90 | 642.000 |
| Rumania | 21.117 | 1.962 | 1.109 | 9.29 | 56.50 | 860.000 |
| Yugoslavia | 21.815 | 1.566 | .797 | 7.17 | 50.89 | 316.415 |
| Bulgaria | 5.097 | .165 | .120 | 3.23 | 72.70 | c |
| Total | 101.193 | 21.293 | 11.100 | 21.04 | 52.10 | c |

[a] For underlying sources, see textual footnotes and the national statistical handbooks for each country.
[b] Arable land, gardens, orchards, vineyards, meadows, pastures.
[c] Data not available.

Like those in Czechoslovakia, the Polish land reforms aimed primarily, though not exclusively, at mass colonization. A decree promulgated in the fall of 1944[7] provided for the confiscation of land owned by citizens of the Reich not of Polish nationality by origin as well as that of Polish citizens claiming German nationality, by traitors, and by corporate entities whose holdings exceeded 100 hectares. The properties of the Church were excluded from the reform until the spring of 1950. Moreover, a special decree provided for the confiscation of forests and woodlands with an area of over 25 hectares, together with all real estate and movables utilized in forestry.[8] The reform affected 13,846,000 hectares of land, of which 10,255,000 hectares were agricultural and forest land. Of these, 7,100,000 hectares were in the newly acquired territories, and 3,089,000 hectares (of which one-fourth was German land) were in the former Polish territories (Table 5.1). In western Poland, over 3,600,000 hectares were distributed to 601,000 new Polish settlers, most of whom were repatriates from eastern Poland and landless peasants from the rest of Poland, families of demobilized soldiers and farm hands.[9] In central Poland the land reform involved 2,300,000 hectares (of which 779,000 hectares were formerly German owned), allotted to 466,000 farms—some of them new farms and some existing dwarf, small, or medium farms which were expanded. The newly created farms accounted for roughly one-third of all peasant farms in Poland. Notwithstanding the availability of land for parcelization in the western territories and the relatively comfortable allotments there for new settlers, many of the peasants on dwarf farms remained attached to their traditional locations in the former Polish provinces and shunned transfer to the west. Thus the expulsion of the German population facilitated the creation of a large stratum of medium-sized peasant holdings in the West, without, however, fully relieving rural overpopulation in the old Polish provinces.[10]

## LIQUIDATION OF FEUDAL REMNANTS

Liquidation of the area's most obtrusive "feudal" vestiges—of large, plurisecular estates in Hungary, and of pastoral, clan, and traditionalist "pre-capitalist" relationships in Albania—was one of the primary goals of the land reforms in those two countries.

In Hungary, the relative share of the large estates in the total farm-land acreage continued to increase rather than diminish during the interwar years. In pre-World War I Hungary, estates of over 100 hectares covered 30.6 per cent of the farmland; in the early interwar period, in 1921, they covered 41.1 per cent of the farmland; in 1935, 43.1 per cent. Privately owned estates of over 500 hectares represented 17.1 per cent of the total farmland acreage; those of over 1700 hectares, 11.5 per cent of the total farmland acreage. The post-World War I land reform in Hungary was the most restricted in scope in Eastern Europe since it could not involve vast landholdings of non-nationals, as it could in the "successor" states. In Hungary, the prewar reform encompassed only some 600,000 hectares, of which less than 400,000 hectares were actually parceled out. The post-World War II reform, introduced in the spring of 1945,[11] provided for the confiscation and transfer into a state land-fund of any estate—including Church estates—exceeding 1000 "cadastral holds" (575 hectares). Also to be confiscated were the estates of Germans, traitors, and collaborators. The reform this time affected a total of 3,200,000 hectares of agricultural and forest land, of which some 1,900,000 hectares were rapidly parceled out to 642,000 claimants. The latifundia were thus annihilated. By 1947, only 21 private properties in the whole country were as large as the new legal maximum of roughly 180 hectares each, and none surpassed this limit. The large estates of the Church, which before the war extended over more than one million cadastral acres, were reduced to less than one-fifth of that amount.[12]

In tiny Albania, of some 1,204,800 hectares of agricultural land (some 42 per cent of Albania's surface), the land in use, excluding woodland, amounted to only 393,000 hectares, of which, before World War II, 3.7 per cent was in the hands of seven big landlord families, 12.7 per cent in the hands of the state, 23.2 per cent in the hands of "rich" peasants, and the rest in the hands of poor peasants. The postwar land reform, in some respects patterned after a 1929 land reform which had never been implemented, affected a total of 155,159 hectares, close to 39 per cent of the total land in use at the time. Private holdings above 40 hectares, belonging to some 19,000 landowners, were expropriated in whole or in part, and some 70,000 families, from a total of 147,000 landholders for the entire country, benefited in various measure from the land parcelization.[13]

## LIMITED LAND REFORMS

Comparatively more limited in scope, the post-World War II land reforms in Bulgaria, Yugoslavia, and Rumania involved, respectively, only 3 per cent, 7 per cent, and 9 per cent of the agricultural and forest area. Those countries had only a relatively small land-fund available for colonization, and, furthermore, they had carried out important land reforms after World War I.

The reform introduced in Rumania in the spring of 1945[14] provided for the expropriation of the lands of German nationals, traitors, and absentee landowners, all properties greater than 50 hectares "which have not been cultivated during the last seven years by their owners themselves," and private holdings in excess of 50 hectares. The estates of the king and the royal family were excepted from the 1945 reform, but at the end of 1947, they were transferred to the state, after the abdication of the king and the proclamation of the republic. Some hundred-odd "model farms" or "agricultural centers," each extending up to 150 hectares, were left to private owners for the production of selected seeds, breeding of thoroughbred animals, etc. These, along with various other holdings, were subsequently labeled "feudal sabotage nests" and were expropriated in the spring of 1949.[15] The 1945 reforms affected 143,000 estates, corresponding to 1,468,000 hectares, of which 1,109,000 hectares were parceled out to 860,000 claimants. The 1947 and 1949 reforms involved the confiscation of close to 500,000 hectares which were added to the state-owned lands.[16]

In Yugoslavia, land reform became law in the summer of 1945.[17] The new constitution limited the arable acreage per holding from 25 to 35 hectares, according to the region, and the total acreage per holding to 45 hectares. Areas exceeding 3 hectares were taken away from those who did not cultivate the land themselves. The reforms liquidated without compensation the large estates of private landowners, land corporations, and banks. Churches and monasteries were allowed 10–30 hectares of arable land and up to 30 hectares of forest area. In Yugoslavia, too, the German settlers were expelled. Notwithstanding these drastic measures, the total land expropriated amounted to only 1,566,000 hectares (far less than after World War I), of which 637,000 hectares represented formerly German-owned land. Of the total, 797,000 hectares were distributed among some 316,000 families of poor, landless peasants and new settlers from other areas.[18]

Finally in Bulgaria, the last of any of the Eastern European countries to need a land reform of the type described above, the reform was designed to liquidate the "big *capitalist* landed property."[19] In accordance with the land reform law, 45,000 hectares were taken from 2,450 "large" owners—18.5 hectares per "large" owner—and 120,000 hectares from the landed properties of the Church and monasteries; of this total of 165,000 hectares, 120,000 hectares were parceled out. The end result was an increase in the already numerous dwarf and small holdings, with a concomitant reduction in the number of holdings exceeding 10 hectares.[20]

## COMMON CHARACTERISTICS OF LAND REFORMS

If these land reforms differed in emphasis from one group of countries to another, they did, nonetheless, have two common characteristics: first, in all the countries of the area, the reforms led to significant expansions in state landholdings; second, in all the countries of the area, substantial numbers of landless peasants could not accede to landownership either because the state was unable or considered it inexpedient to make more land available for parcelization or because the peasants themselves refused to be settled in areas other than those in which they had always lived.

Summarizing these reforms, we may note several basic results. (1) The land reforms affected over 21 per cent of the total agricultural and woodland areas (21,000,000 hectares). However, over 48 per cent of this total was within new Polish boundaries and was attributable to the mass colonization of former German lands. Furthermore, Czechoslovakia, Poland, and Hungary together accounted for 82 per cent of the total land involved in the reforms, the other countries, where the reforms had a more limited scope, for only 18 per cent (see Table 5.1). Mass colonization of "alien" landholdings is typical in any process of "nation building" by successor states; it occurred particularly in Rumania and Yugoslavia after World War I and in Poland and Czechoslovakia after World War II, where the German-held lands became pivotal in land reforms. Communist policies—in Poland, for instance—did not differ in this respect from the "bourgeois" policies after World War I in the rest of Eastern Europe.

(2) Compared to the post-World War I land reforms, the new reforms encompassed a larger land area only in Poland and Hungary. In Bulgaria, Yugoslavia, and Rumania the mass of land expropriated and redistributed was smaller than that after World War I. The same was

true for Czechoslovakia, although there a substantial part of the land expropriated after World War I was actually returned to its previous owners. In Albania, no land reform had occurred in the interwar years.

(3) The immediate effects on the size structure of private holdings were the following: the "consuming units," up to 5 hectares, accounted for as much as 70 to 85 per cent of the total, except in Poland where they accounted for roughly 60 per cent; the medium-sized exploitation, from 5 to 10 hectares, accounted for 10 to 20 per cent of the total; the medium-large and large holdings, corresponding to ranges of 10 to 20 hectares and 20 to 50 hectares, remained significant only in Czechoslovakia, Poland, and, to a lesser extent, Yugoslavia.

(4) The respective shares of these groups in the total private agricultural lands became as follows: the consuming units covered from 25 to 35 per cent of this land in the countries of the area except Hungary and Albania, where they accounted for over 50 per cent; the medium-sized holdings occupied from 30 to 40 per cent of this land in all the East European countries; medium-large and large holdings remained truly significant only in Czechoslovakia, Poland, and Yugoslavia.[21] The redistribution of land led not only to a significant increase in the number of dwarf holdings but also to the spread of consuming units.

While being responsible for the further fragmentation of the land, the reforms also allowed a marked expansion of the public domain. The relative share of the state in the total agricultural and woodland areas now exceeded the combined shares previously taken by private estates greater than 50 hectares and by the old public domain. Therefore, the relative share of land held by all private farms diminished rather than expanded at the end of the 1940's, even though there were more landholders. The new public domain henceforth included virtually all the forests and an augmented share of the agricultural land. As in industry, where the "commanding heights" had been nationalized, so in agriculture, a state-owned core of large-scale undertakings arose among a vast number of private or peasant small-scale undertakings. But there the analogy stops: in industry, small-scale industries have depended strongly on the machines, tools, and even raw materials which the nationalized core has made available to them, whereas in agriculture, peasant endeavors have depended limitedly on the selected seeds, pedigreed livestock, fodder, and marketing services of large-scale farms but strongly and directly on certain products of industry and the towns. The expansion of the state farms had other purposes than to provide assistance for small-scale agricultural undertakings. Rather it was directed toward the immediate establishment of new divisions of labor in the countryside to supplant private farming in various ways and eventually to create the conditions for decisive technological advances in agriculture.

## THE COLLECTIVIZATION PROCESSES

Once in power and therefore in a position to formulate their own ambitious plans for industrialization, the Communists in the East European countries abandoned their policy of land parceling and concentrated their efforts on effecting a number of new economic institutional and technological changes which they considered indispensable for a sustained industrialization and urbanization drive. They attempted first to cooperativize and then collectivize the villages, to appropriate most of the land from peasant tenancy, and thus to acquire a large share of the marketed grain at a lower cost to the state than would obtain if private tenancy prevailed. Additionally they wanted to prepare conditions for eventual large-scale cultivation, mechanization, and electrification in the agricultural sector as a whole.

The first wave of reorganization, however, ran into a number of serious snags much sooner than had been expected. Yugoslavia, which was then struggling with the consequences of its break with the Soviet Union, halted its collectivization process in 1953. The other countries ran into various difficulties in the early or mid-1950's, and Poland, which could not easily collectivize its newly settled western territories, was finally forced to halt its drive in 1957.[22] After the short and uncertain respite of the "New Course" (1953–54), the rest of the countries renewed their efforts to complete collectivization. The goal was finally reached in these latter countries by the end of the 1950's. Cooperativization and collectivization of the countryside were thus finally accomplished in roughly a decade.

The extension of state controls over peasant agriculture was considered essential both for raising certain agricultural crops and for determining consumption, investment, and overall savings in the countryside, since the latter were crucial variables in the indusrtial plans. Expansion of grain outputs was to be secured by introducing mechanization onto the state farms and cooperativized lands. The patterns of consumption and investment were to be modified by transformation of collectivized peasants into residual claimants to their collective output. Under the conditions of deliberate emphasis on producer goods and the ensuing severe scarcity of consumer goods, the policy-makers believed that higher prices alone could not stimulate a noncollectivized peasantry to market enough of their grain output to sustain rapid industrialization and urbanization. Furthermore, the policy-makers obviously assumed that, until the domestic producer goods sector was able to revolutionize the technology of both the light industries supplying the countryside and agriculture itself, collectivization of the countryside would be the only effective means to ready the countryside for new techniques and eventual mechanization and to squeeze sufficient agricultural produce out of the villages.

The gigantic process of cooperativization and collectivization throughout the whole of socialist Eastern Europe relentlessly drew into its vortex some 30 per cent of the population of East Germany, 50 to 60 per cent of the population of Czechoslovakia, Hungary, and Poland, and close to 80 per cent of the population of Albania, Rumania, and Yugoslavia. Over the course of the 1950's, some thirty million agricultural workers were forced to reorganize both their lives and their property. The drive developed along two main axes: the isolation, restriction, and elimination of the "rich" peasants, and the collectivization of the rest of the peasantry gradually enough to avoid the terrible consequences of the Soviet Union's swifter collectivization in the early 1930's (viz., massive destruction of livestock and a sharp drop in agricultural output).

As the policy-makers' industrialization objectives became more and more ambitious and as their impatience with "lagging" deliveries from the countryside increased, the policy of isolation and restriction and of forcing the "rich" peasants to hand over their grain "surpluses" was replaced simply by their ejection from the land. In some countries, "rich" holdings were defined, without qualification or consideration, as holdings above 25 hectares, then above 15 hectares, then above 10 hectares. As the drive progressed, even holdings of less than 8 hectares were branded as "large," and the term "rich peasants" was alleged—in Hungary under Rukosi—to apply to a "state of mind" rather than to a socio-economic status. As taxation on the "rich" holdings steeply increased, the owners sought escape by secretly selling or leasing their land, by liquidating their livestock, by seeking jobs in the towns to pay their land taxes, or by surrendering the land to the state, which then often had to leave it fallow as more and more peasants sought refuge in factories from the harsh conditions prevailing in the countryside.

In principle, a flexible program was to be devised and implemented to draw the small- and, particularly, the medium-landed peasants into collectives. While it is easy to lure the landless and the poor peasants into such organizations—particularly if the state endows the newly formed collectives with land and capital—it is not so easy to attract the medium-landed peasant, who is attached to his own farm. In theory, the policy toward them was to be entirely different from that toward the rich peasants: it was to be a policy of patience and persuasion, designed to cajole them into a voluntary changeover from individual to collective farming. Accordingly, the policy-makers in each country devised "producers' cooperatives" of four basic types. Three transitional, or "lower," types of cooperatives were to prepare the peasants to accede to the fourth, "superior" type of collectives. In the lower-type cooperatives the peasants would, first, jointly till the land while retaining the ownership of their respective plots, draft animals, and implements and receive a share of the crop proportionate to their inputs; second, jointly till the common acreage whose former boundaries had been abolished, the draft animals and the implements alone remaining in private ownership, while the collective would pay rent for the use of the land; and, third, care collectively for both crop and animal production, while the former owner would receive a proportionate rent for his inputs of land, animals, and tools. Finally, these transitional cooperatives would be transformed into the allegedly superior Soviet-type of collectives (*kolkhozy*) where land, major livestock, and implements would belong to the collective and where rent would be abolished as "unearned income."[23] But if, in theory, a wide range of cooperatives was to be presented to the peasants, in practice, in certain countries such as Hungary, the policymakers and their agents in the field were more impatient than their theory intended. The lower types of cooperatives were hardly used as transitions toward the "superior" stage. Peasants were haphazardly organized into this or that type of collective, according to the predilection of the agents, and then "promoted" to either the next or the final stage depending upon the administrative pressures received from the center. In some years either plain bungling or changes in plans increased these pressures and gave the whole process a highly spasmodic character.

Contemporaneously with the collectivization drive, the policymakers pushed the development of state farms, either by establishing new farms on state-owned land or by acquiring hitherto privately owned "rich" peasant farms, and publicly owned machines and tractor stations (MTS) in which they concentrated a large share of the available agricultural machinery and draft animals. One of the early objectives in the fight against the "rich peasant" was to break his alleged "draft-power monopoly." During the early phase of the collectivization, a ceaseless conflict over draft animals indeed took place between the state and the upper and middle layers of the peasantry. The peasants disposed of their draft animals and cattle in any way they could.

The concentration of both machines and draft animals in the public sector left the private farms in a precarious condition. In principle, the MTS were meant to insure service to both collectives and private farms. Actually, the tractor stations seem often to have been grossly mismanaged and the machines rendered unusable when most needed. Even in the collectives, use of machinery increased only slowly, accompanied by much waste of material and human energies. A distressing picture of the disproportions, squandering of resources, and inner tensions engendered by the 1949–53 phase of the collectivization drive can be pieced together from information released during the "New Course." The most significant item emerging from the balance sheet of that period is the fact that the entire agricultural output —crop and animal—had either fallen below or barely reached the "preliberation" level.

To reverse the falling output trends, correct the most flagrant sectoral imbalances, and alleviate some of the tensions created by the early collectivization drive, policy-makers throughout the area decided on new measures for 1953–54: they would encourage the use of all land available and hence stop the process of expulsion of the medium-landed peasants from their property; adopt a more "liberal" attitude toward the peasants ready to rent state-owned land and release from their contracts or other obligations to plants or factories those peasants working part-time in industry and part-time on the farm; liquidate the inefficient collectives and temporarily halt the drive toward massive collectivization (in short, productivity became an important factor); enhance incentives through increased prices, lower quotas of obligatory deliveries, and lessened burdens on the collectives; increase investment in agriculture as a whole and eventually supply credits, technical aid, and seeds even to the individual peasants.

The reappraisal of agricultural policies in mid-1953 was undertaken by all the countries of the area, including Soviet Russia. As always, this important political reversal coincided with a series of significant events—the death of Stalin, the outburst of street revolts in East Germany, and the open admission that the agrarian policy of the Soviet Union itself, during the last two decades (1933–53), had led to a sharp drop in both agricultural output and livestock breeding.

Although the New Course lasted only a short period and the second round of collectivization soon began, commands and incentives thereafter were intermingled much more subtly than they had been in the early 1950's. In addition, local industry was able to supply more small agricultural machinery and consumer goods to the villages now than during the early industrialization. The emphasis on heavy industry continued unabated, and investment in agriculture fell far short of the New Course promises, but the second wave of collectivization did progress more smoothly than the first wave had.

Finally, from a socialized (state- and cooperative-owned) agricultural land "base" of 20–25 per cent in Czechoslovakia, Hungary, and Rumania and 60 per cent in Bulgaria in the mid-1950's, socialization was extended by the early 1960's to 83–93 per cent of these lands in all the countries excluding Yugoslavia and Poland, where the socialized "base" had shrunk to roughly 10 and 13 per cent of the land, respectively (see Table 5.2).

TABLE 5.2. PERCENTAGE DISTRIBUTION OF AGRICULTURAL LAND AFTER COLLECTIVIZATION IN SELECTED EAST EUROPEAN COUNTRIES AROUND THE MID-1960's[24]

|  | (1) STATE FARMS | (2) COLLECTIVE FARMS | (3) AUXILIARY FARMS[a] | (4) PRIVATE FARMS | SOCIALIST SECTOR (1)+(2) | PRIVATE SECTOR (3)+(4) |
|---|---|---|---|---|---|---|
| East Germany | 6.4 | 76.7 | 10.4 | 6.5 | 83.1 | 16.9 |
| Czechoslovakia | 28.3 | 56.4 | 4.3 | 11.0 | 84.7 | 15.3 |
| Hungary | 16.5 | 77.1 | 3.4 | 3.0 | 93.6 | 6.4 |
| Rumania | 30.3 | 55.0 | 6.5 | 8.2 | 85.3 | 14.7 |
| Bulgaria | 11.4 | 76.0 | 12.0 | 0.6 | 87.4 | 12.6 |

[a] Plots of collective farms (and, for some countries, also plots of workers on state farms).

## LARGE-SCALE VS. HOUSEHOLD FARMING

As in the USSR, an uneasy symbiosis has developed in the East European countries, during and since collectivization, between large-scale collective farming and small-scale individual farming, with respect to agro-technical changes, output patterns, income, and growth prospects. In the countries whose collectivization has been completed, farms of 2000–5000 hectares have been established in the state sector (except in East Germany, where their size is smaller) and of 500–2000 hectares and more in the collectivized sector. Each member of the collectives retains a household plot of about an acre (half a hectare) and works on roughly five hectares of common land.

The combination of giant farms and dwarf household plots is the result of a number of economic, sociological, political, and historic exigencies. As a Hungarian source puts it, once they get land holdings, the peasants "cling to them . . . and still consider them to be partly their basis of existence and a security of their personal freedom."[25] Furthermore, large-scale collective farms cannot properly use the private houses, small plots, scattered animal sheds, and small equipment inherited from the peasants who joined the cooperatives. Large farms and small private household plots thus arose side-by-side through the collectivization process itself.

A certain division of labor has gradually developed between the large state and collective farms and the household plots. The technological advantages opened to large farms and the investments made there led primarily to the development of field crop mechanization and only limitedly to livestock raising and the beginnings of an integrated agricultural-livestock husbandry. Complete mechanization of crop work (plowing, seeding, cultivation, harvesting, and storing) and scientific and mechanical assistance to livestock husbandry (breeding, feeding, milking, refrigeration, and shed construction) along with closer integration between agriculture and the food-processing industries to mitigate seasonal labor fluctuation, and finally, the transformation of the village itself to meet modern standards, including electrification, require enormous investments indeed. (Hungarian calculations reveal that, if cooperatives were to take over the raising of the country's entire livestock, they would have to build stables costing about twenty times as much as they now spend yearly on buildings for animals.)[26] On the other hand, the small homestead farms have taken up the cultivation of vegetables, fruits, and potatoes, as well as some subsistence crops, and the raising of certain types of livestock (poultry, pigs, and cows) for both personal use and marketing.

With variations from country to country and from region to region, a three-way pattern of specialization and competition has finally emerged among state, collective, and homestead farms. In contrast to the capital-intensive state farms, the labor-intensive collective farms have been able to develop not only somewhat mechanized field crops but also labor-intensive cultures, such as vegetables, vine crops, and fruit, competitively with the household plots. However, the household plots, notwithstanding their tiny share of total farm-land, have succeeded in maintaining an important place in the supply of vegetables, fruits, eggs, milk, and meat to the towns. Although Soviet collectivization has wrought significant shifts in the relative shares of the state farms, collectives, and household plots in outputs and marketing of agricultural produce, in the mid-1960's—three decades after the completion of collectivization—the private plots still accounted for the largest shares in the overall outputs of vegetables, meat, milk, and eggs, and for significant shares in the marketing of these products as well as wool and potatoes.[27] Data available for various East European countries reveal similar patterns in both output and marketing.[28]

Given this type of specialization and the low investments priority of agriculture, the policy-makers of the socialist countries have constantly been faced with the following dilemmas: should they encourage and deepen the division of labor between collectives and household plots or should they, through restrictions, undermine the productive positions held by homestead farms and finally eliminate them?

Since the 1960's, the Soviet Union and the East European countries with full collectivization have moved toward long-range policies that would erase at least some of the differences between the state farms and the collectives. Formerly only a residual claimant to his own output after all the farm's obligations were met, the collective farmer has now been raised to the position of guaranteed wage earner, somewhat like the state farm worker. In the disbursement of collective earnings, funds for wages are now to be allocated first; when wage funds are lacking, credits are obligatorily granted by the state bank. Increases in the price of farm deliveries, direct purchasing of farm machinery, development of intercollective cooperation, and liquidation of "weak" collectives (by their transformation into state farms) have substantially improved the situation of the collective farmers. The collectives, however, remain an institution compelled to support low-productivity, marginal workers for whom no other job opportunities exist.

It is, however, in the future relationships between the large-scale state and collective farming and homestead farming that the Soviet

Union and the East Europeans have seen one of the key issues in the restructuring of the countryside. Traditionally, the Russians have looked upon the private plot as an unfortunate vestige of precollectivization, an unwarranted competitor for the labor time of the collective worker, and an illegal claimant to the collective land and fodder on which some of the privately owned livestock must be raised. At certain times the Soviet leaders have threatened to "nationalize" all livestock—the mainstay of the private homestead—and have prohibited the raising of certain crops in the small plots or have stringently enforced the obligations of each collective farmer toward collective work and property.

A totally different approach has started to emerge, particularly since the 1960's in Hungary. The new policy is based on the concept of the complementarity of plot and collective farm rather than their unrelenting competition: the private homestead is viewed as an integral part of the cooperative sector, with a significant productive capacity, whose optimal utilization would appreciably improve overall agricultural performance. A number of determinations must therefore be made about the optimal size of the land to be given to the household, the best ways of developing cooperation in utilization of fodder, the best means of soil amelioration, pest and disease reduction, and plant care for the small plots, and the most appropriate marketing methods for their produce.[29] Several policies consonant with this orientation have already been implemented in Hungary, viz., the provision of state credits to stimulate planting of vineyards and orchards by the household farmsteads, the sale of small farm machinery to them, and the increase of certain prices which "give more support to the household plots than to the collective farms."[30]

The Yugoslavs have, of course, maintained since the 1950's that the preconditions for truly modernizing agriculture—namely, the availability of large investments, complex machinery, buildings, electrification, etc.—were not at hand in their country, and that consequently the individual peasant homestead had to continue to play a major role in the production and marketing of agricultural produce. The Yugoslavs, who disbanded most of their agricultural collectives many years ago (these shrank in one year, 1953, from 1,998,000 hectares to 327,000 hectares), and their spokesman, Edward Kardelj, asserted that the true importance of collectivization was measurable not by relative shares in landownership but by relative shares in output and marketing of agricultural produce. "If . . . modern technology is non-existent or insufficient, it is highly questionable which is more productive: the individual holding or a productive organization based on simple cooperation of laborers which the state must sustain by force." And Kardelj added that the socialist state could influence developments in agriculture not only through landownership but through the "volume, technical structure and type of ownership of other means of production" along with other levers.[31] One should note, however, that in spite of the utilization of these levers, the Yugoslavs have been unable to cope with the perennial problems already facing the countryside in the interwar years: on the one hand, continuous land fragmentation and, on the other, land concentration. Indeed, notwithstanding a law fixing the maximum limit of private landownership at 10 hectares, fictitious divisions of larger holdings and land-leases from small-plot peasants have created significant conglomerations of land in the hands of the most enterprising peasant families.[32] The effect of such rental arrangements is to convert the title holder into a tenant under the management and control of the lessee—a development which may be partially controlled by limiting product sales per ownership to the output potential of 10 hectares.

The Poles, who for reasons other than those of the Yugoslavs have also shied away from collectivization, stress the importance of various fiscal and monetary instruments for determining overall market conditions, relative prices of various agricultural produce, and overall profitability of agriculture. Through the utilization of state credits channeled through agricultural associations (so-called agricultural circles), through the purchase of equipment, fertilizers, insecticides, etc., by the "circles," and through the circles' productive servicing of the agriculturists and contractual purchases of the farmers' produce, the Poles hope to influence strongly the "structural transformation" of agriculture, at least at the present stage. Some Polish theoreticians seem to believe that perhaps in the future the country might even "skip" the stage of collectivization if the state would start systematically appropriating peasants' land through "defined forms of purchase and turning it into state farms." The trouble with this kind of land socialization is, of course, "the great scattering of peasant land and difficulties inherent in its unification, and, above all, the very high social cost of its realization."[33]

The spokesmen of the socialist countries where collectivization has been carried out naturally reject the idea that a high level of industrial development is a precondition for efficient collectivization. They view collectivization itself as a means for bringing about this higher development level, through its squeezing an increased share of marketed produce from agriculture at a lower real cost than would otherwise be possible. Nonetheless, even those theorists continue to be confronted, as we saw, with the complex problems of the private homestead, however small its percentage of the total agricultural land.

# [ CHAPTER 6 ]

## *Problems in Foreign-Trade Management*

IN A CENTRALLY organized, Soviet-type national corporation, foreign trade is a state monopoly. This monopoly encompasses not only all export-import operations (concentrated exclusively in the hands of state-chartered foreign-trade corporations) but also all international accounts and credits, thus creating also a monopoly of foreign exchange.

The functions of the foreign-trade monopoly are to protect the growth and expansion of national industries and provide maximum assistance to domestic capital formation; to ward off "capitalist" economic penetration, via rigorous import controls and avoidance of direct contacts between domestic producers and foreign firms; to insulate the economy from world market fluctuations; and to facilitate the eventual coordination of the economic plans of socialist countries.

The maintenance of the foreign-trade monopoly, with its complete central controls on the volume, prices, structure, and direction of foreign-trade transactions, has gone unchallenged in countries with a large domestic market, such as the USSR, and in countries not heavily dependent on foreign markets for the capacity expansion and output growth of their own large-scale industries, not heavily dependent on imports (i.e., whose rate of growth of national income has not been associated with a high rate of growth in imports), and not inclined toward competitive pricing within their domestic markets. The monopoly has, on the other hand, become an increasing hindrance to the growth and development of small-sized countries, such as Czechoslovakia and Hungary, where domestic markets are small, industries are geared toward larger markets, dependence on imports is substantial, realistic relationships between domestic and international prices must obtain, and the inclination toward competitive pricing domestically has increased.[1]

Here we will examine the administrative organization of these monopolies, the nature of inter-socialist trade agreements, the determination of price within the framework of these agreements, the results of plan coordination, and the problems arising when countries attempt to discard the monopoly and change their management of foreign trade, and liberalize trade relations with the West while the old trade relationships with centrally directed socialist countries remain in force.[2]

## ADMINISTRATIVE ORGANIZATION

The foreign-trade system is headed in all socialist countries, excluding Yugoslavia, by a ministry of foreign trade, which plans all the essentials of foreign transactions, as dictated by the domestic output plan, various policy considerations, and existing commitments. The ministry prepares and participates in the negotiation of foreign-trade agreements, and controls and directs the organizations engaging in the field of trade.[3] The ministry is usually organized into "functional" and "operational" sections or departments. The customary functional departments are planning, foreign exchange and finance, contracts, bookkeeping and auditing, arbitration, personnel, and capital construction. The operational departments and/or administrations generally are import, export, tariffs, and forwarding. In many cases, some of the departments are split into several subsections, one concerned with the socialist countries, one with the developed capitalist countries, and one with the less-developed non-socialist countries.

Working in close contact with the state planning committee (SPC), the ministry's planning department prepares the draft plan and submits it to the state-chartered, foreign-trade corporations. The draft is drawn up within the directives of the SPC regarding planned output targets and sectoral relations, existing commitments, import requirements, and the available foreign exchange. The draft plan specifies the volume, prices and transport costs, structure, and direction of foreign trade. The importing and exporting corporations, in turn, formulate their specific plans on the basis of the physical balances (output and its anticipated allocations in physical terms) submitted to them by the selling and purchasing departments of the producing organizations. The foreign-trade corporations make suggestions to accommodate the actual conditions with the basic blueprint and return the revised blueprint to the planning department of the foreign-trade ministry. There a coordinated yearly or long-term (five to seven years) plan is developed and drawn up by the ministry and submitted to the SPC. The opinions of the SPC are usually conclusive in the framing of the final draft, which is then placed before the council of ministers for final approval.

Among the functional departments, the foreign exchange and finance department, in collaboration with the state bank, has responsibility for balance-of-payments problems. The administrative-economic department prepares the budget of the ministry and plans and supervises expenditures by the foreign-trade corporations. The contracts department studies market conditions abroad, prepares the international-trade projects to be negotiated, and drafts instructions to the foreign-trade organizations concerning the implementation of contracts once they are signed. The accounting and auditing department checks and controls the financial accounts of the ministry and its organs.

Among operational departments, the import and export departments tend to be divided into sections for planning and finance and into sections corresponding to the major industrial branches (metallurgy, chemicals, textiles, leather, food and agricultural products, etc.). Each of the sections is, in turn, subdivided by specific commodities, and, for certain basic commodities, the subdivisions are further subdivided, according to countries; such subdivisions exist in Poland for coal, in Rumania for oil, and so on. In some countries, a special department for capital goods, distinct from the departments of imports and exports, handles the import of capital goods. The other operational departments are named for and are responsible for the policies and economics of tariffs and forwarding; each is subdivided into sections for planning, finance, accounting, personnel, etc.

In all the socialist countries the foreign-trade ministry has conducted its activities only through foreign-trade commissioners and/or through the monopolistic foreign-trade corporations. The commissioners, usually members of the regional or central planning bodies, propose measures for trade expansion and supervise implementation of the ministry's instructions and regulations for the operational agencies. The monopolistic corporations are governmental agencies, each operating as an independent legal entity, created by an individual charter for the pursuit of its assigned business. Each is expected to attain planned or above-plan profits while following precisely all the tasks prescribed by the plan. Since the corporations are independent legal entities, their relationship with the producing enterprises is that of customer to supplier, regulated by special contracts specifying prices and terms of delivery. Once the overall economic plan is approved, these contracts are consummated, within the framework of the plan, between the corporations and the selling and purchasing organizations of the economic ministries.

The functional and operational offices of each importing, exporting, and forwarding corporation are subdivided along the same lines as are their counterparts in the ministry of foreign trade. Basically, the importing and exporting corporations specialize according to the main industrial branches and their needs, while the offices of the corporations specialize by type of commodity. Thus, importing corporations are established in each and every CDSE for capital goods, basic raw materials, metals and goods of mass-consumption, household appliances, textiles, and food. The exporting corporations are diversified according to the principal exports which the country has to offer. By and large, there are some twenty corporations in each CDSE. (In most countries, a selling organization for the agricultural cooperatives is also authorized to enter the field of foreign trade.)

In each country, a chamber of commerce, which is not directly included in the ministry of foreign trade or its system, assists foreign customers, sends delegations abroad, arranges participation in foreign-trade fairs, obtains patents for citizens, and so on. To it are also attached arbitration commissions.

The ministry of foreign trade carries on its operations abroad through trade delegations. These delegations are regarded as state delegations and enjoy full diplomatic immunity in the other CDSE's.

They supervise the commercial activities of their national foreign-trade corporations abroad, issue the documents needed for commercial operations, and study general business and trade possibilities in each country. In countries where the delegations are not accepted as state delegations, the socialist countries maintain commercial agencies directly responsible to the ministries of foreign trade.

## TRADE AGREEMENTS

Commercial treaties concluded between socialist countries are based on agreements of "friendship and mutual aid," and have both a political and a commercial purpose. The stated political goal is to help the signatory countries "construct socialism," while the commercial aim is to establish a comprehensive framework for their commercial agreements. The commercial agreements include formal provisions for unconditional, most-favored-nation treatment with respect to export and import operations, transport, and custom duties. They also contain provisions concerning exchange of specialists, organization of trade fairs, and other points of secondary importance.

Among the countries of the Council for Mutual Economic Assistance (variously called CEMA, CMEA, or COMECON), including the USSR and the socialist East European countries except Albania and Yugoslavia, bilateral negotiations of commercial treaties are preceded by multilateral bargaining discussions concerning respective outputs and foreign-trade plans in physical terms (since domestic prices are distorted). These preliminary multilateral bargaining discussions are conducted under the restriction that fuels and raw materials, machinery and equipment, and consumer goods be exchanged on a one-to-one basis, as much as possible. In the bargaining sessions, each country tries first to cover its own important needs and "sell" the products it has in excess. Since the socialist countries have not engaged in meaningful divisions of labor based on comparative advantage, their import needs have been very similar and their export availabilities often overlapping. As a consequence, none of them could fill its primary import needs through CEMA if each one of them were not ready to give in exchange certain goods which it could normally trade in hard-currency markets. This so-called mutual-socialist-help system leads to unexpected export-import recommendations: for instance, to obtain scarce Bulgarian copper, Czechoslovakia, let us say, might have to take Bulgarian vegetables, and add to the bargain some of its rolled steel, considered valuable for the Bulgarian output plan. In the scheduled exchanges of products among all of these countries, strangely assorted groups of goods are thus bartered. The oddity of such "prices" and the crudity of the procedure which determines them are the costs of not using a price system.

The recommendations[4] are translated into five-year bilateral trade agreements and are reflected in the revised national investment, production, and trade plans. The trade agreements state the value of the envisaged trade turnover in roubles and specify that the prices of the goods will be fixed "on the basis of world prices." This price estimation is meant to translate into value terms the exchanges planned in physical terms. A quota list indicates the specific quantities of the commodities to be exchanged. The long-term trade agreements are undertaken to insure for each country the basic minimum supplies needed for its outputs under its "perspective" plan. Additional bilateral yearly agreements are used to adjust the flows of trade to the precise needs of the annual "operational" plan of each country. Upon the signing of such bilateral agreements, the state banks of the two signatory countries open non-interest-bearing credit accounts for the trading partner in the amount of the trade turnover. To implement the agreements, contracts are negotiated between the appropriate foreign-trade corporations of the two countries, specifying the quality, assortment, price, date, and place of delivery of each item.

Let us now follow a foreign-trade operation as it is carried out in practice in the centrally directed socialist economies. On the basis of the plan, contracts are concluded between the exporting corporations and the appropriate domestic organizations selling the commodity ear-marked for export. The price paid by the exporting corporation is f.o.b. factory, exclusive of turnover tax (a sales tax which varies according to the item). For certain commodities, a special purchase authorization may also be needed. The domestic producer is paid when the purchasing exporting corporation accepts the documents indicating that the producer has sent the goods. The commodity is then shipped by the exporting agency to the country of destination, whose foreign importing agency accepts it. The settlement between the exporting and importing agencies is made in foreign-trade prices in their respective bank accounts through a system of "direct payment": upon receiving the accepted export documents, the central bank of the exporting country pays the export organization from the account of the importing country. The bank then sends the documents to the central bank of the importing country, which, in turn, credits the account of the exporting country and then presents the documents to the importing organization for payment. In case the buyer refuses to accept the goods, the banks notify one another and adjust their accounts accordingly. Any discrepancy between foreign and domestic prices is covered by the state budget of the importing country.

Trade agreements with nonsocialist countries are consummated in the same way, but the values in the exchange are expressed in the currency of the outside partner, in dollars, in some other currency, or in "clearing roubles." These are, again, bilateral agreements, with accounts carried in clearing, just as they are carried in trade with the CDSE's. The balance of such accounts can be covered either by gold or foreign exchange or by the agreed shipment of additional commodities. In trade with countries lacking reciprocal clearing accounts, the payments are made through international banks; the exporter receives his payment from a predetermined bank upon the presentation, under specified conditions, of the export documents. Some triangular arrangements involving one non-socialist and two socialist countries have also been established. In one case, certain Finnish exports to the Soviet Union were offset by Polish exports to Finland in exchange for Soviet exports to Poland, and in another case, Burmese exports to the Soviet Union were offset by Czechoslovak exports to Burma in exchange for Soviet exports to Czechoslovakia.

Up to June 1957, the "clearing rouble" was no more than a bookkeeping unit of account. From that time until 1964, the state bank of the Soviet Union acted as a clearing house for CEMA's multilateral compensations. Since 1964, such compensations have been cleared through an *ad hoc* International Bank of Economic Cooperation (IBEC), but, because the bulk of CEMA trade continues to flow bilaterally, the amounts handled by IBEC have been small. IBEC also handles purchases over and above those stipulated in the bilateral agreements, purchases of various consumer goods, and sundry obligations arising from services.

## PRICE DETERMINATION

Payments within CEMA are made, through the trading countries' central banks, in domestic currencies—roubles in Russia, zlotys in Poland, korunas in Czechoslovakia, and so on—at domestic prices. In each country, all gold and foreign exchange and all foreign accounts are the exclusive province of the central bank. Each government defines the gold content of its domestic currency as a universal standard for exchange rates. However, no foreign currency, of either a socialist or a non-socialist country, circulates within these countries, and it is legally prohibited to take the domestic currency abroad. Officially, the rate of exchange of the domestic currencies is established in a "planned fashion." Actually, the rate is fixed at an arbitrary level, since changes in the domestic wholesale and retail prices or changes in the world prices of the goods exported or imported by these countries usually do not affect the "planned" rate of exchange.

In certain cases, foreign-trade organizations act as a simple channel of foreign-trade operations without receiving special consideration for each and every operation involved, i.e., without applying any pre-established profit mark-ups. In other cases, foreign-trade organizations take an established "profit norm"—a mark-up ranging from 1 per cent to 50 per cent of the domestic wholesale price of the item traded. For imported goods, the mark-up is added to the domestic wholesale price at which the goods are sold to an industry; for exported goods, the mark-up is added to the domestic wholesale price, net of the turnover tax. Since the domestic price level is usually higher than the foreign trade price level at the official rate of exchange, imported goods are sold at a higher price than that paid abroad, and the difference (minus the trade organization's mark-up) is transferred to the budget. The price of the commodity sold abroad is often below the domestic price at which the exporter purchased it, and the difference is covered by a subsidy from the budget. Since the mid-1950's, certain socialist countries, like Hungary and Czechoslovakia, have used either variable exchange rates or a higher exchange rate than the official one for these calculations.[5] The purpose of this *de facto* devaluation has been to help planners and producers determine which exports and imports should be encouraged or discouraged and thus "rationalize" foreign-trade choices to echo the new "rationalized" domestic price structure. But the usefulness of these "realistic" exchange rates is severely limited by the fact that the underlying domestic price structure continues to reflect administrative manipulations more than it does opportunity costs. The choices in foreign trade are therefore no more "rational" because of these domestic distortions.[6]

In accordance with an agreement of the early 1950's against intra-CEMA price discrimination, each country in principle charges all CEMA trading partners the same price for the same commodity, with variations only for differences in transport cost. Although there is no assurance of price uniformity for goods exported by more than one country in the area, a limited tendency toward such uniformity does exist because of the limited mobility of buyers and sellers. As already stated, the prices at which the goods are traded in the CEMA are based on "world prices"; these prices, however, are "cleansed whenever possible of the distorting effects of cyclical deviations." The "cleansing" process leads simply to a "lagged" world-price constellation in CEMA. Thus, according to K. I. Popov, trade in the period of 1951–56 was based on the world prices at the end of 1949 and the beginning of 1950; 1958–65 trade was carried on at 1957 world prices; and post-1965 trade was based on the "average price of the main world commodity markets" for 1960–64.[7] Why "lagged" prices should be judged better than those which follow them has never been clearly revealed except by the one explanation that, through this device, the socialist market "excluded" the speculative impact of the Korean war in the early 1950's. Even though these "lagged world prices" are supposed to be accepted by all CEMA partners, price deviations for comparable commodities can be included in their contracts by a mutual agreement to use "prices on different world commodity markets as a base."

The use of the world price pattern creates many misgivings for Marxian economists, since, according to Marx, any developed country is always in a position to exploit a less-developed country. Restating Ricardo's theory of comparative advantage, Marx noted that "an advanced country is enabled to sell its goods above their value even when it sells them cheaper than the competing countries," while a less-developed country "may offer more materialized labor in goods than it receives, and yet it may receive in return commodities cheaper than it may produce them."[8] Since 1948, the theory of an implicitly unequal exchange (more materialized labor of the underdeveloped area against less labor of the highly developed country) has been heavily stressed, first by the Yugoslav Communists, to suggest that unequal relations might also arise among socialist states.[9] Though the Yugoslavs have been expelled as "revisionists," the use of the world price pattern within CEMA is still under question by the CEMA economists. At various conferences concerning price determinations, the Czechoslovak and East German economists decidedly favored use of the world price pattern, while the representatives of the less-developed countries seemed agreeable to world prices only under numerous restrictions. Thus, the representative of Czechoslovakia noted that it would not be "feasible to build a separate price system completely severed from world prices," whereas the Rumanian representative claimed that the application of world prices to CEMA trade "leads to effects harmful to the economy of industrially less-developed countries."[10] However, no agreement has been reached among the less-developed countries as to how these harmful effects could be avoided by the manipulation of prices in foreign trade. Some socialist economists claim to be studying a number of methods for "cleansing" the "cost of production" or the wholesale prices prevailing in particular CEMA countries or in all of them, for use as intra-CEMA foreign-trade prices. An average weighted base price for the socialist market could be calculated, for instance, from the national wholesale prices in the socialist countries, "cleansed" of differences in methodology, recomputed in some common unit, and then weighted by each one's volume of production of the given commodity.[11] The domestic distortions of prices could hardly be "cleansed" by these procedures, however, and such a calculated price can be no more "rational" than its components. Obviously, the CEMA countries cannot create a rational price system of their own if each one of them does not develop along market-socialist lines. Only if every member country adopted a rational domestic price system would rational intra-CEMA prices develop; the intra-CEMA prices would differ from the foreign-trade prices of the rest of the world only to the extent that discriminating trade practices prevented the socialist countries from normal trading in all world markets.

## INTRA-SYSTEM COORDINATION AND RELATIONS

CEMA has used a variety of methods to foster economic cooperation and coordination in both trade and output planning. From 1949 to 1953, the first years of its activity, which coincided with the first development plans of the East-Central European countries, coordination was effected primarily through long-term trade agreements designed to guarantee the minimum supplies of basic materials needed for each country to implement its independently-drawn national output plans. During that period, technical and scientific cooperation also began through the circulation of technical documentation, exchange of experts and technical consultants, training of technicians and skilled workmen, and the like. After the death of Stalin, further development of a "socialist division of labor" received increased attention. During the short period of the "New Course" (1953–54), economic coordination was envisaged not only in trade, as during the preceding period, but also in domestic output. Thus, the activities of CEMA were oriented toward the dovetailing of the second long-term development plans of the East European countries, scheduled to start in 1956, with the Sixth Five-Year Plan of the Soviet Union. While these plans were still in the initial stage of implementation, the upheavals in Hungary and Poland in the autumn of 1956 threw them out of gear and forced substantial changes in their basic design. The Soviet Union itself stopped short of the completion of its Sixth Five-Year Plan and shifted to a new Seven-Year Plan, subsequently also abandoned. It was then proclaimed that CEMA would not only help coordinate the new output plans for 1961–65, but also determine appropriate means for correlating the plans for raw materials, fuel and power, capital construction, and transportation for the whole fifteen-year period extending from 1961–75.

Although there has been much talk about a socialist division of labor, the division has progressed little, not only because each of the countries of the area has long conceived its industrialization as an essentially autarkic process—a process which has been prolonged within each country, region, sector, and industry by a tendency to accumulate stocks or even produce spare parts to avert shortages that might interfere with the achievement of one's "output plan"—but also because no meaningful relation between distorted internal prices and international prices can be established, as we have already observed. Finally, a decisive factor which has operated against the division of labor is the special position of the Soviet Union in relation to the East European countries, because of its size, economic power, political influence, and reluctance to agree to any scheme which might weaken its direct controls either over each transaction with every country of the area or over its own plans for, say, sharing its investable resources. Hence, the CEMA has gained no executive power and each specific division of labor must be achieved via a bilateral or, at best, triangular arrangement.

As a result of all these factors, the division of labor presents a somewhat haphazard pattern, shaped by political and technical-engineering decisions rather than by cost and price considerations. CEMA's permanent commissions of experts laboriously examine each type of product, taking into account plant capacity available in this or that country, and recommend a specific technical-engineering apportionment among the members. The experts propose, CEMA recommends, and the various countries involved implement, if they so decide, the recommendations made via bilateral agreements. Thus, in some cases, given plants in a specific country are earmarked to produce for the whole area; in other cases, outputs of given specifications (e.g., trucks of so and so many tons) will be produced in one particular country; in other cases still, two countries may establish a joint company with one country furnishing the raw materials and the other the industrial facilities, and so on. It is difficult to know in what measure direct bilateral agreements follow or contradict recommendations of CEMA commissions.

The Communist leaders who try to improve the centralized planning system are committed to the maintenance of the monopoly of foreign trade and the system of cooperation prevailing in CEMA, a system which, according to them, is insuring "equality" among partners, "equivalent exchange," and "mutual help." But the partisans of *dirigisme,* or guided-market socialism—like Hungary inside CEMA or Yugoslavia outside CEMA—reject the monopoly of foreign trade and the patterns of intersocialist relations which the monopolistic practices have, in part, conditioned. "Equality," of course, does not flow from cooperation in bookkeeping of mutual transactions. "Equivalent exchange"—even in terms of the labor theory of value—does not follow from the fact that CEMA borrows the opportunity costs from other countries, "lags" them, and "cleanses" them in various ways: a "just price" may indeed be known, as the Justinian codex claimed it, to God alone. Finally, the "mutual help" extended via barter bargaining (rather than via cost-price considerations) is difficult to evaluate, in practice, by economic criteria only.

In either socialist *dirigisme* or socialist *liberalism* the abandonment of most administrative methods is fundamental in foreign trade, just as in the domestic economy. But processes of "decontrol"—even outside CEMA—are long, delicate, and difficult. Only after the introduction of the so-called "Reformed System," since the mid-1960's, did the Yugoslavs proceed to the complete liberalization of exports and to the liberalization of roughly 50 per cent of imports.[12] Western liberalization of imports in intra-European trade, freeing private trade from quantitative restrictions, progressed over the whole decade of the 1950's.[13] Discarding export controls, dismantling either general or selective import restrictions, liberalizing foreign exchange controls, and, above all, gradually adjusting the combinations of these during the tapering-off period to avoid unbearable pressures in the balance of payments and in the domestic economy require astute management under any circumstances. Within CEMA, the difficulty of dismantling controls is enormously increased by the multiple barriers which CEMA, as a body, places on the freedom of action of any of its members, particularly the smaller ones. No member country could now afford, in physical terms, to extricate itself from the preliminary coordination bargaining discussions concerning long-term output and foreign trade plans. Since, as we shall see in the following essay, the Soviet Union is the main supplier of raw materials to all these countries, only a complete break with CEMA could free a country from the necessities of framing its plans in physical terms, establishing the main physical flows on which its plans will be based with other CEMA partners, and implementing certain intra-CEMA recommendations.

On the basis of unit-cost pricing, more realistic exchange rates, and some other considerations, such as the marked retardation in technology of certain socialist industries and their lack of competitiveness in the advanced markets, Hungarian, Czechoslovak, and even East German planners have clearly seen that certain of their exports are unprofitable and should be discontinued; certain imports from the West, particularly capital goods and raw materials, should be encouraged; and certain major shifts should be effected in the import-export patterns which these countries have established from the mid-1950's to the mid-1960's, in regard to the advanced economies market, the socialist markets, and the underdeveloped countries' markets.

However, a CEMA country cannot easily discontinue certain exports whose disappearance would affect not only its own capacity utilization and employment but also the output and foreign trade plans of the other CEMA countries; neither can it substantially liberalize the imports of certain capital goods and raw materials when some CEMA countries would oppose such a move, nor can it easily map out major shifts of volume, structure, or direction in its foreign-trade pattern since the shifts might disrupt the basic patterns of supply within the area as a whole.

Under these conditions, all the system directors of a liberalizing CEMA country can do is retain the system of the monopoly of foreign trade while building next to it new mechanisms for conducting *some* foreign-trade operations, not necessarily the most decisive ones. Thus, without changing the "old ways of trade within CEMA," as a Hungarian policy-maker and economist has called them, a country intending to decontrol its foreign trade may encourage the progressive development of direct agreements (both within and outside CEMA) between producing enterprises, support the expansion of multilateral agreements (both within and outside CEMA), support inter-CEMA competition in third markets, and try to find some new avenues of co-operation in the West.[14] The opening of direct agreements between producing enterprises do not, of course, alter the "principle" of state trading: a producing company may indeed enter foreign trade, in the same way as a foreign-trade corporation, simply because it enjoys specially delegated government authority. The change, rather, lies in the fact that such contracts would bypass the ministries of foreign trade, a development which the countries committed to the maintenance of the monopoly of foreign trade might want to discourage. The expansion of multilateral agreements within CEMA—e.g., Soviet iron ore shipped to Rumania, offset by Rumanian oil exports to Poland, counterbalanced by Polish coal exports to the USSR—along with a systematic increase in multilateral agreements with non-CEMA countries, may require more gold conversion or use of convertible currencies by some countries' accounts than the CEMA's bank, IBEC, and the other CEMA countries may be willing and ready to handle. Increased competition among CEMA countries in third markets would probably generate new and heightened tensions within the CEMA itself, a situation which some countries might want to avoid, no matter how salutary expansion into a new, competitive market might appear to the partisans of decontrol. Finally the opening of new avenues toward the West—for instance, "co-production" or "joint investment ventures" within a CEMA country (the Western partner supplying machinery, technical assistance, management, and marketing facilities and the Eastern partner the plant, workers, and materials); purchases and exchanges of patents, whole plants, and parts; common cooperation in third markets[15]—would have to surmount not only serious difficulties in the West but also possible vetoes from within CEMA.

The processes of decontrol—limitation of state trading to certain branches only, abolition of foreign-trade plans for enterprises, utilization of indirect rather than direct instruments for stimulating the producers, along with the aforementioned measures to break the isolation of the producers from their external markets, arrest their technological retardation, and end their disinterest in their costs and earnings[16]—no matter how useful internally, may turn out to be politically inexpedient and externally dangerous. CEMA's ties are indeed not only economic, but also political and military; organizational as well as economic foreign-trade changes may therefore acquire unwanted overtones. Only very careful management of a country's foreign trade may succeed both in expanding and shifting some CEMA patterns and in moving toward cooperation with Western firms. With the differences existing among countries, the states of their industries, and the intricacy of CEMA's web which they have fashioned, what may prove feasible for one country, such as Hungary, may prove impossible for another, such as Czechoslovakia. Everything is not equal in the eventual transition to decentralized foreign-trade patterns within CEMA, no matter how overwhelming the domestic pressures toward such changes may be. The dilemmas facing the liberalizing policy-maker may perhaps turn out to be more formidable in foreign trade than in any other field.

# III

## DEVELOPMENT
## AND THE
## INTERNATIONAL
## ECONOMY

# INTRODUCTORY NOTE

SOCIALIST theory and practice have long been torn between two opposing tendencies: one political, revolutionary, class-conscious, and cosmopolitan; the other economic, reformist, bureaucratic, and nationalist. As Roger Berg pointed out before World War II, the cosmopolitan tendency plays an ostentatious role before the social-democratic parties accede to power; the nationalist tendency predominates after the parties gain power. The *"socialistes de gouvernement,"* according to Berg, are forced to use the nation state, however they may modify its structure, to organize the nation, direct its economy, and deal with other nations.

The cosmopolitan tendency was dominant in the ideological development of Communism, also, before or immediately after its protagonists' accession to power in a single country, the USSR. The anti-cosmopolitan, nationalist tendency asserted itself not only in the USSR with Stalin's rise to power, but also in a number of other states after their Communist parties' attainment of authority. Like the social-democrats, the Communists, *mutatis mutandis,* have become *"socialistes de gouvernement,"* prisoners of the unavoidable fact that societies develop within nations. Like their predecessors, the Communists have been compelled to identify "class" interests with "national" interests. The policies of each of the countries of the socialist world—with respect to movement of labor and capital, output and foreign-trade coordination, development of backward countries and regions, and so on—reflect national interests. Differences in size, level of development, and factor endowment are as important among socialist countries as they are among non-socialist ones. What maintains the primacy of the Soviet Union among the socialist countries of Eastern Europe is not its birthright as the "first socialist state" but its tremendous economic and military power. If Peking rejects the "Great Russian chauvinist power," it nevertheless does not abandon its own *socialisme de gouvernement.*

A number of decades ago, Leon Trotsky, in his *The Third International After Lenin,* rejected Stalin and Bukharin's contention that, once the "proletariat" had "built socialism" in a number of individual countries, "a world socialist economy" would be built, as Trotsky caustically phrased it, "after the manner in which children erect structures with ready-made blocks." In Trotsky's view, "world socialist economy will not at all be a sum total of national socialist economies. It can take shape in its fundamental aspects only on the soil of world-wide division of labor. . . ." It was already clear that any "sum total of national socialist economies" was bound to be rent by national conflicts; what is still not clear, however, is how a "world socialist economy" could arise from "the soil of world-wide division of labor."

The essays which follow examine various aspects of the conflict between pressing national interests and "cosmopolitan" inclinations. The first essay examines some of the perennial problems of what Stalin called "the second world market"—intra-socialist trade—pushed in various directions by the conflicting interests of its participants and "embargoed" by the West. The second essay discusses the economic mainsprings of a number of socialist disputes: the Soviet-Yugoslav, the Soviet-Albanian, the Soviet-Chinese, and the Soviet-Czechoslovak conflicts. The third and final essay, which concludes the book, focuses on socialist efforts toward economic "modernization" in Eastern Europe and on some broad problems of convergence or divergence between socialism and capitalism once certain levels of development have been reached.

# [ CHAPTER 7 ]

# A "Second World Market": Expectations & Reality

AFTER THE formation of the CEMA in the late 1940's, Soviet and East European policy-makers entertained the hope that the intersocialist council would become the nucleus of a "second world market," one rapidly embracing all socialist countries, vigorously competing with a disintegrating capitalist world market, easily solving its industrialization problems, and forcefully drawing into its orbit the underdeveloped countries. In his last theoretical work, *Economic Problems of Socialism in the USSR*, Stalin averred that "the most important sequel of the Second World War and of its economic consequences" was "that the single all-embracing world market disintegrated, so that we now have two parallel world markets . . . confronting one another."[1] For a while, many East European policy-makers and economists affirmed with Stalin that the socialist countries, after "dropping out" of the capitalist system, had joined together economically, established cooperation and mutual help, and secured the "cheapest possible and technically superb assistance" of the Soviet Union, superior to what any capitalist country could have tendered.

In fact, even two decades after its formation, CEMA has been able to embrace no more than half the Communist-ruled socialist countries. By the end of the 1960's, its share of world trade, including its mutual trade transactions and its trade exchanges with the rest of the world, accounted for about 12 per cent of world trade, a hardly imposing "second world market." Its need for imported technical competence, machinery, and equipment from the West have increased rather than diminished, notwithstanding strenuous industrialization efforts toward self-sufficiency and allegedly superb assistance from the USSR. Finally, its attraction for the underdeveloped countries has remained weak except for a very few cases in which military assistance has been involved. CEMA has turned out to be a regional East European market, one capable of sustaining the industrialization efforts of its members and the expansion of their foreign trade, but only under patently lagging technological conditions. The results, far short of the original expectations, have been achieved under the commandeering influence of the Soviet Union, an influence continuously adjusted to the changing moods and tensions of the smaller CEMA partners.

In the present essay, we intend to examine how CEMA's trade relations, shaped by a common pattern of structural transformation, have reinforced the dependence of some of its partners on the Soviet Union, notably for fuels and raw materials; how Soviet influence has been maintained and reasserted when needed; why relations with the West have become stalemated since the late 1940's; which factors have weakened or strengthened centripetal and centrifugal tendencies within CEMA; and, finally, how CEMA has tried to close technological gaps and provide technological assistance in the past and what it may do in the future.

## STRUCTURAL CHANGES IN CEMA'S MEMBERS

The systematic development of self-contained "socialist industrial bases" within each CEMA country—the crux of industrialization strategy, according to the Russian procedure—led to massive growth in and absorption of capital goods outputs through the 1950's and 1960's in the area as a whole. Within each country rapid development of both backward linkages (raw materials bases) and forward linkages (industries processing materials previously exported in raw or semi-finished states) took place. Efforts were made, on the one hand, to develop fuels, power, and raw materials and, on the other hand, to create or expand certain industrial branches for producing machines, chemicals, plastics, electronics, and even nucleonics. The efficiency with which the linkages were developed and their effects on the industrial structure differed in degree. Nevertheless, as we shall document statistically later, the relative developmental levels of the countries—industrialized (East Germany and Czechoslovakia), interme-

TABLE 7.1. Net Shifts in Industrial Employment throughout Eastern Europe, 1950–64

(*by thousands*)

| COUNTRIES | GAINFULLY EMPLOYED MANPOWER IN INDUSTRY | | "STANDARD GROWTH"[a] | ACTUAL GROWTH | NET SHIFT | PER CENT |
|---|---|---|---|---|---|---|
| | 1950 | 1964 | | | | |
| | (1) | (2) | (3) | (2)−(1) | | |
| Bulgaria | 251 | 878 | 169 | 627 | 458 | 35.0 |
| Czechoslovakia | 1,634 | 2,468 | 1,098 | 834 | −264 | −20.2 |
| East Germany | 2,256 | 2,727 | 1,516 | 471 | −1,045 | −79.8 |
| Hungary | 666 | 1,317 | 447 | 651 | 204 | 15.6 |
| Poland | 2,049 | 3,493 | 1,377 | 1,444 | 67 | 5.1 |
| Rumania | 814 | 1,588 | 547 | 774 | 227 | 17.3 |
| Yugoslavia | 578 | 1,319 | 388 | 741 | 353 | 27.0 |
| Totals | 8,248 | 13,790 | (67.19%) | 6,148 | +1,309 −1,309 | +100.0 −100.0 |

[a] Application of average area growth rate of industrial employment to country employment.
SOURCES: National statistical yearbooks for respective countries.[2]

125

diate (Poland and Hungary), and less developed (the rest of the area)—are still unchanged.

The transformations in each country from its efforts to develop self-contained "industrial bases" may be better visualized if one considers the changing patterns of industrial employment for the area as a whole. Although not all of the employment figures are fully comparable because of variations in definitions, it can be estimated that total industrial manpower rose by some 67 per cent between 1950 and the mid-1960's (from over 8.2 million gainfully employed for all of socialist Eastern Europe, including Yugoslavia, but excluding Albania, to nearly 13.8 million). Following a technique developed by H. S. Dunn and others,[3] one can compare the increment in industrial manpower in each "subregion" (for our purpose, in each country) to the increment in total industrial manpower for the area as a whole, expressing the positive or negative difference in either absolute or relative terms. Contrasting the "standard" gains in manpower, or those which would have been registered if each country had grown at the rate of the East European area as a whole, to actual changes in each country, we obtain comparable data on the so-called net or proportional shifts in employment (see Table 7.1). The calculations show that the largest positive proportional shift occurred in Bulgaria, the other positive shifts, by order of importance, being in Yugoslavia, Rumania, and finally Hungary and Poland. Conversely, the largest negative proportional shift took place in East Germany, followed by Czechoslovakia. Characteristically, a strong demand for new labor inputs and an abundant manpower supply have led to higher-than-average rates of growth in employment in the less-developed countries of the area, whereas a more moderate demand for fresh labor inputs coupled with an increasing labor shortage has made the most-developed tier register rates lower than the average.

The growth of any industrial subgroup in a country may be contrasted to the growth of the whole industry over the entire East European area or to the growth of the same subgroup over the entire area. Following Lowell D. Ashby, we may define the growth change in a whole industry as *structural* (i.e., a change caused by shifts in industry mix) and the growth change in a subgroup as *competitive* (i.e., a change resulting from better access to raw materials, outside markets, technology).[4] If we consider changes in employment by industrial subgroups, viz., engineering (machinery construction), other "leading links" (mining, energy, metals, chemistry, constructoin materials), and other industries (textiles and foodstuffs), we may ascertain the impact on employment of structural or competitive effects. This analysis reveals that the structural effect had a positive impact on the demand for labor in certain developed or "intermediate" countries (like Hungary) and a negative impact in the less-developed tier of the area. The competitive effect, on the other hand, operated negatively on the demand for labor in the developed tier and positively in the less-developed tier (see Table 7.2). It can be inferred

TABLE 7.2. STRUCTURAL AND COMPETITIVE EFFECTS ON INDUSTRIAL
EMPLOYMENT THROUGHOUT EASTERN EUROPE, 1950–64

*(by thousands)*

| COUNTRIES | STANDARD GROWTH | STRUCTURAL GROWTH | COMPETITIVE EFFECT | ACTUAL GROWTH[b] |
|---|---|---|---|---|
| | (1)[a] | (2) | (3) | (1)+(2)+(3) |
| Bulgaria | 169 | −25 | 484 | 627 |
| Czechoslovakia | 1,098 | −3 | −260 | 834 |
| East Germany | 1,516 | 101 | −1,146 | 471 |
| Hungary | 447 | 38 | 165 | 651 |
| Poland | 1,377 | −66 | 132 | 1,444 |
| Rumania | 547 | −17 | 245 | 774 |
| Yugoslavia | 388 | −28 | 381 | 741 |

[a] As in column (3), Table 7.1.
[b] As in column (2)–(1), Table 7.1.

from the structural effects that the developed countries moved toward more labor-intensive industries relative to their industrial structure in the 1950's, while the underdeveloped countries moved toward more capital-intensive industries: the more industrialized countries developed new backward linkages and the less-developed countries pushed the creation and growth of forward linkages.

Moreover, it can be inferred from the competitive effects that, since 1950, gains in productivity and related factors dampened the demand for labor in the developed countries; conversely, slower productivity gains strengthened demand for new labor in the less-developed tier. These different changes are illustrated in Figure 7.1. The less-developed countries are all located in octant 3, where their competitive effect is greater in a positive direction than their structural effect is in a negative direction; thus they exhibit a positive growth in total employment. The most-developed countries are either in octant 5 or in octant 7 where they exhibit a negative competitive effect larger than the positive or small negative structural effect and, hence, a negative net total shift in employment growth as compared to the area as a whole (see Fig. 7.1).

It should be noted that, whatever the initial level of development, the changes in the ratios of industrially employed manpower to total population did not alter the countries' positions in the three-group ranking mentioned earlier. In the 1940's, before the long-term plans, these ratios fluctuated in the less-developed tier from 3.5 to 5 per cent; in the middle tier, around 7 per cent; and in the upper tier, around 13 per cent. After three quinquennia of intensive industrialization, the ratios have shifted in the lower tier to 7–10.5 per cent; in the middle tier to 11–13 per cent; and in the upper tier to 16–17 per cent. At the same time, the uniform application of the same strategy led to the expansion within each country of both backward and forward linkages, generated duplication of relatively small-scale manufacturing facilities, and, in the light of more restricted trading patterns with the West, increased the dependence of all these countries on the only source of export surpluses of fuels, iron, and grain in the area, the USSR.

From the point of view of energy resources, the East European countries are very unequally endowed. The area can be divided into three basic energy groups: the energy deficient (Hungary and East Germany); the energy sufficient, either in solid and liquid fuels or in hydroelectric resources (Albania, Bulgaria, Czechoslovakia, and Rumania); and the energy-surplus countries (Yugoslavia and Poland).

The countries in the first and second groups have traditionally pushed the development of low-quality coal output and the substitution of lignite for higher grade fuels. Their long-term plans foresee large utilization of low-quality fuels in various branches of industry and in domestic use. If certain technical problems could be solved, lignite would also be used for the production of coke. Some countries of the second group—Czechoslovakia and Bulgaria, for instance—

## Fig. 7.1
### IMPACT OF "FORWARD" AND "BACKWARD" LINKAGES IN STRUCTURAL CHANGE IN EASTERN EUROPE
Combined "Structural" and "Competitive" Effects on Industrial Employment
(in thousands of gainfully employed) (1950–1964)

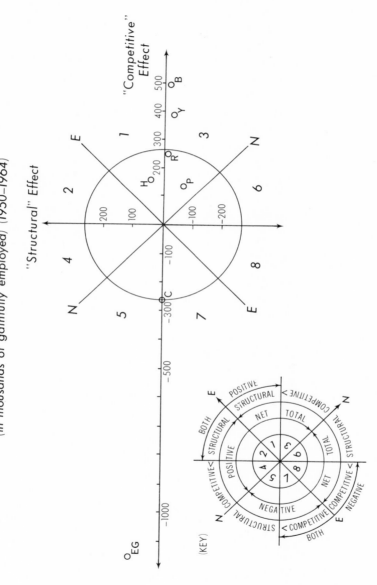

could expand their exports of high-quality coal if they succeeded in increasing domestic consumption of briquettes. Even Poland, through increased utilization of brown coal for the production of thermoelectricity, could export a larger quantity of hard coal, much in demand in the area. Further, Polish output of brown coal could be rapidly augmented since in various zones it is cheap to mine.

Against these possible output increases and substitutions of low-grade for high-grade fuels, one must consider the expanding needs for energy, certain to be far larger in the 1970's and 1980's than in the 1950's and 1960's. Under these conditions, the dependence of the energy-deficient countries on imports will increase sharply. Countries of the second energy group, like Bulgaria and Czechoslovakia, will have to intensify the pressure on their domestic output capacity. The countries of the third energy group will be able to increase their energy exports but only if they find the massive capital investments necessary for the development of their coal and hydroelectric resources.[5]

The ambitious long-term plans of industrialization for the 1970's and beyond will require substantial increases in both output and consumption of fuel and power. During the preceding two decades of structural change and rapid industrial growth, the ratio between increase in energy consumption and increase in energy output has been greater than one only in Rumania. Now it is estimated that, by 1980, the consumption of energy in Eastern Europe will have grown by a factor of 2.3 to 2.5 over that of 1965, and by a factor of 5.5 as of the year 2000.[6]

During the first long-term development plans in the early 1950's, coal was the predominant source of energy for the countries of Eastern Europe. Dramatic changes have taken place in this respect since the early 1960's: in the Soviet Union, for instance, coal has become significantly less important in total energy supplies, while oil and gas have registered rapid increases in use. A system of pipelines of crucial strategic and economic importance, including the "Friendship Pipeline" which has carried Soviet oil into the heart of Europe since the early 1960's, has already substantially increased the share of oil in the energy balances of East Germany, Czechoslovakia, and Hungary particularly. As consumption of fuel tends to grow faster than output of fuel in Eastern Europe, an ever-increasing dependence of the CEMA countries on Soviet oil seems inevitable, unless imports from the Middle East could be appreciably expanded and atomic energy could be made an important public source of energy.[7]

Furthermore, notwithstanding the full utilization of available capacity for electrical power production, the allocation of large shares of power output to industry, and the stringent rationing of electricity for transportation and household uses, a lagging output of electrical energy has put a serious brake on mechanization and industrialization in some East European countries. As much as 75 to 80 per cent of the power produced during the 1950's was assigned to industry and only 15 to 20 per cent was reserved for household use. However, even under these conditions, the consumption of electrical power per industrial worker remained very low. Today, even greater mechanization and automation make enormous demands on electrical energy. Normally the pace of growth in power production should surpass the pace of growth in industrial output. But, according to Czechoslovak calculations, the ratios of the index of power output to total industrial output were already below unity for most of the countries of the area during the 1950's, varying from a low of .59 for East Germany to a maximum of .89 for Poland and .96 for Czechoslovakia.[8] Efforts to increase power capacity have been remarkable, but electrical energy continues to fall short of the domestic needs. The development of a power grid among all CEMA countries has alleviated some peak electrical energy supply problems but has not solved the long-run electrical scarcity.

Even in the 1950's, countries such as Hungary and East Germany already needed substantial imports of electricity, on the order of 10 per cent of their total energy consumption, and this percentage is bound to rise dramatically. In spite of efforts to expand output and improve its utilization, severe limitations will have to be placed for a long time to come on the development of industries which require high power inputs, on power consumption in the countryside, and on various agricultural operations.

Against this background, the role of the USSR as purveyor of fuel to the energy-deficient countries of the area should increase significantly. Yet the USSR cannot fulfill all expected CEMA requirements.

Its own domestic needs are expanding and its own interests compel it to sell a certain share of its exportable surpluses in the hard-currency markets; moreover, the USSR will certainly be tempted to manipulate one CEMA country against the other to scale down their competing requirements and induce at least some of them to participate, through capital exports, in the expansion of its own increasingly costly oil extraction facilities and pipelines, in exchange for the fuel they receive from the USSR. Since even under optimistic assumptions the Soviet Union could supply only a part of the projected energy requirements of the area, pressures for expanding trade arrangements, particularly with the oil-producing countries of the Middle East, already very strong, may be expected to gather further momentum in the future.[9]

## MAINTENANCE AND ASSERTION OF SOVIET INFLUENCE

During the first two decades of its development, CEMA's total foreign-trade turnover increased roughly five and a half times, exceeding by some 30 per cent the overall growth rate of world trade. The key element in this expansion was the growth of CEMA's mutual trade, half of which was accounted for by trade with the Soviet Union. Intra-CEMA trade throughout the period absorbed roughly 65 per cent of its total trade, trade with the developed capitalist countries about 15–20 per cent, and trade with the underdeveloped countries 10 per cent. Trade with the non-CEMA socialist countries played only a modest role in CEMA's trade expansion even before the Soviet break with China. The structure, as well as the direction, of CEMA's exports reveals both a capacity of the CEMA countries to contribute substantially to their own industrial transformation even under a Western "strategic embargo" and an incapacity to break into the more demanding, advanced capitalist markets or to shake off the predominance of the USSR.

Within the overall export structure, the divergent characters of the exports to CEMA countries, to the developed countries, and to the underdeveloped countries clearly emphasize the extent to which mutual trade contributed to the area's industrial transformation. Typically, the shares of machinery and equipment were far larger in the exports toward CEMA and the underdeveloped countries than in the trade with developed countries (see Table 7.3). The relative shares of foodstuffs and raw materials in the exports directed toward the developed countries were far larger than those in the exports toward the CEMA and underdeveloped countries. In the early 1960's, machinery and equipment comprised about one-half of the overall exports from the industrialized countries of the area, one-third of those from the middle tier of countries, and one-fourth of those from the least-developed tier. In contrast, fuel and raw materials accounted for roughly one-half of the lowest tier's exports and for one-third of exports from the middle and upper tiers, with foodstuffs particularly significant for the middle-tier countries. For Czechoslovakia, 57.1 per cent and 59.4 per cent of the total exports toward CEMA and the underdeveloped countries, respectively, were machinery and equipment, but they constituted only 14.2 per cent of the total exports toward the developed countries.[10] Data for a middle-tier country like Hungary, during about the same period, reveal a similar pattern: 43.5 and 35.6 per cent of the total exports toward CEMA and toward the underdeveloped countries, respectively, were machinery and equipment; only 4.5 per cent of the total exports toward the developed countries were accounted for by this type of product.[11] Certain CEMA countries are concerned about their incapacity to break into the technologically demanding, advanced Western markets. During the short-lived period of Czech liberalism, Professor Ota Šik noted bluntly that the "insufficient" quality of the Czech goods was "the main reason why Czechoslovak enterprises seek easier sales in less demanding markets and why our exports to the developing countries are quite high, where we are compelled to sell through granting medium- and long-term credits. . . . The fact is that our exports to these countries are in far too great a ratio to our total exports, so these credits also take up too large a share in our exports."[12] Remonstrating on the fact that, in the mid-1960's, the share of machinery and transportation equipment exports from Hungary toward the convertible-currency markets reached only one-tenth of their share in CEMA exports, the Hungarian Professor I.

TABLE 7.3. EASTERN EUROPE'S EXPORTS, IN RELATIVE SHARES, BY
COMMODITY GROUPS AND AREAS, 1963–64

| | EXPORTS BY COMMODITY GROUPS AND AREAS | | | | | COMMODITY STRUCTURE BY AREA | | | | |
|---|---|---|---|---|---|---|---|---|---|---|
| COMMODITY GROUPS | World | Eastern Europe[a] | Western Europe[b] | Developing countries | Rest of world | World | Eastern Europe[a] | Western Europe[b] | Developing countries | Rest of world |
| Total | 100 | 64.8 | 17.7 | 10.4 | 7.1 | 100.0 | 100.0 | 100.0 | 100.0 | 100.0 |
| Food | 100 | 53.7 | 31.9 | 9.9 | 4.5 | 12.3 | 10.2 | 22.2 | 11.6 | 7.9 |
| Raw materials | 100 | 58.7 | 30.0 | 5.0 | 6.3 | 12.0 | 10.9 | 20.4 | 5.7 | 10.6 |
| Fuels | 100 | 53.9 | 30.7 | 7.8 | 7.6 | 11.9 | 9.9 | 20.7 | 8.9 | 12.7 |
| Chemicals | 100 | 63.6 | 19.7 | 9.0 | 7.7 | 4.9 | 4.8 | 5.4 | 4.2 | 5.3 |
| Machinery | 100 | 73.2 | 5.2 | 15.9 | 5.7 | 29.5 | 33.3 | 8.6 | 45.1 | 23.8 |
| Other manufactured goods | 100 | 71.3 | 14.3 | 9.1 | 5.3 | 27.3 | 30.0 | 22.1 | 23.8 | 20.4 |

[a] Eastern Europe: including the European CEMA countries and Albania.

[b] Western Europe: includes all the rest of Europe.

SOURCE: Reduced from basic data in United Nations, Economic Survey of Europe 1966 (New York: United Nations, 1967), Ch. III, p. 31.

Vajda observed that the prospects for selling more "value added" to the West were rather dim; worse still, the relative share of these exports was falling even in the trade with CEMA partly because of the "efforts at import substitution in the individual CEMA countries."[13] Lack of Western demand for Eastern Europe's machinery and equipment and diminishing interest within CEMA itself for its own machinery and equipment reflect the increasingly evident lagging of its technology, a problem to which we shall return below.

With regard to imports, the fallacy of "quantitative planning without market orientation"—as Professor Vajda has succinctly defined the basic approach of CEMA countries to foreign trade—combined with the Western embargo has caused far larger relative shares of intermediate goods (raw materials, semifinished products, and chemicals) to be imported from the West than from CEMA. Thus, again in the case of Czechoslovakia, organic raw materials and chemicals together accounted for 36.8 per cent of imports from the West as against 20.8 per cent of all imports and 12.0 per cent of imports from CEMA.[14] Similarly, the bulk of "industrial production" imported by Hungary from advanced-economy markets has consisted of semifinished intermediate products which, along with chemicals, have claimed a share twice as large as that of machinery in the overall imports from these markets—exactly the reverse of the pattern of the imports from CEMA.[15] Hungary is therefore in the awkward situation that intermediate goods bought in hard-currency markets have been absorbed in the production of finished goods sold, not back in these same markets, but within CEMA or to less-developed countries on long-term credits, thus aggravating Hungary's balance-of-payments problems.

The biggest "constant" of CEMA's trade has been the USSR, to which from one-third to one-half of the foreign-trade turnover in each CEMA country may be attributed. In turn, CEMA's role in the Soviet Union's foreign-trade turnover has risen from some 41 per cent in 1946 to 57 per cent in 1950 and, after a dip to 49 per cent in the middle 1950's, up to 58 per cent in the mid-1960's.[16] Significant changes, however, have occurred during these years, both in the trade relations of the USSR with the various tiers of East European countries and in the structure of overall trade. Throughout CEMA's existence, the relative share of trade with the upper East European tier in the Soviet Union's total trade has tended to increase, that with the lower tier to decrease, while that with the middle tier has remained roughly stationary. The most important trade partners of the USSR are East Germany and Czechoslovakia, who absorb close to one-third of the Soviet trade. The Soviet Union delivers mostly intermediate products to the upper tier, and intermediate products and raw materials (some simply for processing and re-exporting to the Soviet Union), as well as equipment, to the lower and middle tiers. In exchange it accepts machinery and equipment, some of which could not easily be sold in Western markets, along with intermediate products and manufactured consumer goods.

The Soviet Union has maintained its ascendent position in CEMA by a variety of means. Between 1949 and 1953, it relied on a large number of *ad hoc* economic levers, such as reparation obligations, restitutions, liquidation of former enemy assets, joint companies, etc., in the formerly enemy countries of World War II (East Germany, Hungary, Rumania, and Bulgaria) and on some special agreements with the formerly "allied" countries (Czechoslovakia, Poland, and Yugoslavia. In the early 1950's, after the liquidation of most of the economic sequels of the war, including the extensive Soviet holdings in the banks and industries of the formerly enemy countries, and after a number of economic and political crises in 1953–54, the Soviet hold tended to weaken. However, the inability of the countries of the area to expand their trade outside CEMA, the direct Soviet military intervention in Hungary in 1956, and finally, the increasing dependence of many of the countries on Soviet fuels and raw materials, led to the reassertion of the Soviet role. Economic stagnation in some of these countries, particularly Czechoslovakia, after the beginning of the 1960's inspired renewed efforts to cast off the restraints of CEMA and simultaneously the dependence on the USSR. However, during the Czechoslovak liberalization movement in 1968, the Soviet Union reasserted its dominance through military intervention and an affirmation of its "right" to interpose itself in any country of the area for the "preservation of socialism." CEMA has thus become virtually a captive Soviet market, even though each country continues to conduct its own national economic life autonomously.

### DETERRENTS TO EAST-WEST TRADE

The need to expand imports from and exports to the West has been dwelt on by the CEMA countries, including the USSR, since the late 1950's. But two complex sets of problems have limited East-West trade flows. The first, relating to exports from the USSR and Eastern Europe to the United States and Western Europe, has involved the difficulty of reducing trade policies and practices to a common denominator for both market-directed and centrally planned economies. The second, relating to the trade flows from West to East, has concerned the West's denial of certain exports which might directly or indirectly strengthen the military potential of a Communist country.

Serious impediments have prevented a compromise in the divergent Western and Socialist views.[17] The basic philosophy of the Western economies toward international trade, embodied in the provisions of the General Agreement of Tariffs and Trade (GATT) and related documents, is that virtually no direct governmental controls are to be exercised over trade in "normal times." Further, tariffs on imports are to be applied without discrimination by place of origin except for certain cases whose arrangements predate GATT and except for custom unions and free-trade areas. Only by explicit exception can quantitative trade restrictions be resorted to; non-discrimination among members, expressed in the most-favored-nation clause (MFN), may be suspended only in the cases of a custom union's preferential tariffs, a temporary need for import controls and payment restraints, or a restriction for income price supports. In addition, the signatory nations under GATT have mutual obligations encompassing nearly all governmental actions that may affect imports and competition.

In the socialist economies, except Yugoslavia, quantitative control of international trade has been the rule, not the exception (as discussed in Essay 6). The import plan, directly linked to the scope, structure, and targets of the national plan, has been the foundation of foreign-trade planning. Tariffs have had hardly any significance; although some CEMA countries have adopted a two-column tariff, no country has been subjected to the higher duty rates. Selection of suppliers has been guided by the planners' need to guarantee deliveries at predetermined prices for specified periods. CEMA trade negotiations have reflected efforts to coordinate import requirements with national foreign-trade plans and production plans without resorting to the formal tariff or policy agreements used in the West.

Western governments have indicated that under these conditions they cannot meaningfully compare their principles and practices with those followed by the CDSE's, and that in the absence of formal agreements, they cannot be sure of effective reciprocity and the application of MFN treatment by the latter countries. Given these differences, the governments of the market-directed economies have been unwilling to apply GATT principles to any of these countries, even when the latter have been full members of GATT. Clearly, the market-directed economies have wished both to insure their access to socialist markets and to protect themselves against certain dangers arising from centralized state trading, such as market disruption from abrupt shifts in large trading orders. From the West's viewpoint, however, the range of imports subject to control, the stringency of restrictions, and the extent to which transferability of earnings is granted to the CDSE's vary for each of them.[18]

The CEMA governments, for their part, have pointed out that their own differential tariff was but a defensive response to the application of such tariffs by certain market economies, that consideration of relative costs is actually becoming more significant among their various planning criteria, and that unconditional MFN with respect to both tariffs and quantitative trade controls must prevail in any and all transactions if international trade is to develop on a healthy course. Economists of certain CEMA countries, such as Hungary, have drawn attention to the fact that since the 1960's, at least, the connection of imports to the national plan, the quantitative regulation of trade flows, and the whole program of sales and purchases abroad have been changing, thus helping to reduce the differences between East and West in principles and trading practices. But, as we noted in Essay 6, even the "liberalized" countries remain constrained by the priority obligations they have toward the other CEMA countries.

Besides the impediment to East-West trade afforded by the basic differences in approach, a number of special trading restrictions have been enacted by the Western countries since 1948–49 regarding their exports to the socialist countries.[19] Changes in the scope and nature of these restrictions have been numerous and have at times sharply affected the volume, value, and structure of East-West trade. Controls over exports toward the "Soviet bloc," including Yugoslavia in the early post-war years, were initiated first by the United States and then by the Western European countries at a time when political bipolarization and trade compartmentalization seemed unavoidable. From 1948 until the end of 1953, these controls interlocked in a tight and complicated mesh covering virtually all the Western exports directed to what became in 1949 the "Sino-Soviet bloc." First, the United States devised unilateral controls and established a number of procedures meant to insure that any country receiving US aid would not ship to the bloc. Then the Western European countries developed their own export restrictions on trade with the bloc. Finally, multilateral export controls by all powers of the developed world, including Canada and Japan, became locked together. At the close of 1953, the embargo efforts had reached their zenith; subsequently, shifts within both Eastern and Western Europe started to bring about increasing differentiation in the restrictions applied to each socialist country by each Western power.

In 1954, a second period opened in the history of the embargo. The Western powers decided to revise sharply the lists of embargoed goods, quota restrictions, and goods under surveillance relating to the Soviet Union and CEMA, while maintaining all controls over exports to China. The United States, once the pacesetter for its allies in this sphere, decided to pursue a unilateral course according to its own evaluations of the changes taking place among socialist countries. As differentiation among the socialist countries increased and generated centrifugal forces, the United States relaxed or tightened its export regulations toward individual countries: Yugoslavia received the same treatment as non-Communist countries with respect to exports; Poland and Rumania were exempted from validated licenses for certain imports. Conversely, the term "strategic" was extended to encompass goods of economic as well as military importance, an extension that led to the denial of certain nonmilitary goods to the USSR itself.[20] Over the course of time, the embargo applied by the Western European countries became increasingly limited, covering only implements of war and atomic energy items and a selective range of the most-advanced industrial materials and equipment, while the range of goods covered by the US export controls remained more comprehensive. As the Sino-Soviet conflict has continued to deepen throughout the 1960's, the United States has slowly moved to bring its control standards into closer agreement with those of the other Western countries. In the mid-1960's and then again at the end of the 1960's Washington announced its decision to remove hundreds of items from its embargo lists.[21] A *de facto* Western consensus was thus re-established, but this time on a limited and highly flexible range of goods. However, the United States continues to apply almost a total embargo against certain countries (viz., Cuba, North Korea, and North Vietnam) under the "Trading with the Enemy" Act.

## EFFECTS OF VARIOUS FACTORS ON CEMA'S UNITY

Political and economic shifts within the "Sino-Soviet bloc" and changes in the Western embargo have interacted in a variety of ways during CEMA's existence. When the "Sino-Soviet bloc" appeared as a menacing political monolith in the late 1940's and the early 1950's, the CEMA countries declined significantly in their relative importance in world trade. Whereas in 1938 Western Europe and the United States had absorbed 72 per cent of East Europe's exports (including those from the USSR but, of course, not from East Germany), in 1948 this share had fallen to 40 per cent and in 1953 to only 15 per cent. Patterns of supply and demand for the East European goods entering foreign trade changed rapidly under industrialization, due to the avowed desire of the socialist countries to trade with themselves, the primacy of the USSR within CEMA, and the import-export restrictions established by the Western countries against the "bloc." It should, however, be noted that while the East-West trade of the smaller CEMA countries contracted sharply at the time. Soviet trade with the West actually expanded. The Soviet Union was able both to expand its trade with the other socialist countries, including China, and to cut through the embargo lines and develop an expanding trade with the West.

As new trading opportunities began to open in the West, the share of intra-CEMA trade in the total trade of each of the socialist countries began to contract, hitting its lowest level in 1956 and affecting simultaneously the Soviet Union's share of their trade. To foster CEMA's internal trade, the Soviet Union introduced the idea of integrating not only the foreign trade of the CEMA countries but also their underlying production programs. After 1956 and the Soviet intervention in Hungary, the intra-CEMA trade started to expand and again reached 65 per cent of the area's overall trade, but this time the expansion took place because of the corresponding contractions in the trade with China.

By the end of the 1950's trade linkages between East and West resumed their traditional forms, with shipments of foods, fuels, and crude materials from the East against steel, machinery, and industrial equipment from the West. Important shifts within these broad groups had occurred, however. East European exports had changed from primarily cereals and coal to oil, pig iron, and timber. Poland's coal exports were squeezed out of Western markets by expanding American coal exports. Finally, after the mid-1950's, Soviet oil exports rose sharply, mainly toward Italy, Germany, and Finland. In turn, the import share of processed steel, metals, chemicals, and equipment from the West increased during these years but only for the Soviet Union and the least-developed tier of CEMA countries, notably Rumania.

Since the 1960's almost all the socialist countries of Eastern Europe have been seeking to expand their contacts with the West, to surmount the traditional difficulties existing between West and East in marketing and merchandising, and to find—with the help of Western businessmen—new ways of circumventing Eastern Europe's shortage of convertible foreign exchange. Countries like East Germany and Czechoslovakia have tried to lessen the steel-intensiveness of their industrial economies and to move somewhat away from heavy products such as large generators and turbines toward machine construction, chemical equipment, precision instruments, and electrical equipment. Their dependence on Soviet exports of fuel, raw materials, and food, however, has rendered such changes possible only insofar as they were undertaken with Soviet acquiescence. Czechoslovakia attempted to go beyond this point and fully revamp its industries through deepening contacts with the West, but it was abruptly stopped in August

1968 by Russian occupation. A number of other countries have en-couraged some of their enterprises to work as subcontractors for Western industries (e.g., Swedish mechanical industries). Others, as pointed out in Essay 6, have organized various forms of industrial technical cooperations: large-scale exchanges of technological in-formation, commercial licensing of specific patents, contracts under special, bilaterally negotiated terms and payment arrangements (in clearing or switch financing and barter), and joint-venture invest-ments.[22]

CEMA trade has thus been pulled in various directions which would enhance its centrifugal tendencies were it not for the Soviet military efforts at holding the "second world market" together. The Western embargo has indisputably sharpened intra-bloc conflicts be-tween the richer and the less well-endowed countries, spurred (at least during some critical moments) policies that would de-emphasize development along autarkic lines, imposed a real cost on the socialist countries by denying them the benefits of foreign trade, discouraged their receipt of long-term credits, and contributed, indirectly at least, toward keeping East-West trade at low levels (though the embargo was intended to deal with the composition rather than the volume of this trade). On the other hand, one may note that whether the main objective of the embargo—the depression of the rate at which the Soviet Union and the bloc would be able to build their capacity "to wage war"—could be approached through trade controls is highly problematical.[23] In the atomic age, military preparedness may de-pend on the availability of specific scientific skills indigenous or im-ported, plus the capacity and will to develop and integrate a set of advanced industries and supporting facilities. The impact of the em-bargo on such factors may have been very limited. As we now know, not only the USSR but also China was able to develop nuclear capa-bilities. Furthermore, a policy applied indiscriminately to a whole set of countries could only accentuate the dependence of the less-endowed on the better-endowed in the area. Indeed, the middle and lower East European tiers have grown more reliant on the USSR and, for a while at least, on the more-advanced East European coun-tries. The embargo hit the poorly developed countries harder than it did the industrialized countries. Until new opportunities for trade with the West were opened, the embargo consolidated the monopoly positions of the USSR and the industrially advanced tier within CEMA and strengthened the emergent trading patterns. The opening of alternative sources of supply for higher quality goods at lower prices "exposed" the inefficiency of certain CEMA industries, forced policy-makers, planners, and managers to reorganize those industries, and encouraged Czechoslovakia, for instance, to attempt to turn boldly toward the West.

## CEMA-STRENGTHENING POLICIES, PAST AND FUTURE

The hopes entertained at the inception of CEMA—of forming an expanding socialist "world market," of successfully solving in isolation any and all problems of modern technology, of achieving "independence" from the West, and of drawing the underdeveloped countries into CEMA's orbit—have proved illusory. Few Soviet and East European economists today refer with conviction to CEMA as the "second world market." What they now stress is the existence of a "socialist world system" of which CEMA is not necessarily the most important element. In certain socialist countries it is recognized that the overall industrialization effort of the area has been lagging behind the world level "mainly because of the low quality of investment goods mutually developed."[24] Modernization processes have been carried out in a number of important directions, but even so the CEMA countries lack the means or the freedom to shift their production patterns according to their own decisions to specialize. The countries that push toward a larger and more meaningful division of labor within CEMA, above all the USSR itself and the countries most dependent on it (East Germany, Hungary, and Poland), are deeply mistrusted by the other countries, particularly the less-developed ones which see, in the supranational integration scheme, a means not only of arresting their industrialization but also a means of wresting control over their planning and, ultimately, over their entire national economic life.[25] In short, CEMA's "integration" with the USSR is fraught with distrust, yet CEMA's "integration" without the USSR is out of the question.

While there is much talk about socialist cooperation, actual technological cooperation within CEMA as a whole has shrunk rather than expanded since, in the words of a Soviet economist, "those nations which selflessly shared their technical achievements not only have often lost their consumers but have also found themselves competing in foreign markets with similar goods built in accordance with their own licenses and documentation."[26] Since the mid-1960's, assistance in research and design work, previously shared freely, has been drastically curtailed, especially when large investments have been involved; spreading research costs among interested CEMA members has been increasingly advocated; exchanges of patents and licenses have been put strictly on a cost basis. What emerges little by little, within the general framework of CEMA's trade coordination for the 1970's, is a closer cooperation within an inner circle of CEMA, formed by the USSR, Bulgaria, Poland, and East Germany—the countries which for political reasons have not been able to turn appreciably toward the West. This CEMA inner circle proposes to accelerate its own technological transformation, eliminate the bottlenecks of the past in its growth processes, unite efforts in purchasing equipment and licenses from the West, and eventually catch up and surpass the West in the contemporary technological race.

Actually, the idea of gaining "independence" from the West is as old as the Soviet system and no more likely to be successful in the 1970's than it was in the 1960's or 1950's. Furthermore, the socialist world is as diverse as its capitalist counterpart: in certain respects Eastern Europe is lagging behind the Soviet Union, perhaps just as Western Europe lags behind the United States, while the socialist camp as a whole lags behind contemporary capitalist technology. This lag—as we shall see in the following essay—in part shapes the tensions and conflicts among socialist countries and significantly weakens the economic attraction of the camp, of CEMA, and the inner circle itself for the vast uncommitted zone of underdeveloped countries. Paradoxically, the spread of socialist influence into some specific less-developed regions, such as the Middle East, has been due not so much to the camp's peaceful deliveries of equipment for industrialization as to its ability to furnish the means of war and destruction.

# [ CHAPTER 8 ]

## *National Development, Foreign Assistance, & Inter-Country Conflicts*

DISAGREEMENTS among socialist countries often involve more factors in more complex combinations than do altercations among capitalist countries. Along with the national, political, social, or economic sources, socialist disagreements also have complex ideological overtones, which obscure the nature and scope of the conflict at hand, much as they do in wars of religion. In fact, a Yugoslav commentator has pointed out that conflicts within the socialist camp are usually couched "in the religious terminology of orthodoxy and heresy, submission or schism." Nevertheless, despite the evangelistic charges and countercharges, the underlying issues which have divided the socialist camp are clear and quite familiar. Basically they are development conflicts among "have" and "have nots," viewed in the context of the century-long claims by Marxian-Leninists concerning imperialist exploitation of less powerful nations.

The socialist camp, like the capitalist world, is made up of countries differing vastly in size, factor endowment, level of development, and growth potential. In the camp, as in the rest of the world, an overarching question is how disparities in development and growth potential can be overcome: how and at what speed can the backward countries overcome their backwardness and rise to "highest" levels of modernity. The traditional Soviet prescription for development, priority development of heavy industry within a centrally planned, edict-managed economy, certainly cannot yield the same results in a small and poorly endowed country, which can never hope to muster the critical investable mass needed to propel it rapidly into the highest contemporary levels of development, as it can in a vast underdeveloped country with large and as yet untapped resources.

Should a small, poorly endowed country apply the traditional Soviet model and press for massive help from better endowed countries, or should it abandon outright any self-sufficiency trials—its "all around" development, in Soviet parlance—and strive toward some broad and meaningful inter-socialist division of labor and economic cooperation? And conversely, should a better-endowed socialist country pour its resources into its poorer allies to help them overcome their backwardness as fast as possible, or should it first further its own growth (up to, say, a level of affluence outstripping the capitalist one) such that it could no longer be threatened when it turned to assist the laggard socialist countries? What is more important for the camp as a whole: more equality in per capita incomes now, or a recognized priority for the better-endowed socialist countries to "reach and surpass" the level of development of the most advanced capitalist countries in order to keep the capitalist world in check?

These are some of the questions that now divide and torment the socialist camp.[1] They are at the root of the most important conflicts and splits which have torn the camp apart, the "revisionist" and "dogmatist" splits: the Yugoslav-Soviet split of 1948, the Albanian-Yugoslav split of the same year, the Albanian-Soviet split of 1961, and the Sino-Soviet conflict which erupted openly in the early 1960's but which had started, in fact, in the mid-1950's. As the largest, best-endowed country with the greatest industrial capacity and output in the camp, the Soviet Union was bound to suffer the preponderance of demands for aid from the most backward countries. On the other hand, as an intermediately developed country itself, with a perennially lagging agricultural sector, an obsolete and inefficient light industry, and an enormous national appetite for "catching up and surpassing" the United States, the Soviet Union and its leadership were forced simultaneously to ward off some of the overly pressing claims of the poorest socialist countries and to extend their controls over the socialist commonwealth as a whole. Under that policy, in the absence of unforeseen technological breakthroughs, the camp would remain as diverse and unequal by the beginning of the twenty-first century as it was at the beginning of the last third of this century. According to projections made in 1965, the per capita gross national product of the US in 1965 could be reached by the upper, industrialized tier of

Eastern Europe in some 20 years, by the middle tier and the USSR in roughly 30 years, by the lowest tier in about 40 years, and by China in 110 years.[2] This prediction is precisely why the Chinese hope not only that they will "advance at leap-forward speed" but also that the capitalist countries will "fall behind," torn by insuperable crises.[3] The revolution of "rising expectations" has gripped all underdeveloped areas, but the urgency to attain the expectations is paramount in the socialist camp, where the leadership is development oriented and where some policy-makers believe themselves able "to use a different way from all Western countries to forge forward at flying speed toward a modern industry, modern agriculture, modern science and culture."[4]

In the present essay we shall examine the approaches taken to the question of national development and foreign assistance by various countries of the camp, and show how these approaches conflicted and eventually caused gaping and probably irreconcilable splits. Specifically we will view the economic rationale of the Yugoslav-Soviet split of the late 1940's, the motivation and impact of the Albanian-Yugoslav and Albanian-Soviet conflicts, the Sino-Soviet conflicts, and the Soviet Union's claims toward the other countries in CEMA. Finally we will consider the prospects for an "evening out" of economic differences within the camp and the problem of economic development under socialism in general.

## THE YUGOSLAV-SOVIET SPLIT

Soviet concepts concerning the economic development of the "first socialist state," worked out during the interwar years, had a decisive influence on the domestic and the foreign economic policies of the USSR immediately after World War II. These concepts, devised for a self-sufficient power encircled by its enemies, were maintained virtually unchanged even after the Soviet isolation had ended and the USSR had become surrounded with a number of friendly "popular democratic" states. The Soviet assumptions that the USSR was the "bastion" of a new economic system which would spread world-wide, that its defense and survival required it to surpass the most advanced capitalist countries militarily and economically; and that, if need be, it should build alone a "superior" communist order based on abundance rather than on scarcity determined not only its strategy of economic development, but also its foreign economic strategy vis-à-vis the capitalist countries and the new "popular democracies" as well. It is precisely these assumptions that were soon to be challenged by some of the other socialist states—first by Yugoslavia, then by Albania, and later by China above all.

In the aftermath of World War II, the Soviet Union requested from its newly acquired allies cessions of large territories, wholesale displacements of certain national groups, "restitutions," reparations, levies on current production, and control over former-enemy assets which subsequently became the basis for a network of joint-companies dominating banking industry and transport facilities in certain countries.[5] The conquered countries in particular entered the postwar liberation period burdened by innumerable Soviet economic mortgages, claims which the Communist parties of those countries willingly accepted as necessary for the "higher aims" of rebuilding the Soviet bastion against the capitalist world. Notwithstanding the Soviet controls, each popular democracy was viewed by Moscow and by its own leaders as a fully autonomous economic entity accountable for both its assets and its liabilities. With each of them the Soviet Union developed mutual trade and aid relations on the basis of each nation's national plan.

Immediately following the war, only the leaders of Communist Yugoslavia dared to question the long-established idea of Soviet preeminence among socialist states and the rights which the Soviet Union assumed flowed from it. The Yugoslav Communists had resisted the Nazis and had acceded to power at the head of a popular national Partisans' army. They felt entitled to formulate some counterclaims of their own against the Soviet Union. Starting from assumptions similar to the Soviet Union's, the Yugoslavs argued that their country was also a socialist bastion which needed to be reinforced, that it was in the Soviet Union's interest to fortify this bastion, and that Yugoslavia's own economic plans, patterned after the Soviet model, could be carried out only with sizable Soviet help. "No matter how much each of us loves the land of Socialism, the USSR," observed the Central Committee of the Communist Party of Yugoslavia, "he can in no case love his country less, which is also developing socialism. . . ."[6] And the Central Committee added:

> Even though we know that the USSR has tremendous difficulties with the reconstruction of the devastated land we rightfully expect the assistance of the USSR in the development of our country and the realization of the Five Year Plan without material deprivation to the people of the USSR, because we feel it is to the interest of the USSR for the new Yugoslavia to be stronger, since it is face to face with the capitalist world which is endangering not only its peaceful development but the development of other countries of people's democracy and even the development of the USSR.[7]

The Communist leadership of Yugoslavia decided to put an end to Soviet interferences in their economic affairs and to formulate a fully integrated theory of their own concerning foreign trade, particularly with regard to prices and terms of trade, and foreign aid, notably its forms and amount. Their arguments, which were to play a crucial role in the economic quarrels that subsequently split the bloc, were bolstered with quotations from Marx, Lenin, and Stalin, but they were, as we shall see on close examination, quite similar in substance to those advanced on this side of the world by other underdeveloped countries.

With respect to foreign trade, the Yugoslavs asserted that world market prices should not be applied to inter-socialist trade, and that the Soviet Union, thanks to its overwhelming power, was able both to secure cheap imports from the East European countries and to deliver exports to them at high prices. Following the Marxian theory of foreign trade (to which we already referred in Essay 6), the Yugoslavs contended first of all that the international price pattern was advantageous for industrialized countries (socialist or not) "by definition" because, given their higher productivity per man in their export goods sector, it allowed them to reap automatic advantages in terms of exchanges of materialized labor.[8] Accordingly, they especially accused Hungary and Czechoslovakia of establishing unfair terms of trade, specifically in their importation of Yugoslav iron ore in exchange for their exports of machinery. The Soviet Union, the Yugoslavs claimed, was able to reap additional profits because of the special terms it was able to impose on the weaker and smaller countries through bilateral agreements. The data adduced by the Yugoslavs concerning trade in general did not fully support their case.[9] On the one hand, the Russians also exported raw materials and imported machinery so that the international price pattern, if applied in their case as in the others, would have worked against them just as it presumably did against the Yugoslavs; on the other hand, there was evidence of a *general* tendency among the bloc countries to inflate prices, at that time of decreasing supplies from the West, as each socialist partner attempted to benefit wherever possible from the particular situation.[10] The facts are hard to pinpoint, in part because of the variability of trade terms, depending upon the individual trade sectors involved and in part because of the lack of adequate statistics. The Chinese have also insisted, as we shall see below, that the Russians have deliberately been rigging the terms of trade against the other socialist countries. Some Western economists are inclined to agree that there has been such Soviet exploitation, although others are skeptical.[11]

Concerning foreign assistance, the Yugoslav Communist leaders asserted that Soviet aid was neither "disinterested" nor "abundant," contrary to Russian allegations. Soviet aid, the Yugoslavs further stated, was actually a strict "commercial transaction based on capitalist principles and on the jungle law of capital,"[12] tied to interest charges, annuity repayments, and other obligations;[13] in short, they accused the Russians of labeling as "aid" any and all exchanges of goods, and particularly those involving "investment agreements."[14] Referring to the formation of Soviet-Yugoslav joint companies—Justa and Juspad, for air and river transport—and to Soviet proposals for other joint partnerships in industry, the Yugoslav leaders contended in an official "White Book" that such companies were a "screen to conceal direct exploitation": the Russians systematically overpriced the assets they transferred to a joint partnership, while they underpriced the Yugoslav contribution; moreover, in the industrial joint ventures, the Russians were requesting not only that a large share of the output be exported free of charge to the USSR but that they should also control the distribution of the remaining output within Yugoslavia.[15] Overpricing of assets, we should note, would fully offset the element of subsidy involved in the relatively low interest rates (compared with similar commercial loans abroad) which the Russians usually charge in capital lending. Referring to other forms of technical assistance, such as the training of Yugoslav experts in the USSR, the Yugoslavs averred that the services rendered were overvalued through manipulation of the rate of exchange and requests of repayment in hard currency, and that salaries requested for Soviet experts on loan to Yugoslavia were far out of line with the salary structure prevailing in Yugoslavia for corresponding services.

There is an obvious parallel between some of the arguments advanced by the Yugoslavs against the USSR and those usually presented against the Western countries by the representatives of the underdeveloped countries. Terms of trade that are presumably adverse for primary producers—for the Yugoslavs because of the intrinsic nature of the goods traded and for the others because of an alleged secular deterioration of primary product prices—have been taken in both cases to justify the demand that the more developed countries, as beneficiaries of the imbalance, transfer back part of such "unearned" income. Though the arguments involved have often been seriously challenged, they have led to further proposals: in the East, that the world price pattern be replaced by some socialist price pattern in inter-socialist trade; in the West, that the industrialized countries "take a political decision in favor of parity for the primary products exported by the developing countries."[16]

Concerning aid, the Yugoslavs, in the early 1950's, both explicitly or implicitly underlined many of the inefficiencies which have since been recognized as common afflictions of foreign assistance, particularly the provisions of bilateral agreements that purchases be made from the donor country: the recipient pays substantially higher prices than those obtainable in a competitive market for aid equipment, assumes an obligation to pay excessively for sub-optimal equipment because the donor might not be the most efficient producer of the equipment or because he might not provide the technology most appropriate to the recipient country, and so on.[17] In the East as in the West, these shortcomings have led to the advocacy of multilateral rather than bilateral aid agreements and to proposals for unrestricted aid. The Yugoslavs were the first to propound the idea that foreign assistance was a kind of "moral obligation" for developed countries, though the argument they adduced then was specifically that Yugo-slavia had "proportionately suffered the greatest human and material losses during the war."[18]

The Soviet leadership rejected the Yugoslav contentions and their underlying assumptions. Such claims represented the first open chal-lenge to a subtle but all-pervasive Soviet hegemony in the name of "higher aims," the first attack on the myth of "superior" forms of so-cialist trade and aid, the first public accusation of Soviet economic exploitation, and the first explosion from the pressures of uneven eco-nomic development under socialism. The Soviet leadership denied any Soviet hegemony, selfish business interests, or crude exploitation of smaller and less developed countries. But it did not waste much time arguing against the first *"communisme de gouvernement"* other than Moscow's. It expelled Yugoslavia from the camp, and invited the "true Communists" of Yugoslavia to rebel and replace Tito and his "clique." The Soviet Union did not choose to intervene militarily, possibly because it hoped that Tito would be easily replaced under the force of the "loyal" Communists. The USSR then broke its com-mercial agreements with Yugoslavia and clamped on a damaging economic blockade from which Yugoslavia escaped only slowly and painfully, and, in no small measure, thanks to American aid.

## THE ALBANIAN-YUGOSLAV AND ALBANIAN-SOVIET SPLITS

Are there some special, superior forms of trade and aid which could prevail among unevenly developed socialist countries? The Communist Yugoslav leadership between July 1946 and July 1948 seemed to believe that it had indeed discovered such forms and ap-plied them in its relationship with Albania. The opinion was soon found not to be reciprocated.

In a bilateral agreement signed in 1946, Yugoslavia and Albania decided to coordinate their economic plans "over the next thirty years," to form a custom union, to achieve currency parity, and to standardize their price levels. It was also decided in that year to create joint partnerships for prospecting and developing Albania's oil and metals, and for operating its electricity, banking, transport, and foreign-trade sectors. In this and other agreements, conventions, and protocols, the Yugoslavs extended to the Albanians various loans and a variety of technical assistance.

The preponderance of Yugoslavia over Albania in terms of population, size, and economic development, reinforced by this close economic association and the network of joint partnerships for the management and development of Albania's principal resources, should have been obvious from the outset. Yet the Yugoslavs proclaimed that they were only helping tiny Albania to fulfill its development goals and cope with its consumption needs, even while Yugoslavia was experiencing an extremely difficult period. The Yugoslavs supplied Albania with rail construction equipment, electrical installation, and other machinery, all on credit, as well as with various kinds of technical assistance for carrying out industrial projects. According to the Yugoslavs, over the two-year period of their cooperation they delivered to the Albanians roughly ten times the value of goods and services that they obtained in exchange (2.6 billion dinars as against 260 million dinars).[19]

However, no sooner did the Soviet-Yugoslav conflict break into the open than the Albanians—traditionally hostile to Yugoslavia for its possession of large Albanian settlements—assailed the Yugoslavs with apparently the same charges as those the Yugoslavs were hurling at the Russians. Overnight, the Albanian Communists broke their thirty-year contractual obligations, proclaimed themselves independent from Yugoslav domination, denounced the joint companies as colonial exploitation, and decried the Yugoslav assistance as a screen for subjugation:

Under the pretext of advancing credit to Albania . . . the Yugoslav Government endeavoured to take over the management of our country's economy . . . Altering in principle as well as in practice the formula of the coordination of economic plans the Yugoslav Government brutally pursued a policy of domination in our country, an economic policy of colonial exploitation. It threatened the sovereignty and independence of the Albanian State . . . As to the joint Albanian-Yugoslav companies, the Yugoslav Government . . . made no investment in them, but on the contrary exploited the riches of our country . . .[20]

The Yugoslav Communist leadership countered that there was nothing in the agreements that limited Albania's independence; that there was nothing in them that could be taken for colonial exploitation; and that their assistance was tendered without interest, annuity repayments, and obligations. The joint-partnership agreements were "a unique example" of economic "selflessness" since they called for unilateral Yugoslav investments, reciprocated only by a very small share in profits.[21] One Yugoslav writer recalled that the joint companies were, after all, a "form already established by the USSR"; the Yugoslavs, he said had used the same "form" but had changed its "content and techniques," allowing for better conditions for their partners.[22] The official documents, however, do not show striking departures from the Soviet methods: the agreements placed the Yugoslavs in key managerial positions in Albania, much as the Russians had in various other East European countries. Furthermore, the Yugoslavs emulated the Russians also in their uncompromising pursuit of reparations claims against their one-time enemies, Hungary and Bulgaria.[23] One cannot discern in their approach any new patterns of aid leading to "progressive unification and fraternal cooperation."[24]

In any event, the Albanians soon replaced Yugoslavian with Soviet economic patronage. This new rapprochement lasted officially until 1960, though strains had appeared in it as far back as the mid-1950's. The evolution of this second Albanian conflict throws further light on the complex stresses and tensions among unevenly developed socialist countries.

During the 1950's, the Soviet Union supplied Albania with roughly one-fifth of the main industrial projects completed there in that decade; such projects accounted for one-fourth of Albania's industrial output at the time.[25] Besides credits or gifts from the Soviet Union and the other socialist countries (the Soviet credits granted up to 1957 were then converted to a gift), Albania was also assisted by technical missions, such as pre-investment surveys and aid in construction and initial operations of factories, and training of Albanian students in various socialist countries.

That the Albanian-Soviet relations would be inherently highly asymmetrical in respective importance to the two countries is readily understood; although Soviet aid relative to the size of the Albanian economy was substantial, it was necessarily insignificant in terms of Soviet aid priorities. During the first half of the 1950's, the main claimants to Soviet aid were some of the Asian CDSE's, particularly China, and during the second half of that decade, the Soviets shifted their interests toward strategically important non-bloc countries, mainly India and later Egypt.[26]

The first signs of strain in the Albanian-Soviet relations appeared after the middle of the 1950's, when the Russians softened their stance against "revisionism" and began to mend their fences with Yugoslavia as a first step toward broadening their interests in what was then called the "third" or "neutral" world. The Albanians viewed this rapprochement with suspicion, reinforced by their hostility toward Belgrade and their claims on the Albanian-populated but Yugoslav-occupied territory of Kosmet (Kossovo-Metojia). Albania then recognized a fresh possibility: the protection of a new and potentially more congenial patron, China, not only would help Albania economically but would also uphold its claims against Yugoslavia. An open, official understanding between Albania and China first took place at the end of the 1950's, but a virtual agreement had come into existence about five years earlier.

The economic accusations set forth by Albania in its quarrel with the USSR concerned primarily the repeated Soviet attempts to interfere in its decision-making processes, the niggardliness of Soviet aid to Albania and other socialist countries (as opposed to "bountifulness" toward non-bloc countries), and, finally, alleged outright Soviet sabotage of Albanian development as soon as Albania made any sign of veering away from Soviet influence. It was claimed that high-paid experts on loan from the Soviet Union had "hidden" their engineering blueprints, had abandoned their work in disorder (including preinvestment geological surveys), and had shown undue haste to return home even though they had been invited by the Albanians to stay on.

The Soviet Union, followed by other Eastern European countries, countered with its usual instruments. It broke all economic relations with Albania, recalled its experts, and expelled the Albanian trainees. It then denounced Albania, in a comprehensive bill of particulars published in the main Soviet theoretical journal on Communist affairs, *Kommunist,* for the "crimes" of "nationalism and narrowmindedness," "inordinate demands on the USSR and the other socialist countries," and "reprehensible actions" against Soviet citizens. *Kommunist* accused the Albanians of manifesting "egoistic" concern with their own interests and resentment for the socialist aid granted to the underdeveloped countries of Asia and of Africa. Albania's demands on the USSR were "in violation of the principle of reciprocity" and demonstrated that it "conceived of socialism as a one-way obligation of the other socialist countries to gratify all its economic needs." Finally, the Albanians had harassed the Soviet experts "without rhyme or reason" and hampered their work by continuous police scrutiny and intelligence surveillance.[27]

This exchange provides an insight into the atmosphere of some socialist mutual assistance. But also, and more important, it reflects the Soviet Union's clear intention to minimize any claims of the East European countries that extend over and above the "principle of reciprocity" so that it can freely direct its main assistance capability outside the bloc in the pursuit of its own long-range strategic interests. It is the questioning of this expansion of influence that the Soviet Union found distasteful and branded as "egoism" and "nationalist narrowmindedness."

Thus Albania became the second country to be expelled from the Soviet bloc. The Soviet Union again did not choose to intervene militarily—paradoxically because "rebel" Yugoslavia acted in fact as a shield for far-off Albania. Albania's expulsion from the camp took place not because "Hoxha and his Myrmidons" (as Janos Kadar derisively called the Albanians and their Communist leader) were really as unimportant to the Soviet Union's strategic designs as Kadar suggested, nor because they were doggedly worshiping the late Stalin. It took place because the Soviet Union was ready to punish, with the most appropriate means at its command, any socialist country which would interfere with the pursuit of its economic policy priorities, and, further, because Albania hoped to fulfill its own aspirations better by exploiting the new bipolarization of the bloc and China's willingness to challenge Moscow's "pre-eminence" in the socialist camp.

## THE SINO-SOVIET CONFLICT

An influential group in the Chinese leadership started to detach itself from Moscow about the middle of the 1950's.[28] Like the Yugo-

slavs and the Albanians, the Chinese began to resent the interferences of Moscow's leadership in China's economic policies and started
to reject the Soviet assertion that each Soviet economic achievement
was a "victory" for all socialist states. Mao and his group seemed
particularly incensed by the claim of the Soviet leadership under
Khrushchev that the USSR was already "building communism"—i.e.,
an economy of plenty—at a time when China and many other socialist states were facing enormous difficulties in their drive to
industrialization.

The Chinese started also to question seriously the underlying assumptions of the Soviet Union's economic policies—namely, that the
USSR was everybody else's advanced bastion, that it must surpass
the USA in economic competition, and that it must successfully create, as soon as possible, the Soviet affluent society. Proceeding from
their own national problems, as have all the other *"communistes de
gouvernement,"* including the Russians themselves, the Chinese proclaimed that China was a socialist bastion at least as significant as
the USSR, particularly since the Russians could not enforce their own
views there through military occupation.

The Chinese refused to be placed in a subordinate position by the
USSR, asserted that a secondary role was precisely what the Russians
were handing them by denying them military help, particularly the
atomic bomb, accused the Soviet Union of putting them and other
socialist countries "on a par" with their enemies by extending aid to
those enemies (viz., India, in China's view), and finally, challenged
what they characterized as artificial socialist divisions of labor that
directly hindered the building of integrated socialist economies.

In a number of increasingly malevolent exchanges of official letters
between the Central Committees of the two parties and articles between their main press organs, the Chinese and the Russians explicitly detailed their divergences on a number of important problems.
The Chinese underscored the strictly commercial or "quid pro quo"
character of Soviet aid:

. . . Pravda and Izvestiia and other Soviet propaganda media again beat the
drum to the same tune. We have not yet made a systematic reply in the
press, but we must point out that, so far from being gratis, Soviet aid to
China was rendered mainly in the form of trade and that it was certainly

not a one-way affair. China has paid and is paying the Soviet Union in goods, gold or convertible foreign exchange for all Soviet-supplied complete sets of equipment and other goods, including those made available on credit plus interest. It is necessary to add that the prices of many of the goods we imported from the Soviet Union were much higher than those on the world market.[29]

In the Chinese view, not only had the Soviet Union "also received corresponding aid from China,"[30] but there were "ulterior motives" in Soviet aid, including the desire to reduce other socialist countries into dependencies while building up those countries' enemies, e.g., India.[31] Under Moscow's control, the division of labor among vastly unequally developed socialist countries was, or could be synonymous with, exploitation:

It would be great power chauvinism to deny these basic principles and, in the name of "international division of labor" or "specialization," to impose one's own will on others, infringe on the independence and sovereignty of fraternal countries or harm the interests of their people.

In relations among socialist countries it would be preposterous to follow the practice of gaining profit for oneself at the expense of others, a practice characteristic of relations among capitalist countries . . .[32]

The Chinese launched their main attacks against a second goal of the Soviet foreign economic policy—that of an eventual Soviet "victory" in the economic competition with the USA. The Russians, China claimed, by transforming the old Stalinist slogan of "catching up with and surpassing the highest indices of capitalism" into a policy based on peaceful economic competition and peaceful coexistence, were, in fact, replacing the alliance of oppressed peoples with a coexistence and cooperation with their enemies, and were liquidating international class warfare. The Soviet contention that economic competition with capitalism would ultimately deliver a crushing blow to capitalist relationships and bring about a peaceful worldwide transition to socialism was vigorously rejected by the Chinese Communist leaders:

This is equivalent to saying that the oppressed peoples and nations . . . should just wait quietly until the production levels and living standards of the Soviet Union outstrip those of the most developed capitalist countries when the oppressed and exploited . . . would be able to enter communism together with their oppressors and exploiters.[33]

The Chinese Communists took issue with the Soviet statements of readiness to start building communism, asserted that *all* "socialist countries are still removed from the higher stage of communism,"[34] and concluded that the Soviet idea of communism in the Khrushchev manner—viz., "a good dish of goulash" for everybody—was actually "bourgeois philistinism" devoid of "an iota of scientific communism."[35]

Whereas the Yugoslav Communists had centered their economic arguments against the Soviet leadership on their own theory of trade and aid, the Chinese centered theirs on a more general theory of economic development. According to them, the socialist countries, and above all China, must and would find new ways of carrying out their technical revolution:

We cannot just take the beaten track traversed by other countries in the development of technology and trail behind them at a snail's pace. We must break away from the conventions and do our utmost to adopt advanced techniques in order to build our country into a powerful modern socialist state in not too long a historical period. Is this impossible of attainment? Is this boasting and bragging? Certainly not. It can be done.[36]

In short, the Chinese reasoned that, in the socialist camp, just as in the capitalist world, those who trail economically could leap to the forefront while those now ahead could fall behind during the long period of transition to communism.[37]

In 1960, the Soviets countered the Chinese criticism in various ways: they broke their economic, diplomatic, and military relations with Peking, withdrew their experts, canceled the projects of scientific and technological cooperation, and expelled Chinese students. The rapidity with which these measures were invoked demonstrates how easily Moscow has used all instruments at its command in any "ideological" conflict and, further, why the socialist countries have been so reluctant to engage in any lasting division of labor with Moscow.

Be that as it may, the Russians set out their own theoretical and practical arguments in a report presented by M. A. Suslov to one of their Central Committee "plenums" in 1964. Concerning first the questions of Soviet hegemony, socialist cooperation, and mutual aid, Suslov affirmed that the Russians had never intended to dominate or exploit others and had never sought "advantage or profit." Rather, it had been the Chinese Communists who set out to "sow discord" among the CEMA and the USSR, build a self-sufficient economy, and abolish socialist trade relations, because they had no real interest in "strengthening the unity of the world socialist system." Referring to Soviet growth and the policy of economic competition with capitalism, Suslov stressed that, in the "struggle against imperialism" for the ultimate destruction of capitalist relationships, the socialist countries were pivotal: it was their achievements which stimulated anti-imperialist rebellion within the less-developed countries. Therefore, Suslov added, "Those who wish the victory of socialism must first of all strengthen the great socialist community and its economic might, must raise the living standards of their people, develop science, technology. . . ." By building up the economic and defense potential of the socialist countries, the USSR was consequently making "a tremendous contribution to its internationalist duty." The Maoist contention that the transition from socialism to communism would extend over a long historical period was not correct: "All the facts indicate that the socialist countries can within a historically short time surpass the capitalist countries economically." Alluding finally to the Soviet's own economic development and pursuit of affluence within its frontiers, Suslov rejected the Chinese concept of "big leaps forward"—actually an earlier Bolshevik idea—the Chinese approach to economic development in general, and the apparent indifference of the Chinese leaders to their own people's living standards:

Neither Marx nor Lenin had anywhere even remotely hinted that the rockbottom tasks of socialist construction may be realized by the method of "leaps" and cavalry charges, overlooking the degree to which the socio-economic and spiritual premises of the advance have matured and ignoring the tasks of improving the living standard of the people.[38]

The several schisms in the socialist camp, notwithstanding their apparent diversity and complexity, have thus ultimately hinged on disagreements over foreign economic policy, foreign aid, and strategies for economic development. For the USSR, its own steady growth, along with that of its most closely associated socialist states, is of paramount importance for the future of all socialism. For Mao's China, however, it is China's growth by a number of leaps over a very long historical period, struggling, along with other countries, against both "imperialism" and "Soviet revisionism," that will eventually bring about a new world-wide relationship of forces. The differences in approach reflect above all the differences in strength and the national policy positions from which the Moscow and Peking bureaucracies act: both, however, reason as *"communistes du gouvernement,"* preoccupied with their respective country's interests.

## SOVIET RELATIONS WITH OTHER CEMA COUNTRIES

If the Russians indignantly rejected the Yugoslav theories on world prices and socialist terms of trade in 1948, they have felt no reluctance to use them in a new version and to their own advantage some twenty years later. Indicating the expanding role of the USSR as a supplier of fuels and raw materials to the CEMA countries, Soviet economists have suggested since the late 1960's that the use of the prevailing world prices of these materials has had a negative impact on Soviet trade and on the Soviet economy in general. Thus the Soviets have turned the earlier Yugoslav arguments concerning the "intrinsic" disadvantage for exporters of raw materials into a modern Soviet version of cost-profit analyses. According to I. Dudinski, for instance, the Soviet Union has had to "transform the desert into blooming oases" in central Asia to produce the cotton required by CEMA, and, to provide oil for the European USSR and thence for Eastern Europe, has had to establish new centers in the "uninhabited and inclement districts of Siberia." To supply just these two raw materials has required enormous productive and infrastructural investments, which, according to Dudinski, are improperly reflected in world prices. Furthermore, the machinery and goods of mass consumption delivered in return by the CEMA countries have not adequately compensated the raw material producers, who, in any event, have had to resort to the hard-currency capitalist markets for equipment and machinery, since CEMA-produced items have not reached "world standards." Given the fact that the socialist countries lack the convertible currency to purchase their requisite fuels and raw materials on the world market, they should be prepared to abide by CEMA conditions and allow CEMA's prices to be adjusted at the marginal producers' level even if they might be higher than the average world prices. In short, Dudinski is proposing to take advantage of CEMA's operation as a closed regional market in the case of fuels and raw materials but as an open, competitive one for machinery and equipment. Dudinski then advocates the allocation of investable resources at the overall CEMA level in such a way that the "increasing cost burden" of the raw material producers would be shared equitably by the importers and adequate "incentives" for such producers would remain.[39]

Another Soviet foreign trade theorist, O. Bogomolov, also affirms that existing foreign-trade prices make the export of fuels and raw materials "less profitable than the export of machinery and equipment." Since CEMA's demand continues to grow, the only solution, he believes, is a joint partnership between the CEMA importer and the producer, usually Soviet, based on long-term investment credits from the former to the latter. This would be neither a "colonial pattern" of investment nor socialist foreign assistance; it would simply be, Bogomolov insists, a stimulus for "a rational international cooperation and increased effectiveness," in view of the heavy investments and long gestation period, as well as high operative costs, inherent in the production of raw materials.[40]

As we pointed out in Essay 6, not only the socialist countries but also certain capitalist countries have been invited to engage in such joint partnerships. The Soviet Union, for instance, has sought Japanese cooperation for the joint development of Siberian virgin timberland; this, plus a partnership to compensate for the labor shortage in Siberia, could eventually develop into a triangular arrangement whereby Japan would supply the capital, some East European country the muscle (e.g., Bulgarian lumberjacks), and the Soviet Union the timberland, or, in other similar arrangements, the mines.[41] The Soviet Union might also persuade the CEMA countries to share "proportionately" in research and development costs, as Bogomolov suggested, and to place the formerly free exchanges of licenses and patents on a commercial basis, with world prices obtaining.

The most significant implication of this new Soviet line is not that there is any true deficit in their foreign trade; actually, Soviet real costs even after the price reforms of the mid-1960's are still hard to ascertain, and, moverover, according to Western estimates, Soviet oil costs are relatively low. Rather, the fact is that the Russians are anxious to take maximum advantage of the increasing leverage which they have in the CEMA markets and to capitalize on the importers' pattern of investment in the bloc. If the Russians so choose, they can sell in the Western markets, whereas the machinery and equipment producers in CEMA find no takers for their goods in the West. The squeeze in CEMA engendered by the upward push in prices of Soviet fuels and raw materials, coupled with the downward push in prices of other countries' equipment and goods of mass consumption, and the heightened pressures for huge investments, particularly in Soviet oil and metals, have deepened distrust of some CEMA countries in Soviet price manipulations, destroyed the hope that some new, *sui generis* inter-socialist price patterns can be devised, and incited some countries, like Czechoslovakia, to try to broaden their contacts with Western capital and markets. But the Czechs themselves knew, even before the August 1968 occupation, what contemplating a break with Russia could entail economically; as a Czech commentator said:

Let us not forget that, among other differences between Czechoslovakia and Rumania, our cars run on Soviet gas, two out of every three rolls are baked from Soviet flour, and our gigantic metallurgical combines would come to a standstill within a few days after Soviet ore supplies stopped.[42]

One can understand why, after the occupation, *Pravda* could reiterate that what Moscow sells to Czechoslovakia it could sell in hard-currency markets, but what Czechoslovakia sells to the USSR it could not easily sell elsewhere.[43]

The Rumanians, who are less dependent on the Soviet market either for their exports or for their imports and who are therefore less vulnerable to the general pattern of Soviet leverage, are in agreement that raw materials prices should be revised upwards in intra-CEMA trade. However, even though, as raw materials producers, the Rumanians side with the Russians concerning CEMA prices, yet, as *"communistes de gouvernement"* of a small, backward, industrializing country, they part ways with the Russians. The Rumanian Communist leadership preaches "all around" industrial growth in each country, i.e., the autarkic development of backward countries, and the primacy of each national economic plan, and opposes any supra-national planning. Thus, they are siding with the Chinese Communists for the "principle of socialist sovereignty and national independence" and against the Soviet doctrine of "limited sovereignty" of the socialist states.[44]

Trying to fit these diverging tendencies into a theory of socialist economic development, the Czechoslovak economist, J. Novozámsky, has suggested that the developed economies (e.g., Czechoslovakia) were "objectively interested in pursuing international specialization, i.e. in 'opening' their production complex," while countries on a lower economic level (viz., Rumania) were "objectively interested in completing their production complex and in introducing new industries, that is, in 'closing up' their production complex."[45] Rejecting this strange use of the terms "opening" and "closing" an economy, which Novozámsky uses to mean almost the opposite of what they seem to mean in the given context, Sir Roy Harrod has answered that the "introduction of new industries" was certainly appropriate in backward countries, but that this did not imply the need of a policy of "omni-competence" analogous to the one which, by virtue of its size, the Soviet Union has pursued. Such a policy would ultimately retard growth.[46] Actually, all small-sized countries must, of course, be "objectively" interested in "opening their production complex"; Rumania's pursuit of omni-competence at the borders of CEMA is by now less an expression of devotion to the traditional Soviet strategy of development than a manifestation of apprehension of the leverage which the Soviets would acquire if Rumania chose to follow the Soviet suggestions for its international specialization. Rumania thus concurs with China's positions, not because of persuasive theoretical arguments, but because of narrow practical interests.

## INCOME-LEVELING AND SOCIALIST ECONOMIC DEVELOPMENT

Many of the questions which have divided the socialist camp are quite familiar. But these questions clearly elicit different answers, at different times, from the various Communist leaderships so that one cannot speak of a unified communist theory of economic development after the establishment of socialism: no recognized theory as such exists.

Since the appearance of a number of diversely endowed and diversely developed socialist states after World War II, the Russians have affirmed that economic equalization would take place among them through the application of a uniform strategy of development, mutual aid, and socialist unity. According to the 1961 Draft Program of the Communist Party of the Soviet Union, in the capitalist world the "law of unequal political and economic development" has led to clashes between states, but in the socialist world, thanks to the "proportional development" of each socialist country, the overall world socialist system would be continuously strengthened.[47]

No sooner was that program written than the Soviet-Albanian and the Sino-Soviet conflicts broke into the open. The Russians have since claimed that these conflicts were the result of "parasitical concepts" taking hold of the minds of the Communist leaderships of the less-endowed countries and that such leaderships, because of their own failures, wanted now to "spread poverty" among socialist countries and stop the advance of the most developed ones. Thus it was stated in the Soviet theoretical journal *Kommunist* in 1963:

It was asserted that the obligation of the socialist countries which had advanced in their economic development allegedly was to "wait" for the lagging countries and to give them everything which the advanced countries had created in comparison with the lagging. Such a parasitical concept of the principles of proletarian internationalism applied to the relations between socialist countries is fundamentally contradictory to Leninism and particularly to the Leninist principle of material interest . . .[48]

*Pravda* added, a year later, that "leveling down" would lead to "communism of the barracks,"[49] and that international leveling would "discredit socialism and at the same time would not have achieved a radical improvement in the position of other countries."[50] In 1968, *Izvestiia*, in a discussion entitled "Problems of the Last Third of the Century," added that the "solutions of the problems of the century" are not "to spread poverty uniformly through all nations" but to create conditions for the growth of wealth throughout the world.[51]

The point at issue is actually more complex. It concerns not only relations among countries at different levels of development but also those among the various strata and regions within a country. The Russian Communist leaders have encouraged what they call "material interest," i.e., individual interests, rather than the "leveling down" of incomes in their society. The Chinese Communists under Mao still claim that gaps between incomes "should be rationally and gradually narrowed and not widened."[52] Both Russian and Chinese leaderships seem to believe in "equalization" of development among regions and national areas within each country. Nevertheless, the disparities among regions within countries have remained as wide as those among countries. Notwithstanding important development efforts over the past decades, the gaps within the USSR between the Soviet Central Asian republics and Russia are probably as great as those, say, between the lower and upper East European tiers. The non-Russian, non-Slav republics have certainly benefited economically, culturally, and socially from their association with a more developed society. Some of the better-endowed non-Slav republics, have benefited more than the other, less endowed republics. But the Russians have certainly not found any magic formula for bridging the distances which separate slowly-growing, low-income areas from the better-endowed, higher-income, and faster-growing areas of the USSR. On the whole, the Central Asian republics "have been relatively much less industrialized than most other Soviet republics, less than the average for the USSR as a whole, whether one's measure is output per head, proportion of industrial (or non-agricultural) labor in the labor force, or any other measure one would care to apply."[53] Such disparities may take decades, if not centuries, to overcome. In the meantime, inter-regional inequalities foster tremendous tensions within certain plurinational states, like Yugoslavia, where centralistic controls have been seriously weakened. What happens at the general level of the camp happens openly or covertly within each socialist country: for example, in Yugoslavia, where the per capita income in Slovenia is about twice as high as the average for the entire country and over six times as high as for Kosovo-Metohija, the representatives of the advanced federated republics do not wish a "leveling down" any more than do the representatives of the advanced socialist countries.[54] The crux of the matter is that interregional as well as international disparities can be overcome only through enormous increases in productivity, and these have failed to materialize under socialism.

There is no reason to assume that these contending forces, both within pluri-national socialist countries and within the camp at large, will weaken over the rest of the century. The expansion of the USSR into East-Central Europe and the expansionist tendencies of China have been, in part, attempts to harness new resources for correcting perennial domestic imbalances. The difference between the two expansions lies only in the fact that the Russians are geographically more fortunate: they can expand toward more developed areas. Indeed, in the early years of the Soviet regime, Evgenii Preobrazhenski believed, in an interesting vision of the future, that Russia could and possibly would undertake a "war of aggression" against the West to sieze its resources for the transformation of agrarian Russian and of Europe itself, a Europe redivided "into economic regions according to production criteria, without taking into account national frontiers."[55]

The abstruse "transition from socialism to communism," a transition once supposed to occur at some time in the future, has become an immediate bone of contention in the socialist camp precisely because it accentuates the inequalities in development and the prospects for overcoming them. The vacillating positions of the communist leaderships on this score are instructive and worth registering.

In 1958, A. Stepanian, among other authors, wrote in the Soviet journal *Problems of Philosophy* that the socialist countries united in CEMA would form a special economic whole and be "the first to enter communism." The Asian countries, on the other hand, which "have a lot in common as regards economic and cultural development," will form "a second regional zone, and will also enter communism all together."[56] A year later, this successive regional accession to Communism being considered unpolitical, Khrushchev assured all the socialist countries that they were "marching forward in one front."

A. Fedoseev added in *Pravda* that the transition would, of course, be "simultaneous," since "inequality of development . . . is an incontrovertible law of capitalism which does not extend to the world system of socialism."[57] By 1961 the Russians had given up hope of carrying everybody simultaneously over to full communism, and the official 1961 program of the Communist Party of the Soviet Union announced that the USSR was already building communism. The secretary of the CPSU central committee, L. F. Ilichev, warned illogically that, in this future affluent society wherein abundance would supplant scarcity, the "sacred principle . . . he who does not work does not eat" would still hold and that those who would "pilfer people's property" would not be spared:

In ancient times, the thief had his hand chopped off—apparently for educational reasons. Of course ancient times are not an example for us; but it is our duty to firmly catch the dishonest hand stretched toward people's property.[58]

The Chinese, as we previously noted, have rejected the idea that communism was anywhere in sight. The Bulgarian Communists, however, with their long-acquired sense of political equilibrium, have reconciled all this in a curious formula authored by their first secretary Todor Zhivkov:

Socialist countries will start their transition to communism more or less at the same time, within the limits of one historic epoch. This Marxist principle reflects the new objective development. By taking national conditions into consideration, every party decides the meaning of the expression "within the limits of one historic epoch.[59]

In the Communist camp, just as in the West, obvious national disparities in development, growth potentials, and pace of growth increasingly dampen the hopes for some universal, simple, and painless means for accelerating the advance of backward areas, for shortening the economic distances between them and the developed countries, and for evening out all these differences at some time in the future. Certain Communists have clearly recognized the futility of such hopes. They must, however, continue to pretend that they do have the miraculous solution which is eluding everybody else.

# CHAPTER 9

# *"Catching Up" & "Converging"*

POLICY objectives reflect not only what a country's current status is but how its policy-makers intend to modify it. The targets they choose inevitably embody their own social value judgments. Provided that those targets are broadly consistent and observe economic, technical, human, and political constraints, the programs built around them are at least initially "realistic." There is, of course, no reason why roughly the same status in different countries—say, the same level of economic development—need elicit the same objectives. Indeed, there are many reasons why it should not. In some stage theories, such as Professor Rostow's famous "stages of economic growth," more or less identical drives are considered to carry countries from one stage to another. A number of years after the "take-off" into sustained growth, a drive toward maturity sets in. Maturity is reached when an economy "demonstrates that it has the technological and entrepreneurial skills to produce not everything but anything that it chooses to produce." Then the economy moves naturally into "high mass consumption, where, in time, the leading sectors shift toward durable consumers' goods and services."[1] This deterministic path is no less ineluctable than the Marxian march from capitalism to communism; the theory has ignored the role of policy and of capability of steering an economy in a variety of directions. The choice of different normative goals (such as more military power, more equality, more leisure, etc.) and different horizons may give rise to different priorities with respect to "maturity" or beyond.

Jointly, the "take-off" into sustained growth and the "drive toward maturity"—or, preferably, "modern economic growth"—have some specific characteristics for the economist. Modern economic growth is defined by Professor Simon Kuznets as "the extended application of science to problems of economic production." The economic growth of any nation—the nation being the unit for which economic growth is studied—is measured by rates of growth in total and per capita product, in output capacity, and in efficiency; by changes in the relative shares of manufactures, public utilities, and agriculture in total product; by changes in the pattern of final demand and in import-export opportunities; and by changes in the growth, skills, and mobility of its population. Modern economic growth has been characterized notably by a sustained growth in total and per capita product —i.e., a consistent rise not overshadowed by short-term fluctuations —by expansion in productive capacity, by a sustained shift toward nonagricultural sectors, by an expanding foreign trade, and by a continuous diversification in a population's skills.[2]

Political scientists and sociologists, in turn, have pointed out that the corollaries of such growth are social mobilization and various processes of structural differentiation. The first term refers, according to Professor Karl Deutsch, to the erosion of major clusters of old social, economic, and psychological commitments and to the ramifications of changes in occupation and residence, urbanization, widespread literacy, and mass communications. Structural differentiation, on the other hand, is equated with certain major changes in social structure, characterized primarily by the development of specialized types of social organization, nontraditional national or supernatural group identifications, and wide regulative and allocative mechanisms and organization in all major institutional spheres.[3]

In this concluding essay, I propose to focus on the narrower aspects of modern economic growth as defined by the economist and on the efforts of the Communist policy-makers to further the economic growth of the diverse and unequally developed socialist countries of Eastern Europe. While the noneconomic corollaries of modernization cannot be legitimately bypassed within such an analysis, they will be touched upon here only to the extent that they merge with specific economic processes, policies, and actions. The general economic framework in which various pre-and post-Communist schemes of industrialization have unfolded in Eastern Europe will be examined, as will the forms and pace of growth, with special reference to productive capacity, output mix, agriculture, and foreign trade. Characteristic changes in employment patterns will be briefly reviewed and the overall results contrasted with contemporaneous achievements in the West. Finally an attempt will be made to assess the prospects of convergence or divergence between socialism and capitalism.

## THE ECONOMIC FRAMEWORK FOR
## INDUSTRIALIZATION IN EASTERN EUROPE

As noted previously, Eastern Europe ranges from developed, highly industrialized countries like East Germany and Czechoslovakia, through primarily agricultural countries with significant industrial facilities such as Poland and Hungary, to less-developed countries such as Rumania, Bulgaria, Yugoslavia, and, lastly, Albania. The main economic goal of the policy-makers of the agricultural-industrial and of the less-developed countries, namely, "rapid industrialization," has not substantively changed since before World War II.[4] On the other hand, the economic goals of the highly developed countries of the area—East Germany and Czechoslovakia—have become qualitatively different: since 1945, these countries have sought basically to restructure, re-equip, and then expand an already appreciable industrial establishment.

The basic similarity both before and after World War II in the thrust toward industrialization among some of the agricultural-industrial and agricultural countries of the second and third tier of Eastern Europe does not imply that the strategies of development and the instruments used to carry them out were also similar in the two periods. There were, however, significant points of continuity, as we shall see.

After the debacle of the Austro-Hungarian empire in 1918 and the emergence of new national states in the area, state involvement in the economy grew abruptly in most East European countries, particularly in the area's second and third tiers. The new states expanded defense-connected industries, provided a variety of stimuli such as protective tariffs, tax inducements, grants, and credits for all industries, and increased the state direct or indirect participation in the provision of developmental infrastructure, i.e., transport, power, public utilities, and education. State ownership expanded in the interwar years through numerous discriminatory measures against "alien capital," and protective measures favoring the enterpreneurs or workers of the new "ethnic majority" in each country. Further, state intervention increased with respect to the collection and sale of agricultural produce at home and abroad, allocation of raw materials, and control of prices and credit.[5] Toward the middle or late 1930's, some countries moved toward the formulation of an integrated, central program for the economy as a whole.

The most decisive effort before World War II toward creating and carrying out a strategy of economic development was made in Poland. Begun in the middle of 1936 and ended abruptly by the Nazi invasion in 1939, a comprehensive industrialization program was focused on what was known as the Industrial Central District (C.O.P.) located in the Warsaw-Cracow-Lwow triangle. The strategy was to concentrate the lion's share of the nation's investable resources in this region, in order to bring about significant economies of scale. The region encompassed between one-sixth and one-seventh of both the area and the population of the country (i.e., some 23,000,000 acres with five and a half million people), and the deliberate choice of this "pole of development," as Professor Perroux would call it, implied the relative neglect of development and per capita income growth prospects in all other regions. The selected region—the most poverty stricken of Poland—recommended itself to the policy-makers because of its location, which was well suited for defense industries, the availability of raw materials and large surpluses of peasant labor, and its good natural transportation axis (the Vistula). The first three years of the program became the beginning of an even more ambitious industrialization scheme scheduled to be implemented over a fifteen-year period, extending from 1939 to 1954, and destined to change the occupational structure of the country's manpower from a 70:30 ratio of agricultural to nonagricultural manpower to a 50:50 ratio. In 1936, to effect its immediate program, the Polish government sharply stepped up its regional investment, increased its foreign indebtedness, and, through a variety of tax exemptions, credits, and grants, attracted a large inflow of private investment toward C.O.P. During the three years of actual plan operation, the industrial enterprises completed in the area absorbed as many as 90,000 workers as compared to a total of 800,000 gainfully employed in all Polish industries. Prominent among such enterprises were state aircraft and munitions factories, foundaries and electrical plants, and the private or mixed state and private motor works, as well as engineering, metallurgical, chemical, and other supporting factories.

In Hungary, a comprehensive scheme of development was announced in March 1938, when the government proclaimed its intention of launching a Five-Year Plan to expand rapidly both the defense capabilities of the country and its productive capacity. Over the five-year period, three fifths of a total investment of one billion pengoes ($290 million at the official, and $190 million at the actual, prewar exchange rate) were to be channeled toward industry and armament production, one fifth toward transport and communications, and one fifth toward agriculture. No detailed plan was worked out, and the government's economic activities were not fully coordinated until 1940, when a Supreme Economic Council was set up under the Ministry of Finance. However, partly because of increases in both territory and population (obtained from Rumania) and partly because of war mobilization, the investment target of one billion pengoes was reached earlier. By 1940, two thirds of the volume of investment had already been collected, and by 1944, when the war reached the Hungarian territory, the effect of substantial government spending in industry in general, and in heavy industry in particular, was clearly visible. Industrial capacity and output had expanded appreciably. In the five years between 1938 and 1943, Hungary's industrial manpower had risen by over 100,000 workers, whereas, during the preceding fifteen years, the industrial labor increment had been of the order of only 90,000 workers.

In the late 1930's, Rumania had also attempted to evolve a comprehensive development program. A serious effort was made to elaborate and integrate policies concerning industrial location and concentration, raw materials, "nationalization of capital," labor, output, prices, and consumption. A detailed official study fixing "criteria of behaviour for the formulation of an economic plan" was published by a Royal Supreme Economic Council in 1939. However, planning efforts had to be interrupted shortly thereafter: the country was forced to cede a large part of its territory and population to Hungary and then became fully involved in World War II.

After the conclusion of World War II and the assumption of power by the Communists in Eastern Europe, each country applied Soviet-type strategy and instruments of centralized planning and management to restructure its economy, vastly expand its industrial capacity, and rapidly increase interchanges with all the industrializing socialist countries. In 1949–52 and 1958–62, investments ranged from 20–25 per cent to as much as 30 and even 35 per cent of the net material product in certain countries. During the periods of extreme economic and social imbalances which followed in the mid-1950's and early 1960's, investment decelerated in irregular and halting steps, leading even to disinvestment in some countries, like Hungary.

Although these accelerating-decelerating patterns have seriously disrupted the equilibrium, the big pushes or leaps of the early 1950's, late 1950's, and (at least for some of these countries) mid-1960's, have substantially enhanced productive capacity and employment. Even in the poor years, investment has generally been above the prewar averages of around 4–5 per cent of the national product. As much as 70–85 per cent of the total investment has gone toward the productive sphere of industry, agriculture, and transport, with the balance allocated to socio-cultural projects, such as education, communal construction, and housing. Industry alone received between 40 and 50 per cent of the total investment.

From the late 1940's to the mid-1950's, expansion in capacity and employment in the leading industrial branches led to significant growth in the national product and to shifts in its composition. Average yearly rates of growth were high during the 1950's in Eastern Europe as a whole, and particularly in the lower tier of countries (see Table 9.1). The relative share of manufacturing output rose, while that of agriculture contracted; within manufacturing itself the relative shares of power production, ferrous and nonferrous metallurgy, and engineering industries output increased, whereas the relative shares in output of food processing and light industries decreased. According to official mid-1960's data—which, it should be noted, tend to exaggerate the share of industry and undervalue the share of agriculture because of price distortions (except for Yugoslavia)—

TABLE 9.1. YEARLY GROWTH RATES OF NET MATERIAL PRODUCT IN
EASTERN EUROPE, 1950–60 AND 1961–65, AND PERCENTAGE
CHANGES FROM PRECEDING YEAR, 1961–65, ACCORDING
TO OFFICIAL DATA

| COUNTRIES | ANNUAL AVERAGES | | PERCENTAGE CHANGES FROM PRECEDING YEAR, 1961–65 | | | | |
|---|---|---|---|---|---|---|---|
| | 1950–60[a] | 1961–65[b] | 1961 | 1962 | 1963 | 1964 | 1965 |
| East Germany | 8.0 | 2.8 | 3.5 | 2.2 | 2.9 | 4.5 | 4.7 |
| Czechoslovakia | 7.7 | 1.9 | 6.8 | 1.4 | −2.2 | 0.9 | 2.5 |
| Hungary | 6.5 | 4.6 | 6.1 | 4.7 | 5.7 | 4.7 | 2 |
| Poland | 7.8 | 6.9 | 8.2 | 2.1 | 6.9 | 6.6 | 6 |
| Bulgaria | 9.2 | 6.5 | 2.8 | 6.2 | 7.5 | 9.9 | 6 |
| Rumania | 10.5 | 9.0 | 10.0 | 4.0 | 10.0 | 11.0 | 8 |
| Yugoslavia | 10.0 | – | – | – | – | – | – |
| Albania | 9.1 | 7.3 | 5.8 | 8.0 | 8.0 | 4 | 3 |

[a] 1955–60 for East Germany, 1952–60 for Bulgaria and Yugoslavia

[b] 1959–65 for East Germany, 1960–65 for Rumania, 1960–64 for Albania

SOURCES: *The Growth of World Industry 1938–1961* (New York: United Nations, 1963) *passim; Economic Survey of Europe in 1965* (New York: United Nations, 1966), Ch. I, p. 3; and *Yearbook of National Accounts Statistics 1965* (New York: United Nations, 1966), p. 474–75.

the relative share of manufacturing in total material product ranged from 40–48 per cent in Yugoslavia, Bulgaria, and Rumania, to 51 per cent in Poland and 63–65 per cent in Hungary, Czechoslovakia, and East Germany. Conversely, the shares of agriculture in total output varied from 28 to 34 per cent in Yugoslavia, Bulgaria, and Rumania, 21 to 22 per cent in Poland and Hungary, and 10 to 14 per cent in Czechoslovakia and East Germany (see Table 9.2). Western computations of the gross national product for the mid-1960's in the countries of Eastern Europe at adjusted exchange rate reflect also the significant income differences between the lower, the middle and the upper tier. According to computations of the World Bank, the gross national product per capita in 1966 was 510–650 dollars in the lower tier, 730–800 dollars in the middle tier, and 1010–1220 dollars in the upper tier (see Table 9.2)[6]

The measurements of industrial growth and its changes over time for Eastern Europe raise a host of problems similar to those confronted in analogous measurements for the USSR: the basic problems are, of course, prices and underlying definitions which need not concern us directly here. Let us note only that Western computations, while diverging from the official ones, do confirm that significant growth occurred through the 1950's to the mid-1960's, the most vigorous growth rates being registered by the countries of the lower tier (see Table 9.3). For the area as a whole, an estimated growth rate of 8.0 per cent per year for 1950 to 1964 compared favorably to an estimated rate of 6.8 per cent for the rest of Europe.[7]

Following the deep dislocations brought about by the war and the unsettling impact of various reorganizational measures which we discussed in Essay 5, overall farm output recovered slowly and sporadically. According to official data, during the quinquennium 1959–64, farm output rose significantly only in Albania and Bulgaria, by as much as 6.4 and 4.6 per cent, respectively. In all the other countries, overall increases varied between 1.4 and 2.2 per cent per annum, with livestock output increasing more rapidly than crop production. According to Western estimates, agricultural output in the early 1960's was still at around 80–90 per cent of prewar figures in the upper tier, at roughly the prewar level in the middle tier, and at around 10–30 per cent over prewar output in the lower tier. These figures contrast

TABLE 9.2. PERCENTAGES OF NET MATERIAL PRODUCT ACCORDING TO SECTOR AND ESTIMATES OF TOTAL AND PER CAPITA PRODUCT IN EASTERN EUROPE AROUND THE MID-1960's

| COUNTRIES | PERCENTAGES OF NET MATERIAL PRODUCT BY ORIGIN[a] | | | | | | GNP[b] | |
| --- | --- | --- | --- | --- | --- | --- | --- | --- |
| | Agriculture | Industry | Construction | Transportation | Trade | Other | Total Billion $ | Per Capita $ |
| East Germany | 11 | 73 | 6 | 6 | 15 | 1 | 20.8 | 1220 |
| Czechoslovakia | 14 | 64 | 9 | 3 | 9 | 1 | 14.3 | 1010 |
| Hungary | 21 | 63 | 10 | 5 | – | 1 | 8.1 | 800 |
| Poland | 22 | 51 | 9 | 6 | 10 | 2 | 23.1 | 730 |
| Bulgaria | 34 | 45 | 7 | 4 | 8 | 2 | 5.1 | 620 |
| Rumania | 30 | 48 | 8 | 4 | 7 | 3 | 12.4 | 650 |
| Yugoslavia | 28 | 40 | 8 | 6 | 12 | 6 | 11.0 | 510 |

[a] Excluding services not connected to production. (For all, national income, Soviet definitions; for Yugoslavia, including depreciation). Underlying data in current price, 1964.

[b] GNP at factor cost, Western definitions, 1966 data.

SOURCES: NMP by origin—*Yearbook of National Statistics 1965*, (New York: United Nations, 1966), pp. 464–65, *passim*; GNP, 1966, *World Bank Atlas, Population and Per Capita Product* (Washington, D. C.: International Bank for Reconstruction and Development, 1968).

TABLE 9.3. INDICES OF INDUSTRIAL PRODUCTION AND RATES OF GROWTH IN
EASTERN EUROPE, PREWAR, 1950, AND 1964, RELATIVE TO 1955 = 100

| COUNTRIES | OFFICIAL ESTIMATES OF GROSS VALUE OF OUTPUT | | | | WESTERN ESTIMATES OF INDUSTRIAL OUTPUT[a] | | | |
|---|---|---|---|---|---|---|---|---|
| | Prewar | 1950 | 1964 | Rate of growth 1958–64 | Prewar | 1950 | 1964 | Rate of growth 1961–64 |
| East Germany | – | 52 | 192 | 7.8 | 80 | 59 | 166 | 7.7 |
| Czechoslovakia | 44 | 58 | 198 | 7.4 | 69 | 80 | 167 | 5.4 |
| Hungary | – | 53 | 203 | 5.0 | 56 | 65 | 179 | 7.5 |
| Poland | – | 47 | 219 | 9.1 | 53 | 63 | 196 | 8.4 |
| Bulgaria | 14 | 45 | 276 | 13.0 | 40 | 67 | 250 | 9.9 |
| Rumania | 33 | 49 | 284 | 13.0 | 49 | 69 | 244 | 9.4 |
| Yugoslavia | – | 41 | 286 | 12.1 | – | – | – | – |

[a] Including construction and handicraft production.

SOURCES: Official indices from the national statistical yearbooks of the respective countries. Rates of growth based on official data from *Mir Sotsialisma v tsifrakh i faktakh 1964 god* (*The Socialist World in Facts and Figures, 1964*) (Moskow: Politizdat, 1965), p. 114. Western data from Maurice Ernst, *op. cit.*, p. 883.

with the vigorous growth of agricultural production in Western Europe, where growth over prewar levels has ranged from 38 per cent (West Germany) to over 65 per cent (Denmark).[8] Misallocation of resources, poor planning, and inappropriate incentives have afflicted the farm sector more than any other. Since the mid-1960's, emphasis has increasingly been placed on promoting the profitability of both state and collective farms, on redressing, at least in part, the terms of trade between agriculture and industry in favor of agriculture, and on helping the farms toward a more vigorous capital formation and expansion than in the past.

The efforts of the developed countries to restructure industry by a shift in priorities from consumer to capital goods and to develop their backward linkages and the attempts of the less-developed countries to industrialize and to emphasize the development of their forward linkages, as pointed out in Essay 8, have affected the volume, structure, and direction of foreign trade. The most profound impacts have been in the volume and structure of the intra-East European trade flows and the trade flows between Eastern Europe and the Soviet Union and, in some degree, between Eastern Europe and the underdeveloped countries. Although overall trade grew rapidly throughout the 1950–65 period, trade per capita remained low, so that the potential for further growth is high. Per capita foreign trade in the 1960's was $320–$365 for East Germany and Czechoslovakia, $286 and $295 for Bulgaria and Hungary, respectively, and as low as $115 and $135 for Rumania and Poland, respectively. If the average per capita trade for Eastern Europe and the USSR is taken as 100 for the early 1960's, the per capita average for the Western European Common Market may be estimated at around 400 and that of the European Outer Seven (EFTA) at around 485. The ratios of foreign trade to income have also remained low in the East European countries, particularly for the lower tier.

## MANPOWER AND EMPLOYMENT OPPORTUNITIES

From 1950 to 1965 in Eastern Europe, persistent efforts have been made to establish rapidly a larger managerial and technical elite, to expand, restructure, and upgrade the supply of artisans and industrial manpower, and to absorb into the growing producer goods industries a vast influx of unskilled labor from the countryside. Appreciable shifts in the ratios of urban population to labor force, changes in the growth rates of industrializing communities versus lagging towns, shifts in the manpower structure (particularly in industrial employment), the rise in the supply of high-level professional power, and the fall in illiteracy—all underline the deep and varied changes brought about by the industrialization drive.

The population of socialist Eastern Europe as a whole, which numbered some 105 million at the beginning of the 1950's, reached a total of over 121 million in the mid-1960's. If growth rates remain unchanged, the total should rise to some 132 million in 1975 and to around 138 million in 1980.[9] Inter-censal rates of population growth point toward decelerating growth rates in the post-World War II years as compared to previous periods; the reduced growth rates have occurred despite lower mortality rates and are attributable to sharp declines in fertility rates caused by the deep dislocations from various postwar socio-economic processes, specifically industrialization and collectivization. In the less-developed countries, excepting Albania, the growth rates have fallen below 1.0 per cent per annum in the period 1958–63 for Rumania and Bulgaria, as compared to 1.2–1.3 per cent before the war, and to 1.1 per cent for Yugoslavia, as compared to 1.5 per cent in the late 1920's and early 1930's. Albania alone within the lower tier is maintaining a rate similar to that of the interwar years, namely, 3.2 per cent. In Poland, the rate has fallen to 1.3 per cent, as compared to 1.7 per cent in the interwar years, a rate now below that of the USSR. In Hungary and Czechoslovakia, the rates have declined to 0.4 and 0.7 per cent, respectively, from a growth rate of 0.8 per cent for both during the 1920's. Finally, in East Germany, there has been a negative growth rate of —0.2 per cent.[10]

The process of urbanization in the less-developed tier of countries, already well underway in the interwar years, accelerated substantially during the 1950's and early 1960's. The available data on urbanization are not strictly comparable on an area basis because of significant variations in underlying definitions. Country by country, however, the rising trend of urbanization is unmistakeable. The ratio of rural to

total population which was on the order of 79–80 per cent in the
lower tier, fell to 66–72 per cent in 1960. In Poland and Hungary it
fell during the same period from 63–64 per cent to 52 and 60 per cent,
respectively. Finally in Czechoslovakia the drop was from over 61
per cent to 50 per cent. Entirely new industrial towns were created,
and, in certain cases, small communities were enormously expanded.
By and large, a west-to-east relocation of industry has taken place as
each country has tried to develop new industrial centers in some
backward areas or in areas which are more sheltered from a defense
point of view. In the traditionally lagging areas (eastern Poland,
Slovakia, southern Hungary, and Moldavia and Dobrogea in Rumania), however, industrial expansion has continued to remain modest; expansion in those areas would require enormous investment and
prolonged periods of time.

We have already examined overall changes in industrial employment in Essay 7. Let us note here that the rise in the proportion of
manpower in both manufacturing and services, along with the fall in
the share of agricultural labor, has been particularly strong in the
less-developed tier of countries. The official data for Yugoslavia and
Rumania indicate that the proportion of industrial to total employment almost doubled in 1950–63, from 10–14 per cent to 22–24 per
cent, while for Bulgaria it went from roughly 10 per cent to over 30
per cent. In Yugoslavia and Rumania, the share of agricultural manpower fell from 75–78 per cent to 57–60 per cent, and in Bulgaria it
fell from 82 per cent to 49 per cent. In the middle-tier countries the
share of industry in overall employment rose from 20–23 per cent in
1950 to 28–36 per cent in the early 1960's and that of agriculture fell
from 55–56 per cent to 35–48 per cent. (The middle-tier percentage
changes closely parallel those occurring in the USSR.) Finally, in the
upper tier, the share of industrial employment rose, in the early 1960's,
attaining about 46 per cent of total employment in Czechoslovakia, as
in East Germany, whereas agriculture absorbed only from 16 to 23
per cent of the labor force in both countries.[11]

In the 1946–55 decade the technical-engineering cadres tended to
be recruited from three groups: former technical specialists; technicians rising directly from the ranks of the party, the trade unions, or
the working classes themselves; and technicians newly trained in the

secondary or higher level polytechnical schools. The problem of quickly creating a group of technical specialists became acute during the early postwar years, with the pressure toward industrialization and development. Former "bourgeois" specialists were often necessarily restored to positions of leadership, and stop-gap measures were applied to increase the technical training of persons recruited from among factory workers. Simultaneously, a sweeping drive was initiated to reduce illiteracy, increase vocational and secondary-school training, develop accelerated evening programs, and expand and diversify graduate studies emphasizing modern polytechnical curricula. Illiteracy fell significantly in the less-developed tier of countries where it had been most prevalent, and the supply of the technically trained rose sharply. Technical talent was systematically developed in one-, two-, or three-year vocational schools (based on eight-year elementary schools) and in four-or five-year secondary technical schools, from which the student could qualify for admission to higher educational institutions. The output of high-level manpower to supply the needs of industry, transportation, education, and health-care increased substantially in every East European country. The adaptation of education to the needs of industrialization and urbanization paralleled that elsewhere in the world, except with much stronger emphasis on polytechnical and mathematical training than is found in Western schools.

Since the late 1950's, graduates of higher-level polytechnical schools in a number of Eastern European countries have insistently backed their own candidates for positions of leadership in industry. Former party executives have increasingly been replaced by young engineers and business executives, first in East Germany, then in Czechoslovakia, and gradually in the rest of the area. A Western journal notes that the casualty rate in the managerial ranks would probably have been even "higher if there had been sufficient talent to fill the posts. . . . There may be sufficient qualified technicians, engineers and scientists. But efficient executives who can command with authority, read balance sheets and deal with labor problems are in 'desperate' short supply.[12]

Modernization has been far less satisfactory in the countryside. Agricultural mechanization (mostly as tractors) has accentuated dis-

guised unemployment and reduced appreciably the number of working hours needed in collectvies. At the same time, since industry has
been unable to absorb the increasing surplus of farm population, the
peasant has had to find a partial outlet for his energies in the more intensive cultivation of the small plot of land allotted to him for his
personal use. Mechanization, by reducing the peasant's claim on the
collective's output, has diverted his interest to his small private production.

To displace the East European peasant by the machine seems
absurd in view of the large surpluses of peasant manpower in the
less-developed tier of countries (although opposite situation exists
now in East Germany, Czechoslovakia, and Hungary). Moreover,
further mechanization, in the absence of increasing employment opportunities in the towns, can mean only further surpluses. But, as is
true in *densely populated peasant* countries, no intermediate way has
been found which would allow both increased output per acre
(thereby strengthening agriculture's relations with industry and the
towns) and, at the same time, increased output per head (and, hence,
achievement of an improved standard of living in the villages).

## COMPARISON OF EASTERN AND WESTERN GROWTH

Applying the Soviet strategy of development, the Communist
regimes, including the Yugoslav until 1955, sought to achieve, and did
achieve, rapid growth both in certain leading sectors and in total
and per capita product. But the Soviet model of edict-management,
with which Yugoslavia was the first to become disenchanted in 1950,
was also supposed to obviate short-run fluctuations, unemployment,
and other types of resource wastage and insure a consistently high
overall rate of growth.

As we saw the East European regimes earmarked high shares out
of total product for investment in industry, generously allocated resources to preferential sectors and branches, introduced up-to-date
technology in the privileged military and industrial establishments,
and achieved remarkable results in the leading sectors. But edict-

management and planning could not stop economic fluctuations, falling rates of growth in total product, and wastage of resources in many forms. Even the official statistics, no matter how deficient, clearly bring out these facts. The data available on investment, industrial output, and net material product point clearly toward two types of variations in economic activity for all the countries of the area, particularly the more developed ones: cyclical variations, with peaks in 1950–52 and 1958–60 and troughs in the middle 1950's and early 1960's; and a secular (long-term) decline in the rate of growth, readily apparent when one contrasts the average yearly growth rates for 1950–60 with those for 1961–65 (see Table 9.1). The data on yearly growth rates of net material product show negative growth in the mid-1950's and early 1960's for Czechoslovakia and unusually low rates of growth for Poland and Rumania. The decline of the early 1960's, heralded in the West as an extraordinary phenomenon, was in fact simply a periodic dip in both the Soviet and East European economies. Growth has been erratic from year to year. The inefficiencies of centralized planning and edict-management with respect to growth have, therefore, been costly.

The pace of growth in industrial output—the largest component of the national product—was more rapid in Eastern Europe than in Western Europe in the 1950's but about the same in the early 1960's. The increases were caused both by a deepening of capital and by the large-scale absorption of labor, particularly in the less-developed tier of countries. Productivity gains, on the other hand, have been erratic and far slower in the lower tier than in the advanced countries. The engineering industries have grown spectacularly though duplication is widespread and the output scale limited by domestic requirements.

In agriculture, the pace of growth has been much slower in the East than in the West. Extensive long-run socialist institutional re-arrangements, precipitated more by political expediency than by calculated economic objectives, have alienated rather than won over certain strata of the peasantry. The rapidity with which de-cooperativization took place in Yugoslavia in 1953, as we noted in Essay 5, and the reluctance of the Polish leadership to press its collectivization drive in the 1960's are significant indicators of peasant hostility to collectivization. Nonetheless, the CDSE's have continued to remain fully committed to these policies, because the planned widespread mechanization cannot be left to individual farmers when the farmers cannot accumulate large reserves of capital. One may expect therefore that Poland will try to renew its collectivization drive in the 1970's.

The pace of growth in services, except those directly connected with production, such as freight transportation, communications, and wholesale distributing and storing facilities, has been extremely slow. Everything connected with the individual consumer—quantity, variety, quality, and distribution of consumer goods, housing and commercial and personal services—has been neglected to enhance the output of capital goods. Investment in human beings has been reduced primarily to investment in education, while many of the amenities associated with modern living have been ignored. However, the progress of the sharply restructured, if perhaps disproportionately technical, educational system has been significant.

The spread of modern technology throughout these economies has been severely limited by rigid emphasis on the privileged industrial branches. Obsolescence in the nonprivileged branches has increased as industrialization on the Soviet model has proceeded. Moreover, resistance to changeovers in production has hampered the rapid spread of up-to-date technology even in the privileged branches. Though technical cooperation among the countries of the CEMA group has facilitated access to various advanced production techniques for the less-developed tier of countries, excluding Albania and Yugoslavia, and has benefited even the industrialized countries, the progress in technology has generally not been comparable with that of the West. The inferior technology and product quality have become increasingly apparent even to the East Europeans themselves, who prefer, when they can, to import machinery from the West.

Technology in agriculture has lagged even more than that of industry behind the achievements of the West. The attempted transformation of agriculture falls far short of the Communist ideal of "factories in the fields"; a complete transformation will be a protracted and very costly process. It is a long path from mechanization of plowing, seeding, and harvesting to mechanization of animal output and development of modern methods for feeding, milking, refrigerating, and storing, and the path is even longer to the widespread use of chemicals and genetic manipulation in plant and livestock breeding. An American agricultural expert, Ronald I. Mighell has noted, perceptively, that four periods are distinguishable in the modern development of agricultural technology in the United States. The first, covering the first half of the nineteenth century, was the period of the axe and hoe; the second, in the latter half of the nineteenth century, was the period of horse-drawn machinery; the third, in the first half of the twentieth century, was the period of mechanical power; and the fourth, starting in the second half of the twentieth century, has been the period of chemical and genetic revolution.[13] In the socialist world, China is still largely in the first or, at best, the second of these periods; the less-developed countries of Eastern Europe have entered the third phase and are barely approaching the fourth period. Their model, the USSR, is still far from full emergence out of the third into the fourth period.

The introduction of modern technology into services has been extremely slow. Widespread commercial distribution of and increased consumer access to modern appliances, radios, television, and automobiles are still to come. According to various estimates, if per capita personal consumption in Western Germany is taken as 100 per cent, that in the upper East European tier would be about 60 per cent; in the middle tier about 50 per cent; and in the lower tier about 40 per cent or less. While per capita personal consumption in the West is accelerating, that in Eastern Europe is limping far behind.

Efforts to improve allocation of investable resources are hampered both by inner difficulties in the concepts and methods of management and planning and by external difficulties involving traditional distrusts and conflicting interests. New disagreements have been superimposed onto old differences: for example, the traditional Hungarian-Rumanian conflict over Transylvania is now being heated by the fact that Rumania does not want Hungary to share in the exploitation of the province's rich raw material resources, particularly natural gas. While neighboring Hungary is starved of raw materials, the Rumanians let the Transylvanian resources lie idle until such time that they alone will be able to put them to full use.

Thus the results achieved under the strategy of "catching up" are mixed. Clearly the Communists have attained few of the "highest indices" of capitalism. They have, however, rooted out certain old barriers to economic growth, changed values and outlook, and succeeded in institutionalizing a high rate of investment, which is an indispensable ingredient for growth. On the other hand, they have erected new and formidable barriers to development, thanks to rigid, wasteful, and often patently incompetent leadership, questionable investment priorities, targets, and commitments, distorted incentives, and dogmatic approaches to the international division of labor. Changes in planning, management, and incentives are underway, but no one would venture to predict how long it will take the Communists to eliminate the new obstacles that they themselves have created. How can efficiency and economic performance be improved and output and investment decisions be decentralized without a thwarting of the policy-makers' preferences? How can consumers' preferences be allowed to influence production without impinging upon the main, long-term directions set centrally for the economy? How can a centrally operated servomechanism be designed that will still encourage lower-level initiative, responsibility at the operational levels, and efficient disposal and use of resources? These are some of the questions which now more pressingly than ever confront socialist policy-makers, executive managers, and planners.

The beginnings of an era of what has been called New Economic Management (NEM) in socialist countries point toward increasing pragmatism in future policies at least in Eastern Europe. An eventual reduction of the party's role in production, a changing scope of planning, and a strengthening voice of the consumer may eventually combine with reduced reliance on physical allocation, price liberalizations, and expanded local managerial authority to remove most investment decision-making from central interference. Not entirely foreseeable, however, are to what extent and in what specific manner each socialist country will move in these directions.

## CONVERGENCE AND DIVERGENCE OF SOCIALISM AND CAPITALISM

The actual "catching up" of the USSR and even of the less-developed tier of countries of Eastern Europe with several highest indices of capitalist development, the continuous emphasis on industrialization and modern technology, and the search of the socialist countries for new methods of management are viewed by some as confirmation of "convergence"—or, as Professor Rostow would have it, of the tendency of all countries to move toward "maturity" and thence to "high mass consumption." "Convergence" under this definition may be taken to imply predictable changes along a path that has already been traveled by the developed capitalist countries and that will eventually lead other countries which have "taken off," including the present-day socialist countries, toward the same final (?) stage of "high mass consumption." Contrariwise, Professor Galbraith, while explicitly dismissing the socialist alternative, seems to discern within the developed "industrial state"—i..e, within the developed capitalist economies—changes that will lead toward the discarding of market mechanisms and to planning on a vast scale. Technology, he asserts, promotes extensions of the role of the state, formation within the modern corporations of "technostructures"—"imperfectly defined collective decision making entities" which have nothing in common with the individual capitalist or entrepreneur—and "planning beyond the reach of the industrial firm."[14] Professor Tinbergen sees both capitalism and socialism developing parallel tendencies that are allegedly impelling them toward an "optimal convergence model" of economic organization with a number of salient characteristics. These characteristics include a large public sector to take care of externalities or indivisibilities of importance, decentralized instrument utilization, and public regulation of aggregate demand, total investment level, market instability, and income distribution.[15]

Official Soviet or East European theorists affirm that, in some respects, the Western partisans of convergence simply subscribe now to what the Marxists have always claimed, namely, that the individual capitalist "has become obsolete," monopolist corporations have "fused" their interests with the power of the state, and centralized programming is inevitable to harness the "anarchy" of the market. But they do not consider such tendencies as leading to "convergence" with their own, also-evolving system. Technological revolution, they claim, is no substitute for social revolution; monopoly capitalism does not challenge the "financial oligarchies" or their claims of profit; governmental programming is really forecasting rather than acting as a directive instrument of central policy imposed on dependent enterprises.[16] On the other hand, certain sections of the Soviet and East European intelligentsia disagree with the official views. The Soviet physicist Andrei D. Sakharov, in an apparently widely circulated document in the USSR, asserts that capitalism and socialism are actually "coming closer to each other" in a number of respects: "The development of modern society in both the Soviet Union and the United States is now following the same course of increasing complexity of structure and of industrial management, giving rise in both countries to managerial groups that are similar in social character." Accordingly he advocates "a rapprochement" between the two systems via "changes in the structure of ownership, of cooperative ownership and of the government" within the capitalist countries and via expanding economic reforms within the socialist countries, leading toward a truly "world government" by the year 2000.[17]

Biologically "convergence" is the phenomenon of lineages of animals growing alike as they progressively adapt to similar ways of life. Industrialization and adoption of modern technology, as substantively argued by the theoreticians of convergence, have a similar impact on various lineages of society, though each one may tend to perpetuate some specific differentiating internal characteristics. I am inclined to believe, however, that processes of both convergence and divergence may occur between and within capitalism and socialism. Differences and similarities between the two systems concern not only the economic structures (technical, behavioral, institutional), and not only the para-economic political, social, and legal environment in which the economy functions, but also the goals of the policy-makers and the instruments they are willing to use for attaining their goals.[18] The goals of the policy-makers of the socialist societies remain affected by their Marxist-Leninist persuasion, and their economic policies concerning priorities, pace, growth patterns, public versus private goods, planners' versus consumers' preferences, and so on are and may continue to be substantially different from the economic policies prevailing in the individualist-oriented Western societies.

Furthermore, since present-day socialism of the Soviet-type—as distinct from the earlier Western and Central European socialist philosophies—has come to power in industrializing societies rather than in already industrialized societies (with the exception only of East Germany and Czechoslovakia), "crash" industrialization has also become a typical "socialist" goal of policy-makers in the "socialist camp."

Finally, Marxist-Leninist-Stalinist socialism has taken root within a number of states which remain autonomous, and whose lives continue to be molded by their own relatively specific histories, aspirations, behavioral patterns, factor endowments, and levels of development. In this regard, neither Marx nor Engels but a German Social Democrat, G. Volmar, correctly foresaw, almost a century ago, the emergence of isolated, autonomous, underdeveloped socialist states, rather than a simultaneous victory of socialism in the developed countries and their willing merger into a fraternal association.[19] Isolation may bring about "geographic speciation," differences that have become fixed and often irreversible. Even with respect to goals, therefore, certain socialist states may converge with, while others may diverge from, the capitalist countries.

Basic institutional differences between socialism and capitalism still exist, notably concerning the generation, distribution, and utilization of profit as incentive, source of income, and criterion of economic decision. In the socialist societies, public or collective profits, rather than private profits, are typical. All-inclusive nationalizations have served to erase or weaken private profit-making, private profit-motivation, and private profit as a criterion of economic decision. However, in the decentralized Yugoslav system, the collectives themselves are profit-motivated: profits are used as incentives and as a preferred criterion of decision-making over a wide field. In the USSR, profits are increasingly being used as incentives, but are still not viewed as reliable guides for resource allocation. Finally, in China and Cuba, profits are not used either as incentives or as criteria of resource allocation.

Traditionally, in considering instruments of economic policy, socialists have believed that planning an economy as a whole would replace the market mechanism. Today, overall planning of production and distribution by a single center no longer appears to all socialists to be attainable even with the help of sophisticated computer technology. In all the socialist countries, planning is undergoing deep-

seated change. In the majority of CDSE's planning is still viewed as
a method of charting a rigorous and detailed course of action for the
economy and for the enterprises over a fixed time period. Within the
"reform centralized" system, the Soviet NEM, adjustments and
changes of planning procedures for volume of orders, incentives, and
so on, have become possible and feasible. Finally, in the decentralized
socialist societies like Yugoslavia, planning is but a broad social accounting framework. Experience has invariably forced socialist planners to use market mechanisms. But one should also note that the
market mechanisms affecting price formation, factor rewards, and
capital or goods markets continue to be variously encumbered in each
of these countries. Few of the socialist policy-makers have fully sur-
mounted their distrust of the market mechanism. In the character of
their incentives and rewards, the socialist countries oscillate, as Fidel
Castro once put it, between Sancho Panza and Don Quixote. In practice, Khrushchev's "goulash socialism," (or as Castro would call it,
"Sancho Panza socialism,") means not only economic incentives but
also concealed privileges subtly attached to the incentives offered in
the USSR and Eastern Europe to keep the bureaucratic, managerial
and professional strata closely tied to the Communist leadership.[20] On
the other hand, the Chinese condemn economic incentives, which they
describe as "vulgar economism," though since the 1960's they have had
to adjust their own official emphasis on selfless, Don Quixotic devotion
to the building of socialism to suit the individualist inclinations of the
peasants in the communes.

As far as management is concerned, some socialist countries are still
run as a single economic entity. Others have deliberately created a
number of corporations with some autonomy in directing their industries. Still others, like Yugoslavia, and, briefly, Czechoslovakia, have
tended to decentralize even more, with the intention of eliminating
direct state interference in the business life of the enterprises. No form
of management, however, is final. Since organizational structures
suffice only for specific periods, tasks, and resources, they continue
to be reshuffled at various crucial junctures.

Even if socialism and capitalism used similar instruments, combining planning and market mechanisms in closely related ways, and
even if both relied on the same management form of truly autonomous

large corporations (whether publicly or privately owned), they could still diverge significantly concerning *goals* (the nature and the mix of public-private preferences), economic *structures* (behavioral and institutional), and overall *performance*. The mode in which a system operates, as Lange has pointed out, is characteristic of that system as a whole, and cannot be simply deduced from the characteristics of its components. Finally, the confinement of socialist systems to isolated states at different levels of development leads to heterogeneity and even "speciation."

In boldly projecting currently observable trends into the future, one runs, of course, into the well-known danger inherent in such exercises: that long-run reactions may turn in opposite directions from immediately ascertainable short-run effects. The increasing search for efficiency in resources allocation, for instance, may lead to increased concentration of investment in certain developed cities, regions, or broader national areas, and to increasing discrepancies between developed and less-developed zones. Such concentration along with the ability to handle increasingly complex systems may generate simultaneously vigorous growth in some areas and centrifugal tendencies within the nation as a whole. This may be the case, not only for plurinational states—like Yugoslavia or the USSR—but even for apparently cohesive polities. Indeed, this could happen in any technologically advanced society in which sharp discrepancies in development arise between various megalopolises and the outer regions. Without setting any specific horizons, one may paint the future, as Alfred G. Meyer once pointed out, according to his own optimistic or pessimistic inclinations as leading toward secular versions of paradise or hell— toward Utopia or a totalitarian Nazi-like (Asiatic) despotic *"univers concentrationnaire."* I for one, am skeptical of the implied assumption that all states, or fractions thereof, would ultimately tend to identify with one another.

# A GUIDE TO THE LITERATURE
# ON ISSUES IN SOCIALIST
# MANAGEMENT AND PLANNING

## On Socialist Economic Models

The nature, origins, and prospects of the increasing differentiation in socialist approaches to management and planning have not been fully explored either in the East or in the West. The complete record of the economic debates which have preceded and molded some of the most significant departures from the "traditional" (Stalinist) model of edict-management, mainly the debates in Hungary, Poland, Czechoslovakia, and Yugoslavia from the early 1950's on, is not yet available in any Western language. Some of the discussions which have taken place in the USSR—for instance, the "Liberman discussion" on prices and profit, the controversies on decentralization and industrial reform, or the discussions on planning and the uses of mathematics—are far better known than the economic debates of the other countries, yet they are relatively less significant for an understanding of potential changes in socialist planning and management.

A cinematic view of an evolving and differentiating economic system is admittedly difficult to present in a scholarly report; what one projects instead are disconnected, still institutional pictures, which reflect a situation at a given moment. Only a few recent analytical studies pursue and enrich the famous Western "academic debate" on the possibility of rational allocation of resources under socialism and on models of socialist economies, conducted in the 1930's and 1940's. Among the most outstanding of these studies are Wlodimerz Brus' *Ogolne problemy funkcjonowania gospodarki socjalistycznej (General Questions Concerning the Functioning of the Socialist Economy)* (Warsaw: Państwowe Wydawnictwo Naukowe, 1961), whose promised English translation was unfortunately prevented by the 1967–68 anti-Semitic campaign in Poland and the expulsion of Professor Brus from the Warsaw University; and a number of articles by the late Professor Oskar Lange, notably, "Political Economy of Socialism," "The Role of Planning in Socialist Economy," and "Basic Problems of Socialist Construction," all in *Problems of the Political Economy of Socialism*, edited by Oskar Lange (New Delhi: People's Publishing House, 1962), pp. 1–15, 16–30, 31–56. Studies of similar import are Czeslaw Bobrowski's "Socialist Economic Patterns," included in the Lange volume (pp. 145–170); Ivan M. Maksimovic's discussion of the rationale of certain Yugoslav changes in "Professor Oskar Lange on Economic Theory of Socialism and Yugoslav Economic Thinking," included in Lange's *Festschrift: On Political Economy and Econometrics* (Oxford, Pergamon Press, 1965), pp. 347–362; Branko Horvat's rambling but illuminating book, *Towards a Theory of Planned Economy* (Belgrade: Yugoslav Institute of Economic Research, 1964); and Ota Šik's most noteworthy and comprehensive theoretical effort, *Plan and Market Under Socialism* (White Plains, N. Y.: International Arts and Science Press, 1967).

Among Western contributions to the continuing discussion of socialist economic models, particularly since the 1950's, are Abram Bergson's revised essays included in the section "Socialist Economics" of his volume, *Essays in Normative Economics* (Cambridge, Mass.: Harvard University Press, 1966), pp. 175–242, and other illuminating essays, notably Leonid Hurwicz's "Conditions for Economic Efficiency of Centralized and Decentralized Structures" in *Value and Plan, Economic Calculation and Organization in Eastern Europe*, edited by Gregory Grossman (Berkeley: University of California Press, 1960), pp. 162–175, those of Benjamin Ward on "Illyrian" market socialism in his volume, *The Socialist Economy, A Study of Organizational Alternatives* (New York: Random House, 1967), and P. J. D. Wiles' variations on "possible socialisms" in his *The Political Economy of Communism* (Cambridge, Mass.: Harvard University Press, 1962).

## On Economic Reforms

### SYSTEM DESIGNING AND STEERING MECHANISMS

The discussion of certain aspects of the socialist economic reforms since the 1950's and 1960's has produced a vast body of literature centered mostly on the USSR. Relatively little attention has been paid to the reforms in the other socialist states. To classify the most important materials available and correlate them to my own essays, I shall survey first the studies on system designing.

Certain Soviet and East European economists and engineers have increasingly stressed what they call the "cybernetics" approach to designing and "redesigning" the traditional edict-managed Soviet economic system and determining optimality (according to various criteria) in either planning or relating the economic system to its environment. The literature on both design and optimality is vast and often parallels the Western literature on systems management and control processes. A great impetus in the welding of cybernetics to socialist economics of control was provided by Oskar Lange with his *Wstęp do cybernetyki ekonomicznej* (*Introduction to Economic Cybernetics*) (Warsaw: Państwowe Wydawnictwo Naukowe, 1965), available in almost all East European languages, and his earlier, illuminating short study, "Elements of a Theory of Systems Behavior" in *Essays in Econometrics and Planning*, edited by C. R. Rao (Oxford: Pergamon Press, 1964), pp. 137–152. The Soviet journal *Ekonomika i matematicheskie metody* is replete with articles dealing with systems design; many are now available in English in the journal of translations, *Studies in Economics and Statistics in the USSR and Eastern Europe*. Among the important Soviet contributors are A. I. Katsenelinboigen, Iu. N. Gavrilets, Iu. R. Leibkind, A. L. Vainshstein, K. L. Gorfan, V. A. Volkonskii, and E. Z. Maiminas. An article representative of an overall systems concept of the economy is Maiminas' "Toward an Analysis of Economic Systems" (translated in *Studies in Economics and Statistics . . .* , vol. II, no. 3, pp. 3–31).

The Russian studies on optimality in planning follow specialty branches like those in the West: computer programming and operating systems, mathematical programming models, optimization methods, and so on. *Soviet Cybernetics Review* (until June 1969 *Soviet Cybernetics: Recent News Items*), a publication of the Rand Corporation edited by Wade B. Holland, contains useful references to the continuing Soviet efforts in these fields. A number of these subjects are examined by various contributors to the volume, *Mathematics and Computers in Soviet Economic Planning*, by John P. Hardt *et al.* (New Haven: Yale University Press, 1967); the volume also contains a useful reference list of the Soviet contributions in this field up to the mid-1960's. Of crucial importance for the study of the planning system as it now functions and of its prospects is Janos Kornai's work, *Mathematical Planning of Structural Decisions* (Amsterdam: North-Holland Publishing Co., 1967). An interesting though sketchy comparison of planning in the East and West is presented by Rudolf Bičanić in *Problems of Planning East and West* (The Hague: Mouton & Co., 1967).

STRATEGIES OF DEVELOPMENT

The greatest innovator on the well-known Soviet strategy of economic development has been, I believe, China. For various "nuances" in China's adaptation of the Soviet model as well as for views exactly opposite from mine, see Alexander Eckstein's "The Strategy of Economic Development in Communist China," *American Economic Review*, May 1961, pp. 508–517; and in the same vein, Anthony M. Tang's "Policy and Performance in Agriculture," in *Economic Trends in Communist China*, edited by Alexander Eckstein *et al.* (Chicago: Aldine, 1968), pp. 459 ff. Apparently supporting some of my own views—that, unlike the Russians, the Chinese strove from 1952 to develop simultaneously a widely dispersed labor-intensive industry (serving primarily agriculture) and a capital-intensive industry serving the modern sector—is N. R. Chen and W. Galenson's book, *The Chinese Economy under Communism* (Chicago, Aldine, 1969), pp. 5, 40–41, 65, 67 and *passim*. Also of interest are Alfred Zauberman's "Soviet and Chinese Strategy for Economic Growth," *International Affairs*, vol. 38, no. 3, July 1962, and Peter Schran's "Some Reflections on Chinese Communist Economic Policy," *The China Quarterly*, July-September 1962, pp. 58–77. The complex organizational background of policy formulation and change in China is presented by Franz Schurman in his *Ideology and Organization in Communist China* (Berkeley: University of California Press, 1966), particularly Ch. VII as well as in his earlier, shorter statement of China's policy development, "China's New Economic Policy—Transition or Beginning," *The China Quarterly*, no. 17, January-March 1964, pp. 65–91. Again Schurman's "Politics and Economics in Russia and China" and K. C. Yeh's "Soviet and Communist Chinese Industrialization Strategies" are competently introduced by Gregory Grossman under the title "Strategies and Tactics of Economic Development," Part V of the volume *Soviet and Chinese Communism, Similarities and Differences*, edited by Donald W. Treadgold (Seattle: University of Washington Press, 1967), pp. 291–363. Finally, for a bird's eye view of China's economic policies, one may refer to Arthur G. Ashbrook's "Main Lines of Chinese Communist Economic Policy," the introductory paper to *An Economic Profile of Mainland China*, vol. I, Studies prepared for the Joint Economic Committee, 90th Congress, 1st Session (Washington, D. C.: U. S. Government Printing Office, 1967), pp. 17–44, and to an earlier Chinese "declaration of intent"—"The Big Leap Forward in Socialist Construction after the Basic Completion of the Socialist Transformation," in *The Transformation of the National Economy in China*, Hsueh Mu-Chiao, Su Hsing, and Lin Tse-Li (Peking: Foreign Language Press, 1960), pp. 238–287.

### SPECIAL DEBATES

The socialist economic reforms of the 1950's and 1960's have generated a number of special debates, some of which have been extensively presented in the West. The principal Soviet articles concerning volume and types of indicators, particularly profits, connections of "actuators" (the supervisory agencies) to the budget office and the banks, and utilization of the market as an "identifier," are available in English translations in the collection *Planning, Profit and Incentives*, vol. I: *The Liberman Discussion*, and vol. II: *Reform of Soviet Economic Management*, edited by Myron E. Sharpe (White Plains, N. Y.: International Arts and Science Press, 1966). The Soviet debates and the reforms of the mid-1960's are examined by

George R. Feivel in *The Soviet Quest for Economic Efficiency, Issues, Controversies and Reforms* (New York: Praeger Special Studies, 1967), and by Eugene Zaleski in *Planning Reforms in the Soviet Union, 1962–1966* (Chapel Hill: University of North Carolina Press, 1967).

Reforms in the other East European countries, some of which have only amended the Soviet-type edict-managed national economy and others of which (like the Czechoslovak reforms) have tried to break out of the confines of this system, are surveyed, usually randomly, in various Western studies, e.g., in Michael Gamarnikow's *Economic Reforms in Eastern Europe* (Detroit: Wayne State University Press, 1968), or in *Wirtschaftsreformen in Osteuropa* (*Economic Reforms in Eastern Europe*), edited by Karl C. Thalheim and Hans-Hermann Hohmann (Cologne: Wissenschaft and Politik, 1968). The outline of the intended Czechoslovak reforms, before the Soviet invasion of August 1968, is presented by Ota Šik in certain chapters of his volume already cited (*Plan and Market . . .*) and in a short pamphlet, *Economic Planning and Management in Czechoslovakia* (Prague: Orbis, 1968, 3rd ed.). A group of nine interesting articles on the "new system" in Hungary are presented in English translation by Istvan Friss (ed.) in *Reform of the Economic Mechanism in Hungary* (Budapest: Akadémiai Kiadó, 1969).

## Sectorial Management

### INDUSTRY

Management organization and the system of controls over industrial enterprises, both in the traditional centralized Soviet setting and under the changes since the 1960's, are amply discussed in the standard books on the Soviet economy, e.g., Alec Nove's *Soviet Economy* (New York: Praeger University Series, 1961, and subsequent editions); Abram Bergson's *The Economics of Soviet Planning* (New Haven: Yale University Press, 1964). An outstanding critique of "overcentralization" is presented in the classical work of Janos Kornai, *Overcentralization in Economic Administration, A Critical Analysis Based on Experience in Hungarian Light Industry* (London: Oxford University Press, 1959); an interesting presentation of the problems arising in information transmission within centralized or decentralized frameworks is presented in a short paper by Pavel Pelikan, "Language as a Hidden Parameter: Some Notes on the Problem of Centralization vs. Decentralization" (Pittsburgh: Carnegie-Mellon University, Graduate School of Industrial Administration, September 1968, mimeo.). Soviet documents and analyses of the mid-1960's reforms ushering in the "New System of Planning and Economic Incentives," or New Economic Management, are presented in the two volumes edited by Myron E. Sharpe cited above. A thoughtful commentary on the Liberman discussion is to be found in George N. Halm's "Mises, Lange, Liberman: Allocation and Motivation in the Socialist Economy," *Weltwirtschaftliches Archiv*, Band 100, Heft 1, pp. 19–39.

The evolving Yugoslav system of management and planning has been examined in a number of well-known books. The specific problems with which we are particularly interested here—namely, the main aspects of the organization and activities of the industrial enterprises—have received special attention in a number of somewhat less-known works. The general background concerning the transition to the "third stage" of Yugoslav reform was sketched by the late Rudolf Bičanić in "Economics of Socialism in Yugoslavia, Transition to the Third Stage: The Reform" (Zagreb: 1967, mimeo.). Also useful regarding the position of the producing enterprise in the planning framework are Rikard Lang and Milan Mesarić, "Planification économique en Yougoslavie," in *Problèmes du dévelopement économique dans les pays Méditerranéens* ("Economic Planning in Yugoslavia," in *Problems of Economic Development in the Mediterranian Countries*), Naples International Seminar, October-November 1962, edited by Jean Cuisenier (The Hague: Mouton & Co., 1963), pp. 225–266; Carl Landauer's "Geplante Marktwirtschaft: Das Beispiel Frankreichs und Jugoslavwiens" ("Planned Market Economy: The Example of France and Yugoslavia") *Kyklos*, vol. XVI, fasc. 4, pp. 543–566; and Benjamin Ward's discussion on the "Illyrian" firm included in his *The Socialist Economy* (chs. 9 and 10, pp. 208–257), cited above. On worker's management and on the management of the enterprise in general, one may refer to two papers by Boris Jelić and Djordje Mijić included in *Le Régime et les institutions de la république populaire féderative de Yougoslavie*, (*Administration and Institutions of the Federal Popular Republic of Yugoslavia*) (Brussels: Centre d'études des pays de l'Est, 1959), pp. 13–28 and 70–80. Significant articles on these problems are to be found in the theoretical Yugoslav periodicals, available in English under the titles *Socialist Thought and Practice* and *Yugoslav Survey*. Books of particular importance are Harry Schleicher's *Das System der betrieblichen Selbstverwaltung in Jugoslawien* (*The System of the Enterprises' Self-Management in Yugoslavia*) (Berlin: Duncker and Humblot, 1961), which examines the economic and legal components of this system in a broad historical perspective covering the whole postwar period up to 1960; Albert Meister's *Socialisme et autogestion, l'experience Yougoslave* (*Socialism and Self-Management, the Yugoslav Experience*) (Paris: Seuil, 1964), which discusses the various types of self-management (communal, industrial, rural cooperative, social) within the country's overall power structure; and Gudrun Leman's *Stellung und Aufgaben der okonomischen Einheiten in den jugoslawischen Unternehmungen* (*Position and Tasks of the Economic Units in the Yugoslav Enterprises*) (Berlin: Duncker and Humblot, 1967), which discusses the role of self-management organs in "the sociology of the enterprise as a whole"—i.e., its industrial organization and functioning. A comparitive analysis of the possible impacts on industrial performance of centralized or decentralized mechanisms in Yugoslavia is presented by Thomas A. Marschak in "Centralized versus Decentralized Resource Allocation: The Yugoslav 'Laboratory,'" *Quarterly Journal of Economics*, November 1968, pp. 561–87.

AGRICULTURE

No comprehensive overall study on the East European agrarian reforms has yet been done. Neither a comparative study of the prereform structures relevant to the policies of land reform nor an examination of the true objectives of these reforms themselves as they were carried out in the immediate post-World War II years has been undertaken. The first part of Essay 5 recalls briefly some of the positions I have already taken in my earlier *The Economics of Communist Eastern Europe*. Much remains to be done, however, in carrying this analysis further and examining in depth both the international and the intraregional differences in agrarian structure, outputs, trade patterns, etc., which preceded the reforms and which are still affecting their results. The forms and pace of collectivization, the changing structure of agricultural inputs and outputs, and the principal indicators of agriculture's performance under collectivization are only partly documented in various national studies on the development of agriculture under the Communist regimes. Certain standard Western studies on East European countries, e.g., John Michael Montias' *Central Planning in Poland* (New Haven: Yale University Press, 1962), and his *Economic Development in Communist Rumania* (Cambridge, Mass.: M.I.T. Press, 1967), and Bela Balassa's *The Hungarian Experience in Economic Planning* (New Haven: Yale University Press, 1959) contain only cursory references to the nature, scope, and objectives of the land reforms but present interesting analyses on the allocation of resources to this sector, its mechanization, planning, etc. Numerous studies also of this type are scattered throughout the United Nations publications, particularly the annual *Economic Survey of Europe*. The scope of rural socialist policies as attempted by Edward Kardelj for Yugoslavia in his interesting and imaginative study, *Problems of Socialist Policy in the Countryside* (London: Lincolns-Praeger, 1962), needs to be fully explored. Furthermore, more extensive evaluation of the impact of collectivization on productivity and income distribution, like the work of Tikomir J. Markovitch in *Le Revenue agricole en Yugoslavie (Agricultural Income in Yugoslavia)* (Geneva: Droz, 1967), is essential. The "Research Project cn National Income in East Central Europe" of Columbia University, directed by Dr. Thad P. Alton, has published a number of occasional papers on output trends in agriculture, expenses, gross and net product, productivity, etc., but these are keyed to the specific national income studies of the project and do not attempt to present an integrated picture of the problems of socialist management and planning in the East European agricultural sector as a whole.

FOREIGN TRADE

The theoretical and practical implications of foreign-trade management and planning have commanded great attention. Foreign-trade organization, planning procedures, price-setting processes, choices of partners, coordination efforts, and so on have been surveyed in Frederic L. Pryor's *The Communist Foreign Trade System* (Cambridge, Mass.: M.I.T. Press, 1963). Other studies have encompassed its statutes, historical evolution, achievements, and prospects: for example, Istvan Agoston's *Le Marche commun communiste, Principes et pratique du COMECON* (*The Communist Common Market, Principles and Practice of COMECON*) (Geneva: Droz, 1964), and Michael Kaser's *COMECON, Integration Problems of the Planned Economies* (London: Oxford University Press, 1965). Others still have examined the underlying doctrines (political, military, juridical) on which socialist "integrations" have been predicated: for example, Teofil I. Kis, *Les Pays de l'Europe de l'Est, Leurs rapports mutuels et le probleme de leur integration dans l'orbite de l'USSR* (*The East European Countries, Their Mutual Relationship and the Problem of Their Integration in the Soviet Orbit*) (Louvain: Nauwelaerts, 1964). Finally, some studies have tried to establish the broad outline of the theoretical framework of centralized planning and international trade, or to fill in the specific details of the "political economy" of Communist trade and of Communist "international economics": notably, "Foreign Trade of Centrally Planned Economies," by Alan A. Brown and Egon Neuberger in their *International Trade and Central Planning* (Berkeley: University of California Press, 1968), pp. 3–28, and especially P. J. D. Wiles' *Communist International Economics* (Oxford: Blackwell, 1968). Of course, various aspects of the management and planning of foreign trade under socialism are discussed in the literature produced in the East European countries, particularly in the volume of theoretical studies, *International Trade and Development Theory and Policy* (Warsaw: Państwowe Wydawnictwo Naukowe, 1966), which contains a number of important articles by Polish economists. Lastly, and of particular interest for the English reader, are the articles published in the periodicals *Acta Oeconomica Academiae Scientiarum Hungaricae* of Budapest and in the *Czechoslovak Economic Papers* of Prague.

## Development and International Relations

### TRADE PATTERNS

A significant number of Western studies have examined the overall patterns of socialist foreign trade, especially the relations within CEMA, between East and West, and between CEMA and the less-developed countries, as well as various problems affecting their balance of payments. Some of these questions have been examined in the Brown-Neuberger volume and by Kaser, Pryor, and Wiles in their books cited above. Specific studies on the direction, structure, volume, and value of intrasocialist trade are to be found particularly in issues of the United Nations *Economic Survey of Europe* and the United Nations *Economic Bulletin for Europe*. Official Soviet or East European data are published in various statistical compendia issued by the individual countries. China's foreign trade has been examined in a number of books, particularly in Alexander Eckstein's *Communist China's Economic Growth and Foreign Trade* (New York: McGraw-Hill, 1966). The West has manifested particular interest in the question of Soviet price discrimination in intra-socialist trade. A guide to an intricate American "debate" on the subject may be found in Frank Holzman's "More on Soviet Bloc Trade Discrimination," *Fletcher School Reprints Series* (Medford, Mass.: The Fletcher School, December 1965). An exhaustive study of the problem is Oliver von Gajzago's *Preisentwicklung und Preispolitik im Sowjetischen Aussenhandel 1955–1963* (*Price Development and Price Policy in Soviet Foreign Trade 1955–1963*) (Cologne: Bundesinstitut fur ostwissenschaftliche und internationale Studien, 1966).

The evolution and problems of East-West trade have been examined in a number of documents of the US Congress published over the last decade. Useful background material may be found in *A Background Study on East-West Trade*, prepared by the Legislative Reference Service of the Library of Congress for the Committee on Foreign Relations, US Senate, 89th Congress, 1st Session (Washington, D. C.: Government Printing Office, April 1965). Other studies to be consulted on this question are Michael von Berg, *Die strategische Bedeutung des Ost-West Handels* (*The Strategic Importance of East-West Trade*) (Leiden: Sijthoff, 1966), and *East-West Trade*, a symposium edited by Philip E. Uren (Ontario: The Canadian Institute of International Affairs, 1966). Finally, the evolution and implications of the Western strategic embargo are exhaustively discussed by Gunnar Adler-Karlsson in *Western Economic Warfare 1947–1967* (Stockholm: Almquist & Wiksell, 1968), in terms often colored by what seem to be personal biases against certain US policies.

Socialist aid and trade relations with underdeveloped countries have yielded only a very limited number of studies. Among the most recent and complete are Marshall I. Goldman's *Soviet Foreign Aid* (New York: Praeger, 1967), and Leo Tansky's "Soviet Foreign Aid to Less Developed Countries," included in *New Directions in the Soviet Economy*, Studies Prepared for the Subcommittee on Foreign Economic Policy of the Joint Economic Committee, 89th Congress, 2nd Session (Washington, D. C.: Government Printing Office, 1966), vol. IV, pp. 947–74.

## ECONOMIC NATIONALISM, MODERNIZATION, AND "CONVERGENCE"

The implications of the economic nationalism of each *"communisme de gouvernement"* have not been explored as fully and systematically as those of the *"socialisme de gouvernement"* (see Roger Berg, *Le Socalisme entre l' economie nationale et le cosmopolitisme* [Paris: Sirey, 1935]). Certain aspects of economic nationalism particularly connected with commercial policies have been examined by John M. Montias in "Economic Nationalism in Eastern Europe: Forty Years of Continuity and Change," *Yale Economic Growth Center Paper No. 82* (New Haven: Yale University, 1966), and by Karel Hobik, "COMECON and East European Economic Nationalism" published in English in the *Zeitschrift fur die gesamte Staatswissenschaft*, vol. 122, no. 4, pp. 721–40. Much remains to be done, however, in the thorough examination and assessment of the impact of socialist nationalist policies on industry (development patterns, location, labor), agriculture (land reforms and collectivization), services (particular professional services), etc. On the other hand, the usual aspects of "modernization" under Communist rule (viz., industrialization, agricultural mechanization, institutionalization of a high saving rate, etc.) have been scrutinized for almost every country of the socialist camp. Special attention has been given to growth in production, consumption, productivity, and efficiency for Eastern Europe as a whole in Maurice Ernst's "Postwar Economic Growth in Eastern Europe (A Comparison with Western Europe)," in *New Directions in the Soviet Economy*, pp. 873–916, and more exhaustively, in *Economic Developments in Countries of Eastern Europe, A Compendium of Papers*, submitted to the Subcommittee of Foreign Economic Policy of the Joint Economic Committee, 91st Congress, 2nd Session (Washington, D. C.: Government Printing Office, 1970).

The question of convergence or divergence between the capitalist and socialist systems is yielding an increasingly rich literature. Of great interest for the partisans of convergence are the numerous papers of Jan Tinbergen and particularly his paper with H. Linnerman and J. P. Pronk, "Convergence of Economic Systems in East and West," published in *Disarmament and World Economic Interdependence*, edited by Emile Benoit *et al.* (New

York: Columbia University Press, 1967), pp. 246–60, which contains not only a systematic presentation of the convergence thesis but also an extensive bibliography. Peter Wiles has espoused both pro and con positions on this subject; he has, however, some useful thoughts on the matter in "Fifty Years After: What Future for Communism," *Lloyds Bank Review*, no. 86, October 1967, pp. 36–48. The official Russian opposition to the theory of convergence has been stated by V. Cheprakov in "Teoriia konvergentsii i deistvitel' nost' " ("Reality and the Theory of Convergence"), *Voprosy Ekonomiki*, no. 2, 1968, pp. 87–96. The non-official acceptance of the convergence theory is given by Andrei D. Sakharov in *Progress, Coexistence and Intellectual Fredom* (New York: Norton, 1968). Finally, a broad confrontation of Western and Eastern ideas on this and related subjects is to be found in *Koexistenz zwischen Ost und West, Konflict, Kooperation, Konvergenz* (*Coexistence between East and West, Conflict, Cooperation, Convergence*) proceedings of a conference held in Austria in 1965, edited by Hans Mayrzedt and Helmut Romé (Vienna: Europa Verlag, 1967).

# NOTES

1 . SCOPE AND LOGIC OF ECONOMIC REFORMS

1. See Lucas Pun and John Peschon, "The State of the Art of Automatic Control," in *Disciplines and Techniques of Systems Control,* ed. John Peschon (New York: Blaisdell Publishing Co., 1965), pp. 3–36.

2. J. Steindl has noted that the market's self-regulatory functions invariably resemble controllers, and that economic theory "presupposes the existence of a controller without, however, demonstrating that it really exists and how it works." On the basis of a cursory analysis of commodity cycles, such as those of hogs or crops, which fluctuate in a "cobweb" manner—i.e., with exploding quantity effects or with dampening effects on output and price—Steindl asserts that the market is not "a very efficient servomechanism" in achieving economic equilibrium. Referring then to the famous "competitive solution" proposed by Lange for efficient allocation of resources under socialism, Steindl adds that the market is not the only controller possible and that "a great variety of controllers can be imagined and they can be shaped so as to serve the purposes which we choose." (See J. Steindl, "Servomechanisms and Controllers in Economic Theory and Policy," in *On Political Economy and Econometrics, Essays in Honour of Oskar Lange* [Oxford: Pergamon Press, 1965], 545–54.) The crucial difference between a centrally managed and a competitive market economy may be not in the existence of visible or invisible "controllers" but—as Hurwicz has suggested—in the *type of communications* prevailing in each one of them. In the centrally managed economy, central preferences, description of technologies, and resources holdings are communicated; in the competitive market, bids and prices are transmitted. (See L. Hurwicz "Centralization and Decentralization in Economic Systems. On the Concept and Possibility of Informational Decentralization," *American Economic Review,* May 1969, pp. 513–524).

3. For general discussions on Soviet "cybernetic" approaches to planning problems, see A. Zauberman, *Aspects of Planometrics* (London: The Athlone Press, 1967), pp. 287–89, and R. W. Judy, "Information, Control and Soviet Economic Management," in *Mathematics and Computers in Soviet Economic Planning,* ed. J. P. Hardt *et al.* (New Haven and London: Yale University Press, 1967), pp. 1 ff. See also V. A. Trapeznikov, "Problems of Control of Economic Systems," transl. from *Automatika i telemekhanika* in Joint Publications Research Service, no. 47 (April 1969), p. 802.

4. See M. Meyer, *L"Entreprise industrielle d'Etat en Union Soviétique* (The State Enterprise in the Soviet Union) (Paris: Cujas, 1966), Ch. III, pp. 693 ff.

5. V. A. Trapeznikov, *loc. cit.*

6. I am referring here to the complex of measures outlined and put into effect by the March and September 1965 plenary sessions of the Central Committee of the Communist Party of the Soviet Union—a complex defined by the Soviet economist A. Birman "as the third all encompassing reform in the history of our country," which "in scope and importance yields nothing to the first two: The transition to the New Economic Policy in 1921 and the reorganization of management in 1930–1932." The new reform—referred to as the "New System of Planning and Economic Incentives,"—has stressed "substantiation" of draft plans, increased responsibility of suppliers for output quality and sales, renewed importance of "profitability," shorter pay-out periods and more stringent procedures of business accounting. (The main aspects of the reform are discussed in Essay 2.) Let us note here that the key overall objective of the reform—a perennial objective in Soviet planning—namely, to bring about plant managers to "disclose" their true output capacities and to undertake "maximal" output tasks, has not been attained. Notwithstanding elaborate rearrangements concerning plant managers' utilization of manpower and the wage fund, shares in profits and other inducements, the reform has failed to break the inertia of the Soviet bureaucratic machine. See A. Birman, "The Reform in Its Fifth Year, Thoughts after the Plenary Session," *Literaturnaia gazeta*, no. 7 (February 11, 1970), p. 10; transl. in *The Current Digest of the Soviet Press*, vol. XXII, no. 7 (February 13–19, 1970), pp. 3–4.

7. See B. I. Iskakov-Pliukhin, "Concerning the Chain Model of Expanded Reproduction," transl. in *Mathematical Studies in Economics and Statistics in the USSR and Eastern Europe*, vol. II, no. 2, (Winter 1965–66).

8. B. A. Volhkov, Iu. R. Leibkind, and Iu. Samokhin, "Certain Problems Connected with the Creation of an Automated System for the Development of the National Economic Plan," *Ekonomika i matematicheskie metody*, no. 1, 1966.

9. A. Berg, "Econmoic Cybernetics," transl. in *Problems of Economics*, vol. XI, no. 2 (June 1968). For a discussion on economic systems analogues, see O. J. Smith and H. F. Erdley, "An Electronic Analogue for an Economic System," *Electrical Engineering*, April 1952, pp. 362–66.

10. E. Z. Maiminas, "Economic Cybernetics," transl. in *Mathematical Studies in Economics and Statistics in the USSR and Eastern Europe*, vol. II, no. 3 (Spring 1966), pp. 3–31.

11. See A. A. Fel'dbaum, "Optimal Systems," in Peschon, *op. cit.*, pp. 317–73.

12. A. I. Katsenelinboigen and E. Iu. Faerman, quoted by M. Ellman, "Optimal Planning," *Soviet Studies*, vol. 20, no. 1 (July 1968), p. 116.

13. Cf. "Decree on State Network of Computation Centers," *Izvestiia*, March 20, 1966.

14. For a discussion of all these reforms in perspective, see R. Bičanić, "Economics of Socialism in Yugoslavia, Transition to the Third Stage: The Reform," 1967 (mimeo.).

15. This has incited—unjustifiably, I believe—some Western economists to assert that Yugoslavia is transiting back from socialism to capitalism. See D. D. Milenkovitch, "Yugoslavia: The Transition from Socialism to Capitalism?" paper pre-

sented at the Northeastern Conference of the American Association for the Advancement of Slavic Studies, April 26, 1969.

16. See *Acta Oeconomica Academiae Scientiarum Hungaricae*, vol. 3 (1968), *passim.*

17. V. I. Lenin, "The State and Revolution," in *Selected Works*, ed. D. Fineberg (New York: International Publishers, *ca* 1933), vol. VII, pp. 48 ff.

18. Roger Garaudy, *Le grand tournant du socialisme* [The Great Turning-Point of Socialism] (Paris: Gallimard, 1969), pp. 33 ff.

## 2. RAMIFICATIONS IN INVESTMENT POLICIES

1. The Marxian schema, presented in *Capital* (K. Marx, *Capital, A Critique of Political Economy*, vol. II, ed. F. Engels [Moscow: Foreign Language Publishing House, 1957 ed.], part III, chs. XX and XXI, pp. 392-523), has been examined innumerable times by Soviet or Western economic authors. Let us recall briefly here only that Marx divides the physical output of the economy, on the basis of its destination, into two categories: producer goods $(I_g)$ and consumer goods $(C_g)$, produced by industries of sector I and sector II, respectively. Each output is, in turn, equated to depreciation plus raw materials used $(c)$, wages $(v)$, and surplus value $(m)$ (i.e., property income, though Marx does not define it thus). Total output under the scheme is equal to $c_1 + v_1 + m_1 = I_g$, and $c_2 + v_2 + m_2 = C_g$. Under repetitive stationary conditions, the output of Sector I must match the capital consumption and raw materials used up in both sectors (that is, $c_1 + c_2$), whereas consumer goods output must match an expanded wage bill (expanded by the wages of the additional workers needed to produce the extra producer goods) and the surplus. Simple and expanded reproduction can be effected smoothly only if certain mutual relationships between the components of the national (physical) product and the components of the outputs of the two sectors are realized. (See Paul M. Sweezy, *The Theory of Capitalist Development, Principles of Marxian Political Economy* [New York: Oxford University Press, 1942], part II, pp. 75 ff.)

2. "Standard Rules for Determining the Economic Efficiency of Capital Investments" have superseded in September 1969 the rules on "Economic Effectiveness of Capital Investments and New Technology" established in 1959. The "Standard Rules" have updated the old methods of calculating economic efficiency and have stressed notably the need, in the case of branch instructions in particular, of comparing overall net output to capital ratios (i.e., ratios of overall net gains to capital investments, called "coefficients of absolute effectiveness") and the "coefficients of relative effectiveness," indicating which specific alternative is to be viewed as more efficient for the solution of a given economic task. Contrary to the 1959 rules, the "Standard Rules" have established a "normative of efficiency for the national economy as a whole" (i.e., a sort of official "interest rate") to be used in calculating these coefficients. This "normative," subject to subsequent change, was fixed for the given plan period at 12 per cent. (This figure is described in a commentary by A. Mitrofanov, as a "working" datum to be corrected in various ways by branches for current or planned work, for long range calculations, etc. See "Tipovaia metodika opredeleniia ekonomicheskoi effektivnosti kapital'nykh vlozhenii" ["Standard Rules for Determining

the Economic Efficiency of Capital Investments"] and the commentary on the Rules by A. Mitrofanov, "Kompas ekonomicheskoi effektivnosti" [The Compass of Economic Efficiency"], *Ekonomicheskaia gazeta*, no. 39, September 1969, pp. 11–13.)

3. See *Ekonomicheskaia gazeta*, nos. 7, 11, 12, 19, and 21, 1965. Certain Western economists claim that growth follows from application of this "law," provided it is interpreted as implying high investment priority for the machinery construction sector. Eventually, the growth rates of the other sectors of the economy would converge on that of this sector. The demonstration is dependent, however, on a number of admittedly unrealistic assumptions. See P. R. W. Preece, "The Priority Given to Heavy Industry in Socialist Economic Planning," *Science and Society*, vol. XXXII, no. 3 (Summer 1968). For a more detailed discussion of the schema and of these schools, see Shumpei Kumon, "The 'Schema of Reproduction' as a Model of Planned Economic Growth" (Ph.D. dissertation, Bloomington, Ind., Indiana University, 1968), pp. 27 ff.

4. Cf. "The Planning and Financing of Investment in the Soviet Union and Eastern Europe," *Economic Survey of Europe in 1955* (Geneva: United Nations, 1956), pp. 96 ff.

5. See *Paper Submitted by the Government of the People's Federal Republic of Yugoslavia*, prepared by S. Blagojevich for the Economic Commission for Europe, Meeting of Senior Economic Advisers, Geneva, March 20–24, 1961.

6. If, by Marxian notations, gross material product equals $c + v + m$, where constant capital, or interfirm purchases and depreciation, is $c$, payroll is $v$, and "surplus," or in Western income accounting, total of interest, rent, and profits before taxes, is $m$, then net material product equals $v + m$. Traditionally, planned prices of producer goods approximated average variable costs in that sector, or $c_1 + v_1$, and the prices of consumer goods, $c_2 + v_2 + m_2 + m_1$, that is, costs in that sector plus the "surplus" of the economy as a whole $(m_2 + m_1)$.

7. If it is assumed that, with the price system selected, the planner aims at equating the total surplus of the society—to be partly collected centrally and partly left in the hands of the enterprises—to the goal of capital accumulation selected as that necessary for growth, then the price system based on the "straight value" concept could be expressed by the equation $p^* = A p^* + w$ $(1 + a)$, where $p^*$ is the new vector of prices in that price system; $A$ is the matrix of input coefficients computed on the basis of initial prices; $w$ is the vector of direct wage inputs per monetary unit of output $a$ the scalar, to be computed, showing, in percentage, the allocation of the "surplus" in relation to wage. Similarly, for the "average value" price system, the price equation would be $p^* = (A p^* + w) (1 + \beta)$, in which $\beta$ is the scalar to be computed, showing in percentage the allocation of the "surplus" in relation with prime costs. Finally, in the producer-type price, the price equation would be $p^* = A p^* + w +$ $(C_{p_i} + V_{p_j}) \gamma$, where $C$ and $V$ are vectors representing the fixed and variable capital per monetary unit of output at initial prices, $p_i$ is a producer-type price index of fixed assets of a representative sector (i.e., a sector whose cost structure best represents that of the tied-up fixed assets), $p_j$ a producer-type price index of working capital of a representative sector (i.e., a sector whose cost structure best represents that of the tied-up working capital), and $\gamma$ is the scalar, to be computed, showing, in percentage, the allocation of the "surplus" in relation to fixed and variable capital. In the three systems, the starred letter is the decision

variable. For a fuller discussion of these and other suggestions, see "The Price Model and its Uses in Practice," a Czechoslovak report in *Macro Economic Models for Planning and Policymaking* (Geneva: United Nations, 1967), pp. 129–33.

8. Cf. Jiří Novozámsky, *Vyrovnovani ekonomicke urovne zemi RVHP (Leveling of the economic levels of the countries of Popular Democracy)* (Prague: Naklad politicke lit., 1964). The title is obviously a deliberate misnomer.

9. As Dr. Richard Hamming of the Bell Telephone Laboratories observed with respect to computer systems, "When any one of the dimensions of a system are changed by an order of magnitude or more, then the system has changed not only qualitatively but also quantitatively." Joseph Weizenbaum, of the Massachusetts Institute of Technology who quotes Dr. Hamming, remarks: "The point is perhaps easier to appreciate when applied to aircraft. An airplane that can carry at most 10 passengers is used very differently from one which can accommodate 100. Similarly, a military airplane capable of sustained speeds of at most 100 mph is a different weapon than one which can cruise at 1,000 mph. A space craft is not merely an airplane that can climb to very high altitudes." (See J. Weizenbaum, "Extrapolations," in *Computer Methods in the Analysis of Large-Scale Social Systems*, ed. James M. Beshers [Cambridge, Massachusetts, The M.I.T. Press, second edition, 1968], p. 51.)

10. See "Enterprise and Socialism," *The Economist*, July 16–22, 1966, p. 238. Commenting on these reforms, the *Economist* notes that Yugoslavia seeks "to add enterprise to socialism" by dropping "much of the 'statism' that throttles orthodox economic systems (and indeed encumbers many capitalist economies too)." An additional factor that may have influenced the Yugoslav decision to abandon investment planning is the impossibility of achieving central agreement because of the diverging interests of the six Yugoslav republics. See D. D. Milenkovitch, *loc. cit.*

11. Ota Šik, "Television Speeches," *Pragopress*, August 1968.


### 3. "CATCHING UP" STRATEGIES

1. This essay draws heavily upon an earlier essay entitled "Contrasting Economic Patterns: Chinese and Soviet Development Strategies," published in *Soviet Studies*, vol. XV, July 1963.

2. Niu Chung-hang, *China Will Overtake Britain* (Peking: Foreign Language Press, 1958), p. 66. See also Hsueh Mu-chiao, Su Hsing and Lin Tse-li, *The Socialist Transformation of the National Economy in China* (Peking: Foreign Language Press, 1960), p. 271: "To catch up with and surpass Britain, strenuous efforts have still to be made. Since China's population is more than ten times that of Britain, to achieve this aim is only the first step in industrialization. Continuous efforts must be made to catch up with and outstrip the most advanced of all capitalist countries."

3. See V. E. Motylev, *Problema tempa razitiia SSSR (The Problem of the Pace of Development of the USSR)* (Moscow: Kom. Akad. Izdat., 1929), p. 144 ff.

4. Cf. *Statisticheski spravochnik SSSR 1928 g. (Statistical Handbook of the USSR, 1928)* (Moscow: Statist. Izd. TsSU, SSSR, 1929), pp. 282, 383, 494–99, and *passim*.

5. L. E. Hubbard, *The Economics of Soviet Agriculture* (London: Macmillan, 1939), p. 120.

6. See my *Soviet Strategy for Economic Growth* (Bloomington, Ind.: Indiana University Press, second printing 1967), pp. 85 ff.

7. Data from *Statistical Yearbook 1961* (New York: United Nations, 1961), *passim,* and *Ekonomika stran sotsialisticheskogo lageria 1960 (Economy of the Countries of the Socialist Camp, 1960)* (Moscow: Mysl', 1961), *passim.*

8. The estimated ratios of their populations have shifted now to 3.3:1. See *Ekonomika stran sotsialisticheskogo lageria, op. cit.,* p. 60.

9. Hu Jui-liang and Yuan Tai-hsu, "On the Handicraft Industry and its Economic Form" *Chin chi Yen-chin,* July 1962, transl. in *Joint Publications Research Service,* no. 15, p. 819.

10. L. E. Hubbard, *The Economics of Soviet Agriculture, op. cit.,* p. 188; and *Narodnoe khoziaistvo SSSR,* 1959, pp. 350, 351; *ibid.,* 1961, pp. 365 ,368.

11. Chao Kuo-chun, *Economic Planning and Organization in Mainland China: a Documentary Study (1949–1957),* II (Cambridge, Mass.: Harvard, 1960), p. 5, mimeo.

12. See *First Five-Year Plan for Development of the National Economy of the People's Republic of China in 1953–1957* (Peking: Foreign Language Press, 1956), p. 16.

13. *Ibid.,* pp. 31 ff. Adam Kaufman has described in detail the results of the absorption of artisans into the Soviet industrial labor force and the incursions of the state industry into the "home" industries of the Soviet peasant population. According to him, during the Soviet First Five-Year Plan, small-scale industrial output and employment fell in both absolute and relative terms. The relative shares of small scale industry in total industral output and employment fell from 28 and 44 per cent to 8.0 and 8.4 per cent respectively (see Adam Kaufman, *Small-Scale Industry in the Soviet Union* [New York: National Bureau of Economic Research, 1962] pp. 6, 71, 81). The same process took place in Eastern Europe. (See my work, *The Economics of Communist Eastern Europe* [New York: Technology Press of M.I.T. and Wiley, 1957] p. 83 and *passim*). Nai-Ruenn Chen and Walter Galenson note for their part the following difference between the Soviet and the Chinese strategy in regard to industry: "The Russian planners gave short shrift to small workshops and the traditional handcrafts. Artisans were herded into cooperatives, whose share in total output declined rapidly . . . In China (and in India as well) the traditional handcrafts retained their significance in both output and employment. One estimate put non-agricultural Chinese handcraft employment at 10 million in 1957, compared with only 5.9 million in factories and mining." (Chen and Galenson, *The Chinese Economy Under Communism* [Chicago: Aldine, 1969] p. 40.)

14. *First Five-Year Plan . . . ,* op. cit., pp. 113, 121.

15. *Ibid.,* p. 122.

16. Mao's emphasis on the role of the "bloc of the four classes" in China's revolution followed, up to a point, the political line laid down by Bukharin and Stalin between the Vth andVIth Congresses of the Communist International. The Left (under Trotsky) opposed this orientation violently and stressed for its part that the Communists must preserve their "complete independence" under all circumstances (even within temporary "alliances" with the Kuo Min Tang) and

that "peasants' soviets *must* be united through workers' soviets in the cities and the industrial centers"—if the revolution was to succeed. (See L. Trotsky, *The Third International After Lenin* [1928], transl. John G. Wright [New York: Pioneer Publishers, 1957], pp. 31, 37, 78, and *passim*.) Mao never forgot to preserve the independence of his movement, but he did not wait for the workers to create their soviets. His resolute reliance on the peasantry, simultaneously downgrading the role of the urban workers in the Chinese civil war—was his own contribution to the strategy of Communist revolutions. His faith in the organized peasantry and his own distinctions between revolutionary phases and the connections among them are now recalled in China to stress that in industrialization, as in the civil war, the first phase depends on "the political consciousness and the organized strength of the peasants." (See Shih Ting-hsiana, "The Distinction and Link-Up Between the Two Stages of the Chinese Revolution," trans. from *Hung Chi* in *Peking Review*, January 20, 1961.)

17. See Yang Ling, "Agriculture: Foundation of the National Economy," *Peking Review*, October 18, 1960, 14 ff.

18. Teng Tzu-hui, "Report to the Rural Work Conference of the Central Committee, New Democratic Youth League, July 15, 1954," in Chao Kuo-chun, *Agrarian Policies of Mainland China: A Documentary Study (1949–1956)* (Cambridge, Mass.: Harvard, 1957), pp. 71–72.

19. See Tan Chen-lin, "Speeding up Mechanization of China's Agriculture," *Peking Review*, September 27, 1960, p. 8. Certain Western scholars, among whom Professor Alexander Eckstein plays a leading role, contend that from 1953 to 1957, the Chinese emulated Stalin's strategy and his emphasis on industry, particularly heavy industry, and later developed a new strategy, the "Great Leap Forward," which involved at its core mass mobilization of unemployed rural labor on a scale never attempted before, even in China. (See Alexander Eckstein, *Communist China's Economic Growth and Foreign Trade*, [New York: McGraw Hill, for the Council on Foreign Relations, 1966] pp. 29–30, 36). I have suggested above (cf. note 13, for instance) that unlike the Russians, the Chinese have already attempted, during their First Five-Year Plan, to develop *simultaneously* small-scale and large-scale industry, the former for meeting peasant demands, the latter for coping with the needs of the modern industrial sector. Further, unlike the Russians, the Chinese used collectivization primarily as a means of mass mobilization of peasant labor for capital construction, rather than as a means for increasing the marketed share of grains. In this perspective the "Great Leap" did not represent a change of *strategy*, but rather an effort on a grander scale to reach the objectives pursued during the First Five-Year Plan. Professor Eckstein, for his part, sees in the "leap" both an unique phenomenon and a means of managerial "decentralization," i.e., a means through which economic decision-making was being placed, as never before, "as far down as the commune or the local party unit" (*Ibid.*, p. 36).

20. See Wang Kuang-wei, "How to Organize Agricultural Labor Power" (August 1957) in Chao Kuo-chun, *Economic Planning and Organization in Mainland China*, vol. I, pp. 143 ff.

21. See *An Economic Profile of Mainland China*, Studies prepared for the Joint Economic Committee Congress of the United States, 90th Congress, 1st Session (Washington, D. C.: U. S. Government Printing Office, 1967), vol. I, p. xi.

22. Ronald Hsia, "The Development of Mainland China's Steel Industry since 1958," *The China Quarterly*, July-September 1961, pp. 112 ff; also Li Fu-chun, "Raise High the Red Flag of the General Line and Continue to March Forward," *Peking Review*, August 23, 1960, pp. 7 ff.

23. According to the study by Adam Kaufman, total employment in Soviet small-scale industry measured in thousand full-time equivalents fell from 2,953 in 1913 to 2,408 in 1927–28 and to 861 in 1933; or, if 1913 is taken as a base of 100, it fell to 82 in 1927–28 and 29 in 1933. (See Adam Kaufman, *Small-scale Industry in the Soviet Union, op. cit.,* pp. 19, 45.)

24. For a discussion of these options see *600 Million Build Industry* (Peking: Foreign Languages Press, 1961), pp. I–II; also Ch'eng Ou-yang, "On Building an Independent Integral and Modern National Economic System," *Ta-kung pao,* June 27, 1962, transl. in *Joint Publications Research Service,* no. 14,714 (August 2, 1962), pp. 28–48.

25. See Yuan-li Wu, in association with Robert J. Barr and K. N. Chang, "Potential and Projections of the Chinese Economy, 1958 and Beyond, A First Report," vol. III, pp. 25–26, mimeo. See also Vasil Magdeski (Peking correspondent of the Zagreb *Vjesnik*), "To the Other Extreme," *Vjesnik,* May 17, 1962.

26. See "Mainland China," in *Economic Survey of Asia and the Far East in 1961* (Bangkok: n.p., 1962), pp. 96 ff.

27. See Ronald Hsia, "The Development of Mainland China's Steel Industry Since 1958," p. 114. But Professor Hsia notes that the massive efforts of 1958 were not entirely lost; they gave a definite impulse to expansion of the industry. Subsequently, some of the small native furnaces were discarded, while others were replaced by modern furnaces of larger size. However, as Prof. Pounds has remarked, "Some of the best steel has been made by craft methods in Asia. Perhaps the most that can be said against the Chinese method of expanding output is that it makes such excessive demands on labor as to be completely impracticable outside China. It most definitely allows the fullest use to be made of the small and scattered deposits of ore and fuel." N. J. G. Pounds, *The Geography of Iron and Steel* (London: Hutchinson University Library, 1959), p. 163.

28. Cf. "Mainland China," *Economic Survey of Asia and the Far East,* p. 97. Beginning in 1961, China imported from the West between four and six million tons of wheat and barley at an annual cost of between 300 and 500 million dollars. One should note, however, as Chen and Galenson rightly point out, that China's agricultural recovery, since 1962, has not changed the policy of importing wheat, which has "valid economic reasons, for rice is being exported as it was even during the crisis years of 1959–61. The policy of substituting imported wheat for Chinese rice has probably yielded a comparative advantage to China." (See Chen and Galenson, *op. cit.,* p. 101.) What has changed from the period of distress to the period of recovery, are the ratios of the quantities of rice to grain exported and imported.

29. See Yang Ling, "Agriculture: Foundation of the National Economy," *op. cit.,* p. 22.

30. *Jen-min Jih-pao,* quoting the decisions of the Ninth Plenum of the Eight Central Committee, January 1961. See "Hold Aloft the Great Banner of the General Line and Strive for New Victories," editorial of *Jen-min Jih-pao,* October 1, 1961, in *Peking Review,* October 6, 1961, p. 7.

31. *Ibid.*, p. 8.

32. See "On to New Victories," *Jen-min Jih-pao*, abridged transl. in *Peking Review*, January 4, 1963, p. 7.

33. An interesting, though not very illuminating discussion on the strategy took place in 1958 between the leading nonparty economist Ma Yin-ch'u and some of the party's young economists. See Kenneth Walker, "Ideology and Economic Discussion in China: Ma Yin-ch'u on Development Strategy and His Critics," *Economic Development and Cultural Change*, January 1963, pp. 113–33.

34. See N. Spulber, *The Soviet Economy: Structure, Principles, Problems* (New York: Norton, revised ed. 1969), p. 221.

35. Ragnar Nurkse, *Problems of Capital Formation in Under-developed Countries* (New York: Oxford University Press, 1957), pp. 37–38.

36. See Alexander Eckstein, "The Strategy of Economic Development in Communist China," *The American Economic Review*, May 1961, pp. 508 ff. I disagree, however, as already noted, with Professor Eckstein's suggestion that this strategy "began to crystallize in 1958" only (*ibid.*, p. 514); for me, the solutions adopted go farther back to Mao's basic approach to revolution in China, rather than to the "frantic search for an escape" caused by a convergence of various pressures in 1957.

37. For a discussion of this point and for an analysis of India's analogous "double-barrelled, heavy-industry and rural emphasis," see John P. Lewis, *Quiet Crisis in India* (Washington, D. C.: The Brookings Institution, 1962), particularly pp. 45 ff.

38. Thus Teng Tzu-hui noted in 1954: "We all know that in the 1930–32 agricultural reform movement of the Soviet Union, collectivization and mechanization were introduced simultaneously. . . . We, however, have not the necessary conditions today. The most important fact is that our standard of quantities-industrialization is too low; we can neither manufacture tractors in large quantities ourselves nor produce a sufficient quantity of petrol. . . ." "We intend," adds Teng, "to try semi-mechanization first. Then later, when we can manufacture large numbers of tractors and pumps and produce great quantities of petrol and chemical fertilizers we can carry out large-scale mechanization." (See Teng Tzu-hui, "Report to the Rural Work Conference . . . ," *op. cit.*, pp. 71–72.)

39. According to Professors L. Schapiro and J. Lewis, two types of leadership systems, and hence two power structures, coexisted in the Chinese Communist Party since the "Yenan period." One, built around Mao in the Communist bases, was predicated on the principle of a direct relationship between the leader and the populace; the other, built around Liu Shao-chi in the towns, was constructed on the principle of a tightly knit professionalized party and bureaucracy. The two types of networks combined eventually but never lost their identity. Finally, after the failure of the "Great Leap," the party split wide open: Mao used the "Cultural Revolution" to smash Liu and the bureaucracy and to turn the party as a whole into the direct propagator of his dogma. In short, like Stalin, though with other means, Mao sought "to break the institution so that it cannot thwart the will of the leaders." (See L. Schapiro and J. W. Lewis, "The Roles of the Monolithic Party Under the Totalitarian Leaders," *The China Quarterly*, October-December 1969, pp. 39 ff.) This interpretation does not conflict

with the one I suggested above concerning Mao's "egalitarian" views and their sources.

40. See "Mainland China," *Economic Survey of Asia and the Far East, op. cit.*, pp. 43, 45, 94.

41. As Professor Wu has stated it, "Food supply conditions of Communist China are incompatible with its recent population history and policy, and something must be altered drastically." Yuan-li Wu *et al., Potentials and Projections . . . , op. cit.*, ch. IV, p. 21.

### 4. PATTERNS IN INDUSTRIAL MANAGEMENT

1. F. Engels, *Anti-Dühring* (Moscow: Foreign Languages Publishing House, second ed. 1959), p. 387.

2. D. Guérin, *Jeunesse du Socialisme Libertaire: Essais (Youth of Libertarian Socialism: Essays)* (Paris: Rivière, 1959), p. 25.

3. M. M. Bober, *Karl Marx's Interpretation of History* (New York: Norton, second ed. 1965), pp. 14, 281 ff.

4. E. Bernstein, *Evolutionary Socialism: A Criticism and Affirmation*, trans. E. C. Harvey (New York: B. W. Huebsch, 1909), p. 100.

5. V. Lenin, "The State and Revolution," in *Selected Works, op. cit.*, pp. 48 ff., and 92–93.

6. *Ibid.*, p. 48.

7. See P. Holden, L. S. Fish, and H. L. Smith, *Top Management Organization and Control: A Research study of the Management Policies and Practices of Thirty-one Leading Industrial Corporations* (New York: McGraw-Hill, 1951) fig. 5, pp. 74 ff.

8. See, for instance, "Central Governmental Structure of the USSR," in D. Galik *et al., The Soviet Financial System, Structure, Operation and Statistics*, International Population Statistics Reports, series P–99, no. 23 (Washington, D. C.: Department of Commerce, Bureau of the Census, 1968), p. 10.

9. M. C. Branch, *The Corporate Planning Process* (New York: The American Management Association, 1962), p. 196 and *passim.*

10. P. F. Drucker, *Concept of the Corporation* (Boston: Beacon Press, 1960), pp. 69–70. See also B. W. Denning, "Organizing for Planning in a Large Decentralized Company," in *Programmes of Long Term—Long Range Planning* (New York: Gordon and Breach, for International Computation Center, Rome, 1967), pp. 61 ff.

11. P. F. Drucker, *ibid.*, pp. 67–68.

12. See my *Soviet Economy, op. cit.*, ch. VII.

13. Cf. A. Dragicević, "Self-Management by the Working Class," *Socialist Thought and Practice* (Belgrade), no. 23, July-September 1966, p. 87; and Z. Jovanović, "Trade Unions and Workers' Management," *ibid.*, no. 22, April-June 1966, p. 70.

14. Jovanović, *ibid.*, pp. 34–35.

15. Dragicević, *op. cit.*, p. 87.

16. Jovanović, *op. cit.*, p. 70.

17. D. Bilandzić, "Workers' Management of Factories," *Socialist Thought and Practice*, no. 28, October-December 1967, p. 43.

18. M. Todorović, "The Working Man, Capital Formation and Investments," *Socialist Thought and Practice*, no. 22, April-June, 1966, pp. 32–33.

19. Jovanović, *op. cit.*, p. 37.

20. E. Kardelj, "Responsibility for the Elections," *Socialist Thought and Practice*, no. 25, January-March 1967, p. 34.

21. Schumpeter calls "associationist socialism" "all the varieties of socialist planning that adopt the principle of running production by workmen's associations—of social reconstruction through producers' cooperatives." Schumpeter refers in this connection to the pre-Marxian "utopian" socialists who were not concerned, as Marx was, with critical analysis, but with definite plans of social organization and "with the means of carrying them into effect." (See Joseph A. Schumpeter, *History of Economic Analysis*, edited from manuscript by Elizabeth Body Schumpeter [New York: Oxford University Press, Seventh Printing, 1968], p. 454. Horvat acknowledges readily the indirect influence of the "utopians" on post-Marxian socialist ideology. For him, however, modern "associationist socialism"—is identical with socialism *tout court* and is antithetic to the managerial organization of any capitalist or state-run enterprise. Under capitalism and "statism" any enterprise represents, according to him, a "bureaucratic pyramid with two loose ends, the unidirectional flow of commands and the workers providing soon a base on which the structure rests." Under "associationist socialism" the "base is directly connected with the top . . . : the Board of Directors is replaced by the Workers' Council . . . By connecting the two loose ends of a formerly bureaucratic pyramid, the economic organizations are transformed into self-governing associations and Capitalism is superseded by Socialism." (See Branko Horvat, *Towards a Theory of Planned Economy* [Belgrade: Yugoslav Institute of Economic Research, 1964], p. 95). Actually, Horvat affirms further that Marx's own "vision of socialism, as inspired by the short history of the Paris Commune" was indeed that of "a federation of self-governing associations." (See Branko Horvat, *An Essay on Yugoslav Society* [White Plains, New York: International Arts and Science Press, 1969], p. 25).

22. Text of "Five Party Letter," *The New York Times*, July 19, 1968. Previously *Izvestiia* wrote under the signature of V. Stepanov: "Communist and workers parties are placed in the leadership in the socialist states by history itself. They are the governing parties and cannot . . . relinquish their role as political leaders . . . they cannot 'be ashamed' to penetrate every sphere of the life and development of society and state and actively influence them." *Izvestiia*, May 11, 1968.

23. V. Lisitsyn, "Management Problems of a Socialist Economy," *Planovoe Khoziaistvo*, no. 4, April 1965, transl. in *Joint Publications Research Service*, no. 31242, p. 2.

24. Shih Tung-Hsiang, "Is Yugoslavia a Socialist Economy," in *Peking Review* (translated from *Hung chi*), no. 24, June 12, 1964, pp. 11–16; no. 25, June 19, 1964, pp. 24–28; and no. 26, June 26, 1964, pp. 7–20 and *passim*.

25. "Refutation of the New Leaders of the C.P.S.U. on 'United Action,'" transl. from *Hung Chi*, no. 12, November 11, 1965.

26. "Czechoslovak Reply" (to "Five Party Letter"), *The New York Times*, July 19, 1968.

27. See, for instance, P. Pelikan, *Language as a Hidden Parameter: Some*

*Notes on the Problem of Centralization vs. Decentralization*, Pittsburgh, 1968, mimeo.

28. G. N. Halm, "Mises, Lange, Liberman: Allocation and Motivation in the Socialist Economy," *Weltwirtschaftlisches Archiv*, band 100, heft 1 (1968), p. 35.

29. Dragicević, *op. cit.*, p. 88.

30. Jovanović, *op. cit.*, p. 70.

31. Stepanov, *op. cit.*

32. Iu. I. Cherniak, "The Electronic Simulation of Information Systems for Central Planning," *Economics of Planning*, vol. 3, no. 1( April 1963), p. 23.

33. Editorial, *Jen-min Jih-pao*, May 26, 1965.

34. "Workers' Councils and Managing Boards of Economic Organizations, 1950–1962," *Yugoslav Survey*, vol. IV, no. 13 (April-June, 1963), p. 1836–40.

35. Quoted by P. Vukovic in "Ernesto Guevara's 'Social Violence,' " *Borba*, June 21, 1965.

36. C. Bobrowsky, "A New Economic Blueprint," in *Polish Perspectives*, no. 1, May 1958, p. 6.

### 5. UNEASY SYMBIOSIS IN LAND TENANCY

1. See Edward Kardelj, *Problems of Socialist Policy in the Countryside* (London: Lincolns-Prager, 1962), p. 10.

2. See N. Cornățeanu, "Cercetări asupra rentabilității agriculturei românești" ("Researches on the Rentability of Rumanian Agriculture"), *Economia Română*, December 1945, p. 104.

3. Decrees: No. 12 of June 21, 1945, on the confiscation of land; No. 28 of July 12, 1945, on the settlement of Slav farmers; No. 63 of September 2, 1945, on the institution of the National Land Fund. See Valer Fabry, *Agricultural Laws of the Czechoslovak Republic, May 1945-March 1949*, vol. 17, Ministry of Agriculture, Library of the Czechoslovak Institute for International Collaboration in Agriculture and Forestry (Prague: Brazda, 1949).

4. J. Kotátko, *Land Reform in Czechoslovakia* (Prague: Orbis, 1948), p. 13.

5. Bill of July 1947, see Fabry, *op. cit.*, pp. 13–14.

6. March 21, 1948. Fabry, *op. cit.*, p. 13.

7. Decrees of September 6, 1944, implemented by Executive Order of the Ministry of Agriculture and Land Reform on March 1, 1945. See Stanislaw Gryziewicz, "Rolnictwo" ("Agriculture"), *Kultura*, 1952, special series (Paris), pp. 306, 307.

8. Decree of December 12, 1944, implemented by Executive Order on January 20, 1945.

9. The peasant holdings created under the resettlement scheme remained indeterminate for a long time as far as boundaries and recorded titles of ownership were concerned. From the legal point of view the situation of these holdings was rather undefined and fluid. Three hundred thirty-eight thousand holdings of this kind (with an area of 2.9 million hectares) were affected in this way up to September 6, 1951, when a decree finally normalized their status. S. Gryziewicz, *op. cit.*, p. 315. See also *The Polish Countryside in Figures* (Warsaw: Polonia, for the Institute of Agricultural Economics, 1954), p. 17.

10. In a rather roundabout way, Hilary Minc states that this overpopulation has only been reduced, thanks to the transfers to the west: "The recovered terri-

tories are now inhabited by about six million Poles of whom five million are new settlers. The ethnical character of these lands has been changed completely and the agricultural overpopulation in Central Poland, materially reduced." Hilary Minc, *Poland's Economy, Present and Future* Documents and Reports on Poland, no. 5 (New York: Polish Research and Information Service, 1949), p. 21.

11. Decrees of March 17, 1945.

12. Out of a total of 1,006,311 "cadastral holds" belonging to churches of all denominations, 862,704 belonged to the Roman Catholic Church. Some were very large estates: the Hungarian Catholic Religious Foundation covered 122,000 acres; the Principal Chapter of Eger, 94,000 acres; the Holy Benedictine Order of Pannonhalma, 84,000 acres; the Archbishopric of Kalocsa, 82,500 acres, etc. The total left to all religious denominations after the reforms amounted to 181,064 "cadastral holds" (about 104,000 hectares), of which about one-half were left to the Catholic Church. See *Gazdasagstatisztikai tajekoztato (Economic and Statistical Bulletin)*, July 1948, no. 9, p. 547. Also Ilona Polanyi, "The Issues in Hungary," *World Affairs*, 1948–49, nos. 2–3, pp. 138–39.

13. See *Anuari statistikator i Republikes Populare Te Shqiperise 1960 (Statistical Yearbook of the Albanian Popular Republic 1960)* (Tirana: Drejtoria e Statistikes [Directorate of Statistics], 1961), p. 126 ff. See also "La République Populaire d'Albanie" ("The Albanian Popular Republic"), *Notes et Etudes Documentaires (Notes and Documentary Studies)*, serie économique (Paris: Secretariat général du gouvernment, 1954), pp. 1 ff.

14. March 22, 1945. Ministry of Information, Director of Foreign Cultural Relations, *La Réforme agraire en Roumanie (Land Reform in Rumania)* (Bucharest: November 1946), pp. 3 ff.

15. "The Feudal Estates, Nests of Sabotage, Are Liquidated," *Scânteia*, March 3, 1949.

16. *Comunicări statistice (Statistical Information)*, no. 17 (Bucharest: 1947), tables 6 and 9. See also *Dezvoltarea Economică a României 1944–1964 (Economic Development of Rumania, 1944–1964)* (Bucharest: Academia R.P.R., 1964), pp. 24–29.

17. Law of August 29, 1945.

18. Official data from *Statisticki godisnjak FNRJ 1954 (Statistical Yearbook of Yugoslavia 1954)* (Belgrade: Federal Statistical Office, 1954), p. 115.

19. T. Cernokolev, "The Agrarian Policy of the Bulgarian Workers (Communist) Party," *For a Lasting Peace, For a People's Democracy*, July 1948. Italics supplied in text.

20. As noted by Cernokolev (*ibid.*), "Land reform has only limited importance. It could not liquidate the scarcity of land or the excess of agricultural population. This problem remains to be solved by the intensive development of industry capable of absorbing the overpopulation from the countryside."

21. See my *Economics of Communist Eastern Europe, op. cit.*, pp. 245 ff.

22. Thus a Polish writer notes, "Also after the war there was a wide-scale division of land caused by the agrarian reform and the settlement of the Western Territories. As a result it was almost impossible to accomplish collectivization of the land while at the same time breaking up the estates for social and political reasons." See Tadeusz Hunek, "New Trends in Agricultural Policy," in *Polish Perspectives*, vol. VI, no. 1, p. 8.

23. See *Economics of Communist Eastern Europe, op. cit.*, pp. 255–57.

24. See *Statistiches Jahrbuch der DDR, 1965* (*Statistical Yearbook of the German Democratic Republic*) (Berlin: Staatsverlag der DDR, 1965), pp. 259, 261. *Statistická ročenka CSSR* (*Statistical Yearbook of Czechoslovakia, 1965*) (Prague: SNTL-SVTL, 1965), p. 262. *Statistical Yearbook, 1964* (Budapest: Hungarian Central Statistical Office, 1965), p. 132. *Anuarul statistic al R.P.R. 1965* (*Statistical Yearbook of Rumania 1965*) (Bucharest: Direcția Centrală de Statisticăe, 1965), p. 224. *Statisticheski godishnik na NRB 1965* (*Statistical Yearbook of Bulgaria 1965*), (Sofia: Tsentralno statistichesko upravlenie, 1965), p. 181.

25. F. Fekete and By. Varga, "Household Plot Farming of Cooperative Peasants in Hungary," *Acta Oeconomica Academiae Scientiarum Hungaricae*, no. 2, 1967, p. 347.

26. *Ibid.*, p. 350.

27. See *The Soviet Economy, op. cit.*, pp. 78, 87.

28. See, for instance, *Statistická ročenka CSSR*, p. 259, for output and marketing; *Statistical Yearbook* (Hungary), p. 138, for livestock output only; *Anuarul statistic al RPR*, pp. 268–77, output only; *Statisticheski godishnik*, pp. 176–77, output only.

29. Fekete and Varga, *op. cit.*, p. 354.

30. *Ibid.*, p. 356.

31. Edward Kardelj, *op. cit.*, p. 19.

32. Between 1953 and 1963 the total number of private homesteads increased from 2.0 million to 2.6 million. The number of owners for the smallest holdings (up to 5 hectares) rose from 1.3 million to 1.8 million, while their share in total land holdings increased from 36.5 per cent to 36.7 per cent. See Tihomir J. Markovitch, *Le Revenu agricole en Yougoslavie* (*Agricultural Income in Yugoslavia*) (Geneva: Droz, 1967), pp. 10–19.

33. Tadeusz Hunek, *op. cit.*, p. 16.

### 6. PROBLEMS IN FOREIGN-TRADE MANAGEMENT

1. Between 1960 and 1965, a 1 per cent increase in the national income has, on the average, been accompanied by an increase in imports of 2.0 per cent for Hungary and Bulgaria and 4.2 per cent for Czechoslovakia, compared to 1.1 per cent for the USSR, 1.2 per cent for Rumania, 1.4 per cent for East Germany, and 1.6 per cent for Poland. The increases in exports have been even higher than the import increases in certain countries of the first group mentioned to cope with balance of payments problems. See "Recent Changes in Europe's Trade," *Economic Bulletin for Europe*, vol. 18, no. 1 (November 1966), p. 10.

2. A preliminary and shorter variant of this essay was published in *Law and Contemporary Problems*, Summer 1959, pp. 420–34, under the title, "The Soviet-Bloc Foreign Trade System."

3. D. D. Mishustin, *Sotsialisticheskaia monopoliia vneshnei torgovli SSSR* (*The Socialist Monopoly of the Foreign Trade of the USSR*) (Moscow: Mezhdunarod. Kniga, 1938); *Pravovye regulirovanie vneshnei torgovli SSSR* (*Legal Regulation of the Foreign Trade of the USSR*) (Moscow: Vneshtorgizdat, 1961); M. F. Kovrizhnykh, A. D. Frumkin, and V. C. Pozdniakov (eds.), *Vneshniaia torgovlia stran norodnoi demokratsii* (*Foreign Trade of the Countries of People's Democracy*) (Moscow: Vneshtorgizdat, 1955); B. S. Vaganov (ed.), *Organizatsiia i tekh-*

*nika vneshnei torgovli SSSR i drugikh sotsialisticheskikh stran (Organization and Techniques of the Foreign Trade of the USSR and of the Other Socialist Countries)* (Moscow: Imo, 1963); S. Shchipiorskii, *Organizatsiia vneshnei torgovli Polskoi Norodnoi Respubliki (Organization of the Foreign Trade of the Polish People's Republic)* (Moscow: n.p., 1957); H. S. Levine, "The Effect of Foreign Trade on Soviet Planning Practices," in *International Trade and Central Planning*, ed. A. A. Brown and E. Neuberger (Berkeley and Los Angeles: University of California Press, 1968), pp. 255 ff.

4. "Some thousands of products in the fuels, raw materials and equipment categories are officially stated to have been covered by such recommendations for the 1961–65 plan period." Work is in progress on perspective plans ending in 1980. See *Economic Bulletin for Europe*, vol. 16, no. 2 (November 1964), p. 45.

5. As of 1957, all CEMA countries had introduced varying premiums on the official rate of exchange in connection with various payments among them. These rates diverge significantly from the official rates.

6. Until the 1960 price reforms, the Hungarian trade corporations, for instance, used a "coefficient of foreign exchange" in export operations and a "coefficient of domestic realization" in import operations. In the computation of both coefficients, the elements were the domestic and foreign prices paid and received and the official rate of exchange. To compute the coefficient of foreign exchange, assume that the rate of exchange is 1 dollar for 6 Hungarian forints, and 1 rouble for 1.5 forints. Assume further that a given commodity is purchased by the exporting enterprise at 1400 forints and sold for 200 dollars—i.e., 1200 forints at the official rate of exchange. The coefficient of foreign exchage is taken to be the ratio of the domestic price to the price obtained as computed at the official rate—i.e., 1400 ÷ 1200 = 1.16. The coefficient is then 16 per cent above parity. If the commodity is sold for 250 dollars, the coefficient is .93 (1400 ÷ 1500), or 7 per cent below parity. The lower the coefficient, the more profitable a transaction was considered to be. The same types of calculations were made for imports. In this latter case the lower the coefficient of domestic realization, the more unprofitable the operation was considered to be. Obviously, it is more profitable to sell an item costing 1400 forints at $250 than at $200, and vice versa for importing an item costing $200. The fallacy in all this is that, to start with, the 1400 forints is not an opportunity-cost price.

For a discussion in greater depth of efficiency analysis of foreign trade from the early 1950's to the mid-1960's in the area as a whole see: United Nations, Secretariat, Economic Commission for Europe, "Methods of Plan Construction in Eastern Europe and the Soviet Union," in *Economic Study of Europe*, part II, *Economic Planning in Europe* (Geneva: 1965), ch. 4, pp. 43–55.

7. K. I. Popov, "Modern Theories of Building Up Price Systems in Trade between Socialist Countries," in *Price Formation in Various Economies*, Proceedings of a Conference held by the International Economic Association, ed. D. C. Hague (London: Macmillan, 1967), p. 147.

8. Karl Marx, *Capital*, transl. Untermann (Chicago: n.p., 1909), p. 278. The paradox is presumed to arise from the fact that "capitals invested in foreign trade come in competition with commodities produced in other countries with lesser facilities of production" (*ibid.*, p. 279).

9. See, for instance, M. Popovic, "O ekonomskim odnosima izmedju socijal-

istickih drzava" ("On the Economic Relations among the Socialist States"), *Komunist* (Belgrade), July 1949.

10. L. Vaněk, "Rentabilita zahraničního obchodu" ("Conference on the Economic Rentability of Foreign Trade"), *Politicka Ekonomia*, vol. 6 (1958), p. 337; "Konference o mezinarodní delbe prace v socialistické světové soustavě" ("Conference on the International Division of Labor in the World Socialist System"), *ibid.*, p. 383.

11. The weighted base price for the CEMA market $(P_m)$ could be calculated from the formula:

$$P_m = \frac{P_a V_a + P_b V_b + \ldots + P_n V_n}{V_a + V_b + \ldots + V_n},$$

where $P_a$, $P_b$, $\ldots$ , $P_n$ are the national wholesale prices of these countries and $V_a$, $V_b$, $\ldots$ , $V_n$ are their volumes of production of the given commodity. See K. I. Popov, *op. cit.*, pp. 148–49.

12. See "Socialist Federal Republic of Yugoslavia," OECD *Economic Survey* (Paris: OECD, September 1967), p. 7.

13. E. S. Kirschen *et al.* (eds.), *Economic Policy in Our Time* (Chicago: Rand McNally, 1964), vol. I *(General Theory)*, pp. 110 ff.

14. See, for instance, J. Bognar, "La conception du commerce éxterieur dans le nouveau mecanisme economique," *Acta Oeconomica Academiae Scientiarum Hungaricae*, no. 2, 1967, pp. 77 ff.

15. See J. Bognar, *op. cit.*, p. 86, and E. Benoit, "The Joint Venture Route to East-West Investment," in *Financing East-West Business Transactions*, ed. J. H. Hickman (New York: American Management Association, 1968), pp. 23 ff.

16. S. Balazsy, "Foreign Trade and the Reform of Economic Management," *Acta Oeconomica*, vol. I, fasc. 3–4 (1966), pp. 313–25.

## 7. A "SECOND WORLD MARKET": EXPECTATIONS AND REALITY

1. J. Stalin, *Economic Problems of Socialism in the USSR* (New York: International Publishers, 1952), p. 26.

2. *Statisticheski godishnik 1965*, p. 114; *Statisticka ročenka CSSR 1965*, p. 189; *Statistisches Jahrbuch, 1965*, p. 125; and *Statistisches Jahrbuch, 1966*, p. 105; *Statisztikai Evkonyv 1965 (Statistical Yearbook 1965)* (Budapest: Kozponti Statisztikai Hivatal, 1966), p. 53; *Rocznik statystyczny 1963*, p. 63 (state industry only); *Anuarul statistic 1965*, pp. 186–87; *Statisticki godisnjak FNRJ, 1965*, p. 97.

3. See "Shifts of Manufacturing Industries," in *Industrial Location and National Resources* (Washington, D. C.: National Resources Planning Board, 1943).

4. Following Lowell D. Ashby, let $b_{ij}$ be the base-year employment figure of one industrial subgroup in one country; $r_{oo}$, the growth rate of employment for all industry in the whole area; $r_{io}$, the growth in employment for one industrial subgroup in the whole area; $r_{ij}$, the growth rate in employment for one industrial subgroup in one country. We may then define adjustment for structural effect as $b_{ij} r_{io} - b_{ij} r_{oo}$, and adjustment for competitive effect as $b_{ij} r_{ij} - b_{ij} r_{io}$. See Lowell D. Ashby, *Regional Change in a National Setting*, Staff Work-

ing Paper in Economics and Statistics, Department of Commerce (Washington, D. C.), no. 7, April 1964, p. 35.

5. The report of Alexander A. Karpov underlines the necessity of very large investments for developing the Yugoslav resources in *Transactions of the Fifth World Power Conference*, vols. 18–19 (*Osterreichisches Nationalkomites der Weltkraftkonferenz*) (Vienna: 1957), pp. 6–279. See also V. P. Maksakovskii, *Toplivny resursy sotsialisticheskikh stran Evropy (Fuel Resources in the European Socialist Countries)* (Moscow: Nedra, 1968), ch. I, pp. 5 ff.

6. A. M. Tomashpolskii, *Neft' i gaz v mirovom energeticheskom balanse (1900–2000 gg.) (Oil and Gas in the World's Energy Balance, 1900–2000)* (Moscow: Nedra, 1968), p. 140.

7. According to Tomashpolskii's hypotheses (*ibid.*, p. 141), the structure of socialist Eastern Europe's energy output should shift as follows in 1980 and 2000:

| | PER CENT | | |
| Output | 1965 | 1980 | 2000 |
|---|---|---|---|
| Oil | 7.5 | 24.4 | 21.0 |
| Gas | 7.5 | 11.5 | 20.5 |
| Coal | 80.0 | 53.5 | 28.5 |
| Hydroenergy | 5.0 | 2.1 | 1.5 |
| Atomic energy | — | 8.5 | 28.5 |

8. *Postavení ČSR ve světovem hospodarství (Position of Czechoslovakia in the World Economy)* (Prague: Statni nakladatelstvi politické literatury, 1956), p. 24.

9. I. Dudinski, "Toplivno—syr'evaia problema stran SEV i puti ee resheniia" (The Fuel and Raw Materials Problem of CEMA's Countries and the Road toward Its Solution"), *Voprosy ekonomiki*, no. 4, 1966, pp. 84–94. See also "When Oil Flows East," *The Economist*, Jan. 10, 1970, pp. 51–52. The Soviet leadership has formulated an ambitious set of projects for the development of oil extraction in the Soviet Union's "Alaska"—the Ob basin of Western Siberia (Tiumen and Tomsk provinces). Output should grow from some 20–30 million tons in 1970 to 100–125 million tons in 1975, and to 230–260 million tons in 1980. The Ob basin is scheduled to become the Soviet Union's main source of oil and gas and its largest petrochemical center: its 1980 output should match the entire Soviet oil production of 1965 (243 million tons) and account for as much as one-half of the projected oil output from all other sources. If these plans are carried out, the Soviet Union could, of course, enhance significantly its oil export abilities. But it should be noted that enormous difficulties are yet to be overcome, and that vast resources are yet to be marshalled before the Tiumen taiga and tundra, and its permafrost and deep rock can be fully exploited for drilling and extracting oil or for laying the pipelines and roads needed for transport. (See *Pravda*, January 15, 1970, on the CPSU decisions, and *Pravda*, February 12, 1970, translated in *The Current Digest of the Soviet Press*, vol. XXII, no. 2 [February 11, 1970], pp. 13 and 33; and vol. XXII, no. 8 [March 24, 1970], pp. 7, 10, 16).

10. *Hospodářské Noviny*, no. 33, 1968 (suppl. on foreign trade). Data for 1967.

11. I.Vajda, "External Equilibrium, Neo-Techniques and Economic Reform," *Acta Oeconomica Academiae Scientiarum Hungaricae*, no. 2, 1967, p. 297.

12. Ota Šik, "Excerpts from the Televised Series of Talks on Czechoslovakia's Economy," *Pragopress*, August 1968.

13. I. Vajda, *op. cit.*

14. *Hospodářské Noviny, op. cit.*

15. I. Vajda, *op. cit.*

16. See "Recent Changes in Europe's Trade," *Economic Bulletin for Europe*, vol. 18, no. 1 (November 1966), p. 28.

17. The literature available on these views is enormous. Let me mention particularly, as background material, the following important United Nations study: "Trade Problems between Countries Having Different Economic and Social Systems," *Proceedings of the United Nations Conference on Trade and Development*, Geneva, March 23–June 16, 1964 (New York: United Nations, 1964), vol. VI (*Trade Expansion and Regional Groupings*), part I, pp. 113–69. For the Soviet views, see *Mirovaia sotsialisticheskaia sistema khoziaistva (The World Socialist Economic System)* (Moscow: n.p., 1967), vol. 2, particularly chs. 13–15, pp. 385–475.

18. Czechoslovakia is the only centrally planned economy whose membership in GATT was established before it came under Communist rule. Poland established relations with GATT by a declaration in November 1959, but only certain members extend MFN treatment to it. Yugoslavia associated itself with GATT by a declaration in May 1959 and acceded to full membership in November 1962, after important changes in its foreign trade and foreign exchange systems. Rumania is authorized to follow the work of GATT as an observer, and Hungary applied for a similar authorization in November 1966. Rumania made a formal membership application in 1968.

19. For a detailed, though not always objective, discussion, see Gunar Adler-Karlsson's book, *Western Economic Warfare 1947–1967* (Stockholm: Almqvist & Wiksell, 1968).

20. "Trade Expansion and Regional Groupings," in *Proceedings of the United Nations Conference on Trade and Development*, vol. VI, part I, p. 121. The United States has denied by law, since January 1952, the application of MFN to the USSR and the East European countries, excluding Yugoslavia. Accordingly, imports from these countries have been subjected to rates under the 1930 Tariff Acts, not the rates as reduced by trade agreements since the 1934 Trade Agreement Act. In 1960, the US Government granted MFN to Poland, and the Administration warded off a number of congressional efforts to rescind MFN treatment for Poland and Yugoslavia. The "Miller Report," released by the White House on April 29, 1965, suggested, as a fundamental tool in "building bridges" to the East, the vesting of "discretionary authority in the President to grant as well as withdraw MFN treatment [to selected Communist countries]." See N. McKitterick, *East-West Trades The Background of the US Policy* (New York: The Twentieth Century Fund, 1966), p. 29 and *passim*. See also G. Adler-Karlsson, *op. cit., passim*.

21. Foreign subsidiaries and affiliates of American corporations are allowed, since December 1969, to trade in non-strategic goods with Communist China. Ultimately, the US policy on trade with China is likely to become similar to that applying to the Soviet Union. However, no rapid growth of such trade seems likely. Even this "indirect" trade, inaugurated in December 1969, remains

strongly subject to complex political and diplomatic considerations. (See "China Trade Welcomed Here," in *The New York Times,* Business and Finance section, Sunday, April 19, 1970.)

22. See *Financing East-West Business Transactions, op. cit.,* pp. 13, 24, 28 ff., 37 ff.

23. In a statement, "U.S. Policy on East-West Trade," made in 1964, Professor Robert Loring Allen suggested that, during the early 1950's, "there were some rather far-out notions concerning economic war and the nature and effectiveness of the strategic embargo." According to him, the thinking at the time was, "Stop the Soviet Union from importing these items, and stop the economy. This seemed to be an easy solution, and, as in the case of most easy solutions, quite incorrect." See Senate Committee on Foreign Relations, *East-West Trade: A Compilation of Views of Businessmen, Bankers, and Academic Experts* (Washington, D. C.: U.S. Congress, 1964), p. 214.

24. S. Ausch, "Mezhdunarodnoe razdelenie truda i sistema khoziaistvennogo upravleniia" ("International Divisions of Labor and the System of Management of the Economy"), *Acta Oeconomica Academiae Scientiarum Hungaricae,* no. 1, 1966, p. 86.

25. See, for instance, S. Gheorghiu, "Coordonarea planurilor de dezvoltare a economiei naţionale, formă principală a colaborarii între ţările membre ale CAER" ("Coordination of Plans of Development, the Principal Form of Collaboration among the Member Countries of· CEMA") *Viaţa economică,* vol. VII, no. 6 (February 14, 1969), p. 12.

26. O. Bogomolov, "Sotrudnichestvo stran SEV na vazhnom rubezhe" ("Cooperation of the CEMA Countries on an Important Line"), *Kommunist,* 1966, no. 18, pp. 38–53. Also R. N'ersh. "Printsipial'nye i prakticheskie voprosy sotsialisticheskoi ekonomicheskoi integratsii" ("Theoretical and Practical Problems of Socialist Economic Integration"), *Ekonomicheskaia gazeta,* no. 6 (February 1960), p. 40.

## 8. NATIONAL DEVELOPMENT, FOREIGN ASSISTANCE, AND INTER-COUNTRY CONFLICTS

1. In Soviet parlance a "camp" cannot be "split," since by definition it encompasses *all* the countries with the same socio-economic system: every socialist country belongs automatically to the socialist camp, just as any nonsocialist country belongs outside it. But which country is socialist? Yugoslavia has been officially "excluded" and "included" in the camp a number of times and by different socialist leaderships. So have the USSR, China, and Albania—with no end in sight for mutual exclusions.

2. See H. Kahn and A. J. Wiener, *The Year 2000, a Framework for Speculation on the Next Thirty-Three Years* (New York: Macmillan, 1967), p. 149.

3. *Long Live Leninism* (Peking: Foreign Languages Press, 1960), pp. 61 ff.

4. *Ibid.,* p. 63.

5. See my book, *The Economics of Communist Eastern Europe,* chs. 2 and 6.

6. See the official documents in *The Soviet Yugoslav Dispute: Text of the Published Correspondence* (London and New York: Royal Institute of International Affairs, 1948), p. 19.

7. *Ibid.,* p. 30.

8. See V. Malenković, "O pitanju ekonomskih odnosa izmedju SSSR a i njemu potcinjenih zemalja" ("On the Question of Economic Relations between the USSR and the Countries Subjected to It"), *Ekonomist*, vol. III, no. 3 (1950), pp. 39 ff.

9. Cf. E. Zaleski, *Les Courants Commerciaux de l'Europe Danubienne au cours de la première moitié du XX<sup>e</sup> siècle* (Paris: Librarie Générale de Droit et de Jurisprudence, 1952), pp. 383 ff.

10. See *The Economics of Communist Eastern Europe, op. cit.,* p. 439.

11. The literature on this score is by now quite impressive; a shortcut to the discussion is to be found in Franklyn Holzman, *More on Soviet Bloc Trade Discrimination* (Medford, Mass.: The Fletcher School Reprint Series, December 1965).

12. See M. Djilas, *Lenine et les rapports entre états socialistes* (Paris: Le Livre Yugoslave, 1949), p. 97.

13. *Ibid.,* p. 98.

14. After giving the details of all the economic and defense agreements with the Russians in the late 1940's, Tito concluded, "Where then is this aid they are talking about? . . . These figures will convince anyone that it was all a matter of exchange of goods, and not some sort of aid, as they try to claim in their propaganda." See Marshall Tito, *For Independence and Equality* ( Belgrade: Jugoslovenska Knjiga, 1950 ), pp. 74, 77.

15. See V. Dedijer, *Tito* (New York: Simon and Schuster, 1953), pp. 277–89. Also Ministry of Foreign Affairs of the FPRY, *White Book on Agressive Activities by the Governments of the USSR, Poland, Czechoslovakia, Hungary, Rumania, Bulgaria and Albania towards Yugoslavia* (Belgrade: Ministry of Foreign Affairs, 1951), p. 37 and *passim*.

16. See H. G. Johnson, *Economic Policies Toward Less Developed Countries* (Washington, D. C.: The Brookings Institution, 1967), p. 29.

17. Compare Dedijer, *op. cit.,* p. 277 ff., and Johnson, *op. cit.,* p. 81.

18. See *Borba's* official reply to *Pravda*, May 17, 1958, in *The Second Soviet-Yugoslav Dispute*, ed. V. L. Benes *et al.* (Bloomington, Ind.: Indiana University Publications, 1959), p. 241.

19. See *White Book . . .,* pp. 304–14. The totals in question allegedly amounted to $32 million and $3 million, respectively.

20. *Ibid.,* pp. 305, 306.

21. *Ibid.,* p. 307. See also E. Kardelj, *La politique extérieure de la Yugoslavie* (Paris: Le Livre Yugoslave, 1949), pp. 51–57.

22. M. Perović, *Ekonomski odnosi Jugoslavje i Albanije (1947–1948) (Economic Relations between Yugoslavia and Albania)* (Belgrade: Borba, 1951), pp. 164–65, 169.

23. Cf. *White Book . . .,* p. 22.

24. See Djilas, *op. cit.,* p. 98.

25. See "Economic Development in Albania and Bulgaria," in *Economic Survey of Europe in 1960* (Geneva: United Nations, 1961), ch. VI, p. 13. At the Fourth Party Congress of the Albanian Workers' Party, Enver Hoxha indicated that of 400 industrial projects completed in the 1950's, the Russians claimed "nearly 80 had been reconditioned, enlarged, or entirely supplied by the USSR." Cf. Moscow radio release, December 26, 1961. At the official rate of exchange,

the total of the Soviet credits to Albania amounted to 110 million dollars. See G. F. Achminow, "Die Sowjetische Albanienpolitik," *Balkan Studies,* vol. 4, no. 1 (1963), p. 97.

26. "Saving for Economic Development in the Centrally Planned Economies," *World Economic Survey, 1960* (New York: United Nations, 1961), ch. III, pp. 123–24.

27. F. Konstantinov, "Raskol'nicheskaia, antimarksistkaia, deiatel'nost' albanskikh rukovoditelei" ("The Schismatic, Antimarxist Activity of the Albanian leaders"), *Kommunist,* no. 17 (November 1961), pp. 38–53. The quotations are from pp. 47–48.

28. "The truth is that the whole series of differences of principles in the international communist movement began more than seven years ago. To be specific, it began with the 20th Congress of the CPSU in 1956." See "Comment on the Open Letter of the Central Committee of the CPSU, September 6, 1963," in *The Polemic on the General Line of the International Communist Movement* (Peking: Foreign Languages Press, 1965) p. 59.

29. Letter of the Central Committee to CPSU, February 29, 1964, in John Gittings, *Survey of the Sino-Soviet Dispute: A Commentary & Extracts from the Recent Polemics, 1963–1967* (London: Oxford University Press, for the Royal Institute of International Affairs, 1968), p. 136.

30. Like the Russians, the Chinese detailed as "aid" the goods traded in exchange for Russian goods—namely, grain, mineral products, and metals, some of which were "indispensable for the development of the most advanced branches of science and for the manufacture of rockets and nuclear weapons . . ." (*ibid.,* p. 137).

31. "Fourth Comment on the Open Letter, October 22, 1963," in *The Polemic . . .,* pp. 194–95.

32. Letter of the Central Committee of the Chinese Communist Party in June 1963, *ibid.,* p. 41–42.

33. "Sixth Comment on the Open Letter, Dec. 12, 1963," *ibid.,* p. 288.

34. Letter of the Central Committee of the Chinese Communist Party of June 14, 1963, *ibid.,* p. 37.

35. "Ninth Comment on the Open Letter, July 14, 1964," *ibid.,* p. 464.

36. "Chou En Lai Report at Third National Party Congress," Peking Press release, December 31, 1964.

37. *More on the Differences between Comrade Togliatti and Us* (Peking: Foreign Languages Press, 1963), pp. 21, 22.

38. All the quotations are from the report of M. A. Suslov to the Central Committee Plenum of CPSU, February 14, 1964, transl. in *On the CPSU Struggle for Cohesion of the International Communist Movement,* External Research Staff, U. S. Department of State (1964), *passim.*

39. I. Dudinski, "Toplivno-syr'evaia problema . . .," *passim.*

40. O. Bogomolov, "Sotrudnichestvo stran SEV . . .," *passim.*

41. *New York Times,* August 18, 1968.

42. "Milan Weiner Commentary," Prague radio release, March 26, 1968.

43. *Pravda,* September 2, 1968.

44. The Rumanian press has often reiterated these points since their inclusion in an official declaration of the Central Committee of the Rumanian Workers' Party in April 1964. For an outspoken restatement, see S. Gheorghiu, "Coordon-

area planurilor de dezvoltare a economiei naționale, formă principală a colaborarii intre țările membre ale CAER" ("Coordination of the Plans of Development of the National Economy, the Principal Form of Collaboration among the CEMA Countries"), *Viața economică,* February 6, 1969, pp. 13, 18.

45. See *Economic Development for Eastern Europe,* Proceedings of a Conference Held by the International Economic Association, ed. M. C. Kaser (London: Macmillan, 1968), ch. 12, p. 147.

46. *Ibid.,* ch. 13, p. 151.

47. *Draft Program of the CPSU, 1961* (Washington, D. C.: Foreign Broadcast Information Service, 1961), p. 14.

48. *Kommunist,* no. 15 (October 1963).

49. *Pravda,* September 11, 1964.

50. *Pravda,* October 30, 1965.

51. "Problems of the Last Third of the Century" reprinted from *Izvestiia* in the *New York Times,* August 19, 1968.

52. "Why Khrushchev Fell," November 21, 1964, in *The Polemic . . .,* p. 475.

53. See A. Nove and J. A. Newth, *The Soviet Middle East: A Communist Model for Development* (New York: Praeger, 1967), pp. 123, 126, and *passim.* According to V. Holubnychy, a comparison of changes in per capita industrial production in the Soviet republics, for the period 1913–65, shows that in relative terms ( i.e., in relation to the speedier development of the Russian republic itself ) the non-Russian·republics are not "more industrially underdeveloped than they were before the Bolshevik Revolution: in 1913, they produced 44 per cent of per capita Russian production, while in 1965 they produced only 29 per cent." See V. Holubnychy "Some Economic Aspects of Relation Among the Soviet Republics," in *Ethnic Minorities in the Soviet Union,* ed. by S. Goldhagen (New York: Praeger, 1968), p. 72.

54. The President of the Slovenian Executive Council, Stane Kavcić, suggests, for instance, that in the 1970's assistance to the Yugoslav underdeveloped areas should remain at the federal level, whereas the developed republics "should in the future orient themselves primarily toward their own resources"—more or less independently of the center. See Belgrade press release, June 12, 1968. For the income data, see F. E. Ian Hamilton, *Yugoslavia, Patterns of Economic Activity* (London: Bell and Sons, 1968), p. 139.

55. E. Preobrazhensky, *De la NEP au Socialisme: Vue sur l'avenir de la Russie et de l'Europe* (1922), transl. from the Russian (Paris: Editions du Centre de la Recherche Scientifique, 1966), pp. 105 ff.

56. *Voprosy Filosofii,* no. 10, 1958.

57. *Pravda,* February 9, 1959.

58. Report of L. F. Ilichev, "The Current Tasks of the Party's Ideological Work," CPSU Central Committee Plenum, June 18, 1963.

59. Todor Zhivkov, "The Unity of Socialist Countries—A Decisive Condition for the Construction of Communism," *Problems of Peace and Socialism,* January 1963.

### 9. "CATCHING UP" AND "CONVERGING"

1. W. W. Rostow, *The Stages of Economic Growth, A Non-Communist Manifesto* (Cambridge, England: The University Press, 1960), pp. 10 ff.

2. See S. Kuznets, *Modern Economic Growth, Rate Structure and Spread* (New Haven: Yale University Press, 1966), pp. 9 ff.

3. S. N. Eisenstadt, *Modernization: Protest and Change* (Englewood Cliffs, N. J.: Prentice Hall, 1966), chs. 1–2.

4. This section and the following one draw heavily on a previous essay of mine, "Economic Modernization," in *The United States and Eastern Europe*, ed. Robert F. Byrnes (Englewood Cliffs, N. J.: Prentice Hall, for the American Assembly, 1967), pp. 57–80.

5. See my *State and Economic Development . . .*, particularly ch. 1.

6. According to M. Ernst, the 1964 per capita product figures at calculated exchange rates, were for East Germany, $1400; for Czechoslovakia $1,470; for Hungry $1,020; for Poland, $890; for Bulgaria, $690; and for Rumania, $680. Official Hungarian sources have, however, indicated that the Hungarian figure is too high.

7. See M. Ernst, *op. cit.*, p. 883.

8. *Idem.*

9. J. I. Scott, *Projections of the Population of the Communist Countries of Eastern Europe, by Age and Sex, 1965–1985*, International Population Reports Series, Department of Commerce (Washington, D. C.: Government Printing Office, 1965), no. 14, p. 91, and *passim*.

10. For the intercensal data, see United Nations, *Demographic Yearbook 1962* (New York, 1964), pp. 276 ff., and *Demographic Yearbook 1964* (New York, 1964), pp. 105 ff.

11. *Mir Sotsializma . . .*, p. 12.

12. *The Economist*, September 3, 1966.

13. R. I. Mighell, *American Agriculture* (New York: John Wiley, 1955).

14. J. K. Galbraith, *The New Industrial State*, (London: Hamish Hamilton, 1967), pp. 20, 33, 71, and *passim*.

15. J. Tinbergen, "Roads to the Ideal Socio-Economic System," *The Oriental Economist*, February 1967, p. 94; and J. Tinbergen, "Convergence of Economic Systems in East and West," in *Disarmament and World Economic Interdependence*, ed. Emile Benoit *et al.*, (New York: Columbia University Press, 1967), pp. 246–60.

16. V. Cheprakov "Teoriia konvergentsii i deistvitel'nost' ("Reality and the Theory of Convergence"), *Voprosy Ekonomiki*, no. 2, 1968, pp. 87–96. See also "Report of Kurt Hager to SED Central Committee Plenum," *Neues Deutschland*, January 30, 1968.

17. Text of "Essay" of Andrei D. Sakharov in *The New York Times*, July 22, 1968, pp. 14–16; reprinted in book form under the title *Progress, Coexistence, and Intellectual Freedom*, with an Introduction by H. E. Salisbury (New York: Norton, 1968).

18. See my *The Soviet Economy . . .*, ch. XV.

19. G. Volmar, "Der isolirte sozialistische Staat" ("The Isolated Socialist State"), *Jahrbuch fur Sozialwissenschaft und Socialpolitik* (Zurich), 1879.

20. A. D. Sakharov, "Essay," p. 16.

# INDEX

agriculture: China's, 43–55; collectivization of peasantry, 43–47, 50, 55, 91–101; cooperativization of, 43–47, 50, 55, 91–101; employment in, 180–83; farm-output increases, 176, 179; periods of US technology, 186; and fragmentation of land, 81–82; growth rates of, 176, 179; growth rates of East and West compared, 184–85; guide to literature on, 199–200; household farming, 96–101; industrialization at the expense of, 41–42, 47–52, 179; and mass colonization, 84–86, 89; mechanization of, 182–83; MTS, 94; "New Course" in, 94–95; state farms, 90–91, 94; technology in, 185–86; urbanization's effects on, 180–81. *See also* land tenancy and peasantry

aid, foreign, 145–86

Albania: growth rates in, 175; investment policies of, 33; land tenancy in, 81–83, 86–87, 92; split with Soviet Union, 154–56; split with Yugoslavia, 152–54

Arzumanian, A., 24

Ashby, Lowell D., 126

associationist socialism, 72–76

Bakunin, Mikhail, 61

Bernstein, Eduard, 62, 63

Bober, M. M., 62

Bobrowsky, C., 78

Bogomolov, O., 162–63

budgets, state, 25–27

Bukharin, N., 40, 46, 51–52, 122

Bulgaria: and Communist theory, 168; employment in, 125–29; growth rates in, 175–79; investment policies of, 33; land tenancy in, 81–89, 96

capitalism: convergence with socialism, 187–92, 202–3; joint enterprises with socialist countries, 162; strategies of "catching up" with, 35–36, 183-87

Castro, Fidel, 191

CDSE's (centrally directed socialist economies): as cybernetic systems, 6–8; definition of, xiv–xv; entrepreneurial function in, xvi; foreign-trade management in, 102–17; planning changes in, 190–91. *See also* management

CEMA (Council for Mutual Economic Assistance): conflicting interests in, 123–44; decontrol problems in, 114–17; and development of self-contained industrial bases, 124–26; division of labor amongst member countries, 113–14; energy resources of, 128–32; industrial employment shifts in, 125–29; inner circle of, 144; inter-country conflicts in, 123–68; intra-system coordination in, 112–17; multilateral agreements within, 116; price determination within, 109–12; as a regional market, 123–24; as "second world market," 123–44; and "Sino-Soviet